DATE DUE

		ETNA
AUG 1 6 1975	MAR 2 3 1979	
HAPPY CAMP		AUG 2 6 1983
		SEP 2 6 1983
AUG 1 8 1975		MC CLOUD
SEP 1 9 1975		
WEED		JAN 1 1 1990
		FEB 2 0 1992
NOV 2 1976		
JUN 3 1977		
JUL 8 1977		
AUG 2 7		
WEED		
OCT 1 7 1977		
NOV 1 1 1977		
DEC 2 1977		

cop.1

646.4   Schwebke, Phyllis W
Sewing with the new knits.

SEWING
WITH THE
NEW
KNITS

SEWING WITH THE NEW KNITS

Today's Techniques for Today's New Fabrics

Phyllis W. Schwebke
Margery Dorfmeister

Illustrations by Ann L. Fuller

Macmillan Publishing Co., Inc.
New York

Collier Macmillan Publishers
London

Book design by Constance T. Doyle

Macmillan Publishing Co., Inc.
866 Third Avenue, New York, N.Y. 10022
Collier-Macmillan Canada Ltd.

Library of Congress Cataloging in Publication Data

Schwebke, Phyllis W
  Sewing with the new knits.

    1. Dressmaking. 2. Knit goods. I. Dorfmeister,
Margery, joint author. II. Title.
TT557.S38   646.4'04   72-11675
ISBN 0-02-607780-9

First Printing 1975

Printed in the United States of America

CONTENTS

INTRODUCTION

Knits,
The Fabric of Our Times

The new knits are the perfect fabric for our highly mobile way of life. Knit fabrics, with their loop construction, are blessed with an elasticity—a "natural stretch"—that woven fabrics do not possess. In a few short years, we have seen the packable, washable, wearable, versatile knits come close to dominating the trade while, at the same time, they have given an enormous impetus to home sewing.

Although the first knitting machine was invented in England in the reign of Elizabeth I, it was not until synthetic fibers were developed nearly four hundred years later that knitted fabrics really came into their own.* Knitted fabrics, produced from yarn spun from natural fibers, could be only as strong as their weakest link. Previous research in textiles had produced yarns that were smoother, stronger, and more even—such as mercerized cotton and worsted spinning wool—but the first synthetic fibers, yielding a long, continuous filament yarn, transformed the future for knit fabrics. There were drawbacks to be conquered, of course. The clammy, "dead" feeling of the original nylon fabrics, for example, and problems of dyeing, necessitated research into texturizing the new thermoplastic fibers. It was discovered that synthetic yarns could be crimped and twisted to resemble natural fibers; heat-set yarns were developed; Lycra, the first spandex fiber, was invented. Finally, fabrics emerged that were pleasant to the touch, comfortable to wear, and with the bulk and coverage of natural fibers. All the advantages of the natural fibers and few of their drawbacks! The age of knits had arrived.

Originally, knits in America were produced for the trade only, but the pressure of consumer demand, the enterprise shown by a number of home-sewing teachers (notably Mrs. Anne Person of Eugene, Oregon, and teachers at the YMCA in Minneapolis), and the activities of a few forward-looking retailers, all helped to promote knits being merchandised for the home-sewing market. Convinced of the durability of this new home-sewing movement, the big pattern companies fell into line. Important,

---

* See Appendix A—The History of Knits.

too, was the improvement in home-sewing machines. Spurred by the import of sophisticated European models after World War II, the latest models now feature self-regulating pressure, pattern stitching, non-tangle bobbins, a free arm, and ballpoint needles, all of which have made a tremendous difference to the home sewer's ability to handle the new knit fabrics.

THE FUTURE FOR KNITS

Where knits once tended to imitate conventional woven fabrics, they now have opened up a world of variety, color, texture, and pattern to the home sewer.

The whole sewing boom—which seems to trace its beginnings to the advent of the shift dress in the early Sixties—has been accelerated by the popularity of knits. When the fashion silhouette became simple, the home sewer found she could turn out fairly sophisticated looking garments without much trouble. Most knits lend themselves well to simple-line fashions.

Pattern companies have tied in with leading fashion designers and speeded up the turnover of fashions, making the new patterns available to retail outlets in all parts of the country within six weeks or so after a new fashion trend takes hold. Pattern companies, too, have become the largest disseminators of sewing news and information about knits and all types of sewing—as witness the check-out counter of any fabric sales department for the array of free, take-home information.

Sewing is increasingly popular with the young. It is now included in the curriculum of most high schools in America. A recent *Seventeen* magazine survey found that 12 million girls between the ages of 13 and 19 now enjoy it as a hobby.

Men, too, have discovered the comfortable two-way stretchability of the new knits. They own knit shirts, pants, suits, and sports coats, and many of them are even trying their own hand at sewing with knits. A man's knit tie is a favorite beginning project.

Most women still look upon home sewing as an economy measure, even though the emphasis has shifted gradually to place more importance on sewing as a means of creative expression. It is estimated that a woman who sews may save 60 to 70 percent on her clothing as ready-to-wear prices keep climbing. The home sewer, too, becomes increasingly critical of the shoddy quality of the sewing in clothing she buys. She usually feels she could do a better job herself.

What does the future hold?

The increased leisure predicted for our future means more time to travel and thus a need for a larger wardrobe of knits. It also means more time to indulge ourselves in making clothes and more time in which to wear the clothes we make.

Advances in textiles are virtually unlimited. Someday, it is safe to say, most women's, men's, and children's clothing will be made of knits.

Right side of fabric

Wrong side of fabric

Right side of lining

Wrong side of lining

Right side of mesh
or power net

Wrong side of mesh
or power net

Interfacing

NOTE TO THE READER

Sewing with the New Knits covers all facets of home sewing with knit fabrics, from the relatively simple construction methods used to make light-hearted lingerie garments to the couture techniques that give that sophisticated touch to fashion garments. Also included are many "Quickie Methods"—those clever little trade secrets that help the busy but fashion-conscious seamstress turn out a wardrobe of knits in the least possible time. All this adds up to the most complete book of its kind.

For the first time in a home sewing book, we have also presented a history of knit sewing (Appendix A); an explanation of the fabrication process (Appendix B); and the details of knit care. These extras will add interest for the more advanced home sewer, the student, and the instructor—whether at the high school, college, or adult level.

Much of the material between these covers has been tested by Mrs. Schwebke in knit sewing courses offered through the Madison Area Technical College Evening Courses Program in Madison, Wisconsin. The high degree of enthusiasm among students and their sustained interest in sewing with knits influenced the authors in preparing this book.

The skillful work of artist Ann L. Fuller will help the reader interpret the step-by-step directions for specific sewing procedures.

Plain knit

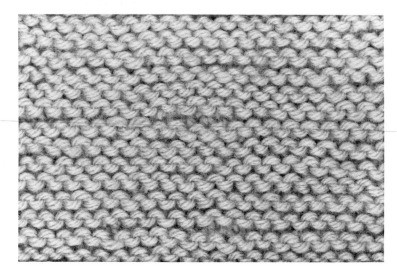

Purl

Rib

1

KNIT FABRICS

The new knits have extraordinary versatility. There are knits that have dimension in the form of blisters which deepen the pattern. There are duo-fabric knits and haute-couture raschel knits—those which are natural and those which are sophisticated. Knits may be silky and soft, as in jerseys, or stabilized for men's wear. They may be bonded, laminated, or combined with plates of plastic. The designs may be printed or piece dyed and as high fashion as those of wovens. There is the tartan warp knit in a 24 gauge for dresses and sportswear. Then there is a luxurious print in a blend of Antron nylon and Lycra spandex which has been used by couture designers for its radial stretch (stretches everywhere). An Arnel triacetate and nylon bias check has been designed for dresses and sportswear. There are even corduroy warp knits for pants and sportswear.

Since knits are so versatile in dimension and design and there is such a variety in knit fabrics, it is important that the home sewer understand some of the basic terms used in the marketing of knit fabric o/c (over the counter). The *construction and fiber content* give knits many characteristics.

KNIT CONSTRUCTION

WARP KNITS: The warp knits which are constructed on flat machines are usually stronger, more resistant to snagging, less elastic and often run-resistant.

> RASCHEL KNITS: offer lacy, open patterns. They are perfect for the sweater look in long vests, T-shirt dresses, and lacy evening wear. Also made in coarse fur cloth.
>
> TRICOT KNITS: are commonly used in lingerie. They stretch more in width than in length and may be textured or brushed. Have fine herringbone rib on wrong side. Printed tricots are used also for evening wear, linings, and blouses. A "wet-look" tricot is suitable for outerwear as well as for garments.

WEFT KNITS: Possess more give and elasticity.

> PLAIN OR JERSEY: is soft and clinging. It is perfect for softness, gathers, and draping.
>
> DOUBLE KNITS: offer a variety of patterns. Have same appearance on both sides. Are desirable for tailored clothing where shape retention is important.
>
> RIB KNITS: are recognized by wales (vertical ridges) on both sides of fabric. They possess considerable crosswise stretch. Used for ribbing and close fit in garments.
>
> PATTERN KNITS: result from variations of basic knit stitches. The fisherman knits are an example.

FIBERS FOR KNITS

The fiber, too, affects the care, warmth, wrinkle resistance, luster, and use of the knit fabric. See chart, *Know Your Knits,* page 3.

NATURAL FIBERS

COTTON:
- Absorbent, comfortable fiber for warm weather. Washable.
- Will shrink if not finished. Read label carefully. Preshrink before sewing.
- Cut tube after preshrinking. Avoid fold line when cutting.
- Available in single knit, double knit, and raschel.
- May bag in knee and seat area.
  VELOUR:
  - Appearance of velvet. Has a nap, so cut all pieces in one direction.
  - Used for robes, tops, and pants suits.
  STRETCH TERRY:
  - Has loops. Cut all pieces in one direction.
  - Used for tops, jumpsuits, and baby clothes.

WOOL:
- Warm, resilient, and holds creases.
- Dry-clean for best results.
- Preshrink fabric. Dry cleaners will preshrink, or yourself use the London-shrink method. Roll carefully in wet sheet and cover with bath towel. Allow to stand for several hours. Unroll and smooth out on flat surface to complete drying and to relax.
- Press with steam and press-cloth.
- Available in single-knit jerseys, double knits, and sweater knits.

SYNTHETIC FIBERS

ACETATE:
- Has a luster similar to silk and is lightweight and wrinkle resistant.
- Some are washable and others need to be dry-cleaned. Read labels. When washing, do not wring fabric. Shake and drip dry. Iron on wrong side with low setting. Fingernail polish deteriorates acetate.
- Available in tricots for lingerie and dresses and raschels for dresses and jackets.
  TRADENAMES: Acele, Avisco, Celanese, Estron, Celaperm, Chromspun, etc.

ACRYLIC:
- Warm and resilient, resembling wool.
- Hand wash or machine wash according to directions. Turn inside out when washing to prevent pilling. Machine dry at low temperature or pat in towel and dry on hanger if hand washed.

KNOW YOUR KNITS
Fibers and Construction

FIBERS AND TRADENAMES	ADVANTAGES AND SPECIAL FEATURES	USES	CARE*
Wool	Warm, resilient, will hold pressed pleats; available in solid colors, plaids and jacquard designs.	Double knits tailor well; select patterns with architectural styling for dresses, suits, coats, sportswear; jerseys—soft styling in separates and dresses.	Careful dry-cleaning; can shrink with too much steam.
Cotton	Wrinkle resistant and absorbent, making it comfortable for warm weather; available in solids, patterns and tweedy, nubby textures.	Double knits — architectural styling for dresses and sportswear. Stretch terry jerseys—soft styling in separates and dresses. Raschels—simple line styles in jackets and dresses.	Hand-wash or machine-wash, check label instructions. Raschel — wash by hand and wrap in towel to remove excess water. To dry, lay on flat surface and block to keep shape.
Polyester Dacron Encron Fortrel Kodel Quintess Trevira	Highly wrinkle resistant, lightweight but firm, strong, great shape retention, won't bag or sag; available in many interesting textures, sculptured patterns and raised surface designs or as a matte jersey.	Pattern selection is the same as for wool, with the addition of the raschels used for jackets and dresses. Polyester double knits do not press as well as the wool ones, so some tailored details should be avoided.	100% polyester — hand-wash; check label for instructions, little or no ironing required. To machine-wash — use warm water, gentle cycle and mild detergent. Dry in dryer, remove immediately and hang on hanger. Raschels—same as for cottons Blends—may need dry-cleaning
Nylon Antron Caprolan Enkalure	Highly wrinkle resistant, lightweight, can be made elastic with great recovery for stretch garments; available in solids, colorful prints, stretch lace and the "wet" looking fabrics.	Tricots and jerseys — lingerie, softly styled dresses and blouses. Stretchy knits and laces—simple garments designed to fit close to body.	Same as for polyester with the exception of the stretch lace which is hand or machine-washable. Drip-dry. Do not put in dryer.
Acrylic Acrilan Creslan Orlon	Warm, resilient and lightweight, resembles wool or fur-like fabric having a soft hand, resists oily stains; available in solids and patterns.	Pattern selection same as for wool with the addition of raschels, used for jackets and dresses.	Hand-wash in cool water. Wrap in towel to remove excess water. Dry on hanger.
Acetate Avisco Celanese Celaperm Chromspun Estron	Wrinkle resistant, lightweight, has a luster giving it a silk-like appearance; available in solids and many colorful prints.	Tricots—lingerie, usually softly styled dresses or blouses but styling depends on firmness of fabric. Raschels — jackets, dresses.	Hand-wash, machine-wash or dry-clean. Check fabric label carefully. Some acetates and triacetates retain appearance best if dry-cleaned. May need touch up pressing when hand-washed.
Triacetate Arnel	Characteristics are like those of acetate; available in solids, prints and the "wet" looking fabrics.	same as for acetate	same as for acetate

FIBER CONTENT + CONSTRUCTION = Knits that have the characteristics you love. They fight wrinkles, are easy to live in and care for. Knits are constructed by interlooping the yarns in various ways to get these types.

Raschels have a lacy, open-work or hand-made crocheted look.

Tricots have vertical wales on the right side and crosswise ribs on the back. They are drapable, run-proof and can be slinky.

Double Knits can look the same on both sides unless a texture has been added on the right side. They are firm and stable.

Jerseys or single knits have a definite right and wrong side and are soft and very drapable.

Two other processes that affect knits are:
Bonding which gives a knit increased stability and makes open knits more sewable. Since it adds warmth and body, fabrics become less drapable. Do not wash unless recommended on the fabric label because the face may separate from the backing.

Yarns can be *texturized* to give increased elasticity, warmth, and bulk to the fabric.

* (Make your own label to sew in with the fiber content so that the dry-cleaner can see what it is, and you'll remember which need to be dry-cleaned or washed.)

- Used for pants suits, tops, dresses, suits, and sweaters.
- Available in plain knits and double knits.
  TRADENAMES: Creslan, Zefran, Acrilan, Orlon, etc.

MODACRYLIC:
- Heat-sensitive fiber. Can be creased permanently.
- Used for wigs, doll's hair, fake furs.
- New, nonflammable Dynel modacrylic knit used for children's garments. It is washable, warm, soft, shrink resistant, nonallergenic. When touched with fire, it does not flare or support combustion.
  TRADENAMES: Dynel, Verel.

NYLON:
- Strong, elastic fiber making it wrinkle resistant and abrasion resistant.
- Most nylon is machine washable in warm water on gentle cycle. May be machine dried at low setting. Always wash white nylon with the white wash, as it picks up colors. A fabric softener may be added at last rinse. Remove from dryer immediately. Press with warm iron.
- Available in stretch fabric for swimwear or ski pants, in lightweight tricot for lingerie, or in Banlon for dresses and tops.
- "Wet-look" finish is applied to nylon tricot.
  TRADENAMES: Caprolan, Enkalure, Qiana, Antron, etc.

POLYESTER:
- Wrinkle resistant, firm so it won't "bag," and is lightweight.
- Most may be machine washed and dried. Fabric softener may be added to the last rinse. Wash by hand if label indicates. Press with warm iron. Use press-cloth on right side. Remove oil-based stains by rubbing with liquid detergent before laundering.
- Available in matte jersey, double knits, in plain or patterned designs in raschels.
- Used for jackets, dresses, tops, pants suits for men, women, and children.
  TRADENAMES: Fortrel, Trevira, Avlin, Dacron, Vycron, Encron, Kodel, Quintess, and Terylene (English).

TRIACETATE:
- Wrinkle resistant and shrink resistant. Often permanently pleated.
- Machine or hand wash according to directions on label. Can be ironed on highest wash-and-wear setting on iron.
- Available in plain, prints, or "wet-look" finish.
- Used for softly styled dresses and blouses.
  TRADENAME: Arnel.

FIBER BLENDS

Many fiber blends are possible for knits. By blending, the desirable characteristics of each of the fibers is utilized. Below are some common knit fabric blends:

POLYESTER/COTTON:
- Wrinkle resistant, washes and dries well. Comfortable to wear. May need to treat oil-based stains.
- Used for sportswear.

POLYESTER/WOOL:
- Appearance of wool but is usually machine washable.
- Used for sportswear and tailored garments.

RAYON/POLYESTER:
- Comfortable and strong. Available in printed single knits for shirts or patterned jacquard knits.
  TRADENAME: Avril/Avlin.

OVER-THE-COUNTER TERMS FOR KNITS

There are several o/c* terms used in the marketing of knit fabrics. The consumer should become familiar with them in order to shop wisely for good quality knit fabric.

FABRIC CONSTRUCTION:
> WALES: loops up and down.
> COURSE: loops running across.
> DENIER: refers to size of yarns.
> WEIGHT: 9 oz. means that fabric weighs 9 oz. to the yard. Common dress weights are 10½ and 11 oz.; 14 to 16 oz. is a good weight for coats.
> CUT OR GAUGE: number of stitches or needles per inch or inch and a half. The higher the gauge, the finer the knit.

YARNS:
> FILAMENT: long, continuous yarns, uniform in size.
> STAPLE: short fibers spun into yarn.

FABRIC FORM:
> FLAT KNIT: fabric which is knitted flat and has two finished edges. Term also used interchangeably to mean a jersey or plain knit.
> TUBULAR KNIT: fabric knitted circular in tube form. May be sold in a tube or slit and sold flat.

PERFORMANCE TERMS:
> RESILIENCE: fiber's ability to stretch and recover.
> RECOVERY: fabric's ability to be stretched and return to original size.

FABRIC DESIGN:
> JACQUARD: knit fabrics with design and texture constructed on a Jacquard knitting machine.
> MORATRONIK KNIT: knit fabrics made with design and texture using a Moratronik machine.

FABRIC PROBLEMS:
> PILL: a ball of fiber formed on surface of knit caused by abrasion.

---

* o/c: over-the-counter

RAVELING: yarns removed from edges of knit fabric. Weft knit may ravel but warp knits usually do not.

RUN: a streak or a ladder caused by a broken yarn.

FABRIC TYPES:

SINGLE KNITS: knit fabric constructed with single yarns usually on a circular machine—i.e., matte jersey, panne jersey, tricot, "wet-look" nylon.

DOUBLE KNIT: knit fabric constructed with double set of needles to make a fabric which is usually alike on both sides.

STRETCH KNITS: stretch may be imparted to a knit fabric by a stretch fiber such as *Spandex*. This is called power stretch, and is found in power net for girdles and in swim wear. *Tradename:* Lycra. Stretch may also be obtained from heat setting the yarns or texturizing the yarns. *Tradenames:* Helenca, Banlon.

STRETCHABLE KNIT: stretch imparted by the type of knit construction and/or type of fiber or yarn. Used for patterns designed for knits only. Includes such fabrics as stretch terry or velour, stretch lace, pucker stretch, sweater knits, and rib knits. Read label for fabric care.

NOVELTY KNITS: constructed on raschel machines. Includes open, lacy knits and crochet knits. Read label for fabric care. If washed, knead in towel. Dry on flat surface.

BONDED KNITS: a knit fabric which is composed of two layers fused together. This provides stability and limits stretch. Most bonded knits are washable by machine. Check care instructions. Some are dry-cleanable only. Handle in sewing like double knits.

VINYL KNIT: a cotton knit fabric coated with vinyl. Many are machine washable. Check care instructions. Handle in sewing like leather or leatherette.

METALLIC KNITS: knit fabrics using yarns which are either plastic-coated metal or metal-coated plastic. Used for dressy or evening wear. *Tradenames:* Lurex, Lamé, Metlon.

ALPACA KNITS: available by the yard in sweater knit in alpaca (hair fiber) or blended with wool. Used for sweaters and two-piece dresses. Dry-clean. Relax before cutting.

FUR FABRIC: available by the yard, imitating almost any kind of real animal fur. Many have knit backs. *Sliver* knitting is one process of inserting and locking staple yarns into a jersey back for making fur fabric. Read labels for care. Fur fabrics may be washed or dry-cleaned or cleaned by the furrier method.

KNIT PROS AND CONS

As consumers today, we are so used to knits in our wardrobes that we no longer think about our reasons for choosing knits—rather than wovens—for many of our garments.

Listed below are some of the advantages of knits, and a few of their limitations.

ADVANTAGES OF KNITS:

COMFORT: knits have been called the original stretch fabric. They allow us to move about easily, lead active lives, lounge on low furniture, and get in and out of automobiles. In addition, the air pockets created by the knitting process serve as insulators and add both warmth and absorbency to fabric. Yet knits are lightweight and may be worn the year round. There are knits suited to almost any climate.

EASY CARE: many of the knits (synthetics) are washable. Some are both machine washable and machine dryable. Most knits do not require special blocking. They have the advantage of packing very well into a suitcase—because of their soft, looped construction—and, when given a little breathing time at journey's end, looking well with little or no pressing.

SEWABILITY: knits tailor well and drape easily. Seams usually do not ravel so the need for seam finishes is almost eliminated. Extra fullness may be eased in without a pinched seam. The necessity for lining and underlining is minimal.

VARIETY AND AESTHETIC APPEAL: the patterns and stitches used in fabricating knits can be varied to produce effects to please any taste. Variety can also be achieved by combining, dropping, or adding stitches. Knits have great appeal in an ecology-conscious age because of their "natural" look.

FASHIONABILITY: knit production is geared to a fast pace. When fashion trends break, knitting equipment is now ready to turn out the newest fabrics in a very short time.

LIMITATIONS OF KNITS:

DIMENSIONAL INSTABILITY: one of the hazards of buying lower quality knits is that they may stretch out of shape during washing or dry-cleaning. This may be particularly true of cottons or acetates.

SHRINKAGE: may occur in cotton knits that are not treated with shrink-proof processing.

NOT WINDPROOF: unless heavily napped or laminated.

COST: knits tend to cost more than wovens of comparable yarn count. That is because it takes more yarn to give the same kind of cover in knits than in wovens of like quality. Double knits are usually more expensive than raschels; the yarns used are the largest element in the fabric cost, while the actual knitting is a mere five or six percent of the selling price.

LADDERING: may result from a broken loop in certain kinds of single knits. A hole may appear, starting a run in the fabric.

STATIC BUILD-UP AND PILLING: current problems of the synthetic yarn knits. The industry is presently developing improved yarns and finishes to combat the problem.

KNIT PICKING

Now that you are armed with the "know-how" about knit fabrics, how do you choose a good quality knit?

It's up to the individual consumer to learn to recognize the type, style, and quality that will suit her needs. On the whole, though, buying good quality is usually the best policy.

Good quality is really a combination of factors: the raw fiber, the firmness and evenness of the yarn; the closeness of the knitting; the artistic interpretation and dimensional stability of the finished fabric, as well as the dyes and special finishes.

Here are some good tips for picking a quality knit:

READ THE LABEL: this is essential when choosing a knit. Manufacturers are required by law to identify the fibers and to give their percentages in every fabric sold. Since it is not otherwise possible—even for a trained person—to recognize fibers made into fabrics today, reading the label or hangtag is the only reliable method of judging how a fabric may be expected to perform.

The label may also offer helpful information about shrinkage control, color fastness, care of fabric, and special finishes that have been used. Some cottons are treated to keep shrinkage controlled to within one to two percent, and this information is usually given on the label. It is important, as shrinkage of more than 2 or 3 percent will have a decided effect on the fit of the finished garment.

CHECK THE FABRICS FOR FLAWS: check to see that the crosswise design is square with the lengthwise rib. Most knits have a finish applied so they cannot be straightened by pulling, washing, or steaming. In the case of bonded fabrics, check to see that the face fabric is bonded straight (at right angles to the edge of the fabric).

COLOR: Look for indications that permanent dyes have been used. "Colorfast" printed on the label is good assurance. (Cottons take dyes well.)

HANDLE THE FABRIC: feel the knit to judge the character and quality of its "hand." Weight, texture, smoothness, softness, drape, and the closeness and evenness of the loops are all revealed by gentle handling. Try crushing the fabric with your hand to test it for wrinkle resistance. Check for *recovery*. A quality knit is one that has good recovery—if you sit or bend, a knit with good recovery will not sag or bag at the knees. Check recovery by pulling fabric in lengthwise and crosswise direction.

BUY AT A REPUTABLE STORE: it is wise to buy at a reputable outlet as not all knits are properly heat-set in the textile mill.

2

CHOOSING THE RIGHT PATTERN

For *loose, bulky knits,* choose a pattern with few seams—a simple design.

Double knits are perfect for suits, coats, pants suits, and A-line dresses which have the tailored look for they do not "bag" or "sag." Seam interest is good. Wool double knits crease better than polyester double knits.

Choose designs which are soft for *single knits*—i.e., jerseys. Skinny turtlenecks, body suits, and garments with fullness are good choices.

For *sheer effect,* use open lace or crochet *raschel knits.*

Two-way stretch knits are used for bikinis, tank bathing suits, ski pants, and body suits.

PATTERNS

There is a knit fabric suitable for any type of garment design, from sportswear to evening wear, from soft, draped designs to crisp, tailored designs. But the pattern design and the fabric must be compatible! Be warned and choose your pattern carefully.

The commercial pattern companies provide special sections in the counter pattern books for patterns for knit fabrics. There are also basic knit pattern designs by smaller companies or designers who specialize in knit fabric designs only.

OVER-THE-COUNTER COMMERCIAL PATTERNS:

- A commercial pattern *designed for woven fabrics* has more ease built into the design than is needed for knits. If you use this type of pattern, you may need to alter the seam allowances or choose a pattern one size smaller.

- Another type of pattern is listed as *recommended for,* or *ideal for, knits.* This pattern has not been made smaller, but the design lines are suitable for knits. Firm knits such as bonded, firm wool, acrylic or polyester single or double knits could be used.

- Patterns designed for *knit fabrics only* or for *stretchable or unbonded* knits may not be used for woven fabrics. They are designed for a close-to-body fit, allowing the fabric to provide additional body ease. Use knits with more stretch such as novelty, single, or stretch knits—i.e., panne knits, tube knits, sweater knits

Fig. 2-1. Over-the-counter patterns. *A,* Vogue (men's knit shirts); *B,* McCall's (knit pants and tops); *C,* Simplicity (knits for children); *D,* Butterick (sweater knits).

Fig. 2-2. Patterns for knits. *A,* Kwik Sew (men's pants), Bonnie Kay Originals (infant patterns), Sew Lovely (lingerie pattern); *B,* Else (knit tops), McDuff (men's knit jacket); *C,* Authentic (western patterns), Sew-Knit-N-Stretch (men's patterns).

(ribbed or cable), tricot, crochet and pucker knits, or stretch terry. Bonded knits would not be suitable.

- Some patterns have an *extra stitching line* for a close fit for stretch knits.
- Some patterns include a *top for stretchable knits* and a *pants* pattern listed as *ideal for knits*. The pants then could be constructed of a double knit *or* a woven fabric.
- Some pattern companies provide a guide for testing the stretch of a knit to assist you in choosing the correct pattern for the knit fabric. (See Chart, p. 27.)

BASIC KNIT PATTERN DESIGNS:

Accompanying the knit home-sewing boom has been the creating and marketing of basic knit patterns by designers and small pattern companies. They are available in some fabric stores or by mail order. Most of the patterns are printed with several sizes in one envelope. These patterns are usually master patterns, and tracing paper is used to trace off the size you wish to use. There are few markings and details on the patterns. The seam allowances on details are usually ¼ inch. Some have a ⅝-inch seam allowance on skirt and pants side seams with a ⅞ inch allowance at CB* for zippers. Others allow ½-inch seam allowances. Hem allowances for shells are often 1 inch and for skirts 2 inches. The instructions may be limited with few drawings. Check pattern carefully for designated seam allowances.

PATTERN SIZE AND PATTERN EASE:

Generally, for home sewing, choose the pattern size you commonly use. The difference in the patterns designed for knits compared to patterns designed for wovens, is in the amount of ease allowed. With knits, additional ease is gained from the "give" of the fabric. A guide for ease for knits in the *bust area is 1 to 2 inches. Three inches* may be allowed for a loose fit or when using firm knits. *One inch* is a recommended amount of ease for *sleeves*. Allow *2 inches for large upper arm or thigh* or when using firm knits. *Hip* ease is usually *1 to 2 inches*. For *sleeve cap, allow ¾–1 inch* ease from notch to notch. To alter patterns, use pattern alteration techniques used in dressmaking. *To remove ease in sleeve cap:*

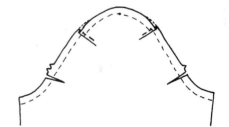

Fig. 2-3. Sleeve pattern alteration.

- Measure the armscye† from notch to notch at the seamline with tapeline on edge. Measure the sleeve from notch to notch on seamline. Compare measurements. If the sleeve measures more than ¾ to 1 inch larger, remove excess ease.
- Fold small tucks in pattern to remove excess sleeve allowances. Put one tuck between notches at front and top of sleeve and an-

---

* CB: center back
  CF: center front
† *Armscye:* another term for armhole.

OVER-THE-COUNTER FABRICS

MACHINE WASHABLE FABRICS

 MACHINE WASH-WARM

MACHINE WASHABLE FABRICS (Dimensional Restorable)

MACHINE WASH WARM
LINE DRY

MACHINE WASHABLE PERMANENT PRESS

MACHINE WASH WARM
TUMBLE DRY
REMOVE PROMPTLY

MACHINE WASHABLE DELICATE FABRICS

MACHINE WASH WARM
DELICATE CYCLE
TUMBLE DRY LOW
USE COOL IRON

MACHINE WASHABLE FABRICS (Pigment Prints)

MACHINE WASH WARM
DO NOT DRY CLEAN

ALL HAND WASHABLE FABRICS

 HAND WASH SEPARATELY
USE COOL IRON

DRY CLEANABLE FABRICS

 DRY CLEAN ONLY

PILE FABRICS

 DRY CLEAN PILE FABRIC
METHOD ONLY

VINYL FABRICS

WIPE WITH DAMP
CLOTH ONLY

Because the Rule requires the Fabric Supplier to

"fully inform the purchaser how to effect such regular care and maitenance
as is necessary to the ordinary use and enjoyment of the article, e.g. washing,
drying, ironing, bleaching, dry cleaning - - - ",

If the above labels do not fully apply to a specific fabric, the complete and correct care instruction should be given.

The following should be considered when selecting the proper care instruction.

1. The definitions of these care terms should be understood by reference to the AAMA Care Guide, Industry Care Guide or ASTM Standard Definitions. For instance label No. 1 means "machine wash in warm water, regular cycle". Bleach may be used on white fabrics. May be tumble dried at any temperature, may be ironed with a hot iron. May be self service - coin op. or professionally dry cleaned and laundered." If any of these care practices should not be used the care instruction should be modified with additional language.

2. Color as well as fabric style must be considered. Dark shades which will stain other fabrics in a wash load should be labeled "wash separately". This could be on a separate second label, if desired.

3. Unless otherwise stated, a fabric may be ironed with a hot iron. If a cool or warm iron is required it must be stated, i.e., some acetates would require "cool iron - reverse side".

4. Permanent Press fabrics require ironing instruction if a hot iron would injure the fabric. "No. Iron" means the fabric should not be ironed at all. We suggest a preferable phrase would be "Do Not Iron".

5. It is assumed the customary care practice is to bleach white goods and to not bleach colored goods. If bleach would harm white fabrics the phrase "No Bleach" should be used. The phrase need not be used for colored fabrics.

6. All washable fabrics are dry cleanable unless otherwise stated.

7. All reference to laundering and dry cleaning includes self service - coin op. facilities unless otherwise stated.

8. The use of a negative term that pertains to only one particular care practice implies that all other customary care procedures involved may be used.

9. The word "only" in any term limits the procedure to the stated instruction.

(Courtesy of Celanese Fibers Marketing Company)

This Guide is made available to help you understand and follow the brief care instructions found on permanent labels on garments. Be sure to read all care instruction completely!

CONSUMER CARE GUIDE FOR APPAREL

	WHEN LABEL READS:	IT MEANS:
MACHINE WASHABLE	Machine wash	Wash, bleach, dry and press by any customary method including commercial laundering and dry cleaning
	Home launder only	Same as above but do not use commerical laundering
	No bleach	Do not use bleach
	No starch	Do not use starch
	Cold wash / Cold rinse	Use cold water from tap or cold washing machine setting
	Warm wash / Warm rinse	Use warm water of warm washing machine setting
	Hot wash	Use hot water or hot washing machine setting
	No spin	Remove wash load before final machine spin cycle
	Delicate cycle / Gentle cycle	Use appropriate machine setting; otherwise wash by hand
	Durable press cycle / Permanent press cycle	Use appropriate machine setting; otherwise use medium wash, cold rinse and short spin cycle
	Wash separately	Wash alone or with like colors

	WHEN LABEL READS:	IT MEANS:
NON-MACHINE WASHING	Hand wash	Launder only by hand in luke warm (hand comfortable) water. May be bleached. May be drycleaned
	Hand wash only	Same as above, but **do not** dryclean
	Hand wash separately	Hand wash alone or with like colors
	No bleach	Do not use bleach
	Damp wipe	Surface clean with damp cloth or spounge
HOME DRYING	Tumble dry	Dry in tumble dryer at specified setting — high, medium, low or no heat
	Tumble dry Remove promptly	Same as above, but in absence of cool-down cycle remove at once when tumbling stops
	Drip dry	Hang wet and allow to dry with hand shaping only
	Line dry	Hang damp and allow to dry
	No wring No twist	Hang dry, drip dry or dry flat only. Handle to prevent wrinkles and distortion
	Dry flat	Lay garment on flat surface
	Block to dry	Maintain original size and shape while drying
IRONING OR PRESSING	Cool iron	Set iron at lowest setting
	Warm iron	Set iron at medium setting
	Hot iron	Set iron at hot setting
	Do not iron	Do not iron or press with heat
	Steam iron	Iron or press with steam
	Iron damp	Dampen garment before ironing
MISCELLANEOUS	Dryclean only	Garment should be drycleaned only, including self-service
	Professionally dry clean only	**Do not** use self-service drycleaning
	No dryclean	Use recommended care instructions. No drycleaning materials to be used.

This care Guide was produced by the Consumer Affairs Committee, American Apparel Manufacturers Association and is based on the Voluntary Guide of the Textile Industry Advisory Committee for Consumer Interests.
The American Apparel Manufacturers Association, Inc. (Courtesy of Celanese Fibers Marketing Company)

Rev. 1972

other tuck between the back notch and the top of sleeve. Redraw seams where necessary.
- May clip pattern at notch to allow the pattern to lie smoothly.
- Keep width of cap of sleeve between notches.

or

- See, *Removing excess ease in cap under sleeves,* Chapter 13, page 89 for two other methods of removing excess ease.

GUIDELINES FOR CHOOSING KNIT DESIGN AND FABRIC

Would you like to check yourself before making the final selection of your pattern and fabric? Below are listed some guideline questions:

SELECT A PATTERN DESIGN:
- Will the design meet the needs for the use of the garment?
- Will the design be suited for the type of knit I wish to use?
- Will the design lines be flattering for my figure?

DECIDE HOW MUCH YOU MAY SPEND:
- How often will I wear the garment?
- Is it for a special occasion or is it for a garment which I will wear for several seasons?

CONSIDER WHO IS TO USE THE GARMENT:
- Is it for a teenager? Is it for a youngster?
- Does the fabric need to be rugged and durable?

CONSIDER THE FIBER CONTENT:
- Considering the use and the wearer, is the fabric durable, inexpensive, or elegant?
- Does it possess wash-and-wear qualities, or does it need to be dry-cleaned?

CONSIDER THE TYPE OF KNIT AND YARN STRUCTURE:
- Is the knit stretchy or firm?
- Is the knit suited to the pattern design?
- Will the knit be durable? Are the yarns loosely twisted and textured so they may snag easily?

CONSIDER THE FINISH ON THE KNIT FABRIC:
- Is the fabric treated so it is washable and will not shrink?
- Is it wrinkle resistant? Stain resistant?
- Is it colorfast?
- Does the fabric require dry cleaning?

CONSIDER THE COLOR, DESIGN, AND DRAPING QUALITIES OF THE KNIT:
- Is the scale of the design of knit suitable for my figure?
- Do the draping qualities of the knit fabric enhance my figure?
- Does the color complement my coloring? Fit into my wardrobe?

CONSIDER YOUR SEWING EXPERIENCE:
- Are there too many details in the design which are new to me?
- Will the fabric be too difficult for me to handle?

SELECT YOUR PATTERN AND YOUR KNIT FABRIC: Get acquainted with your knit—handle it—feel it—and enjoy it as you progress with your fashion garment.

3

THE PROPER SEWING EQUIPMENT

The proper choice of equipment, supplies, and trimmings is important for either the "quickie" or couture sewing of knits.

MEASURING:

FASHION RULER: a plastic ruler which is a combination hip curve, armscye curve, straight ruler and which has a cut-out slot. Used for "truing" pattern alteration lines, guiding tracing wheel, and squaring the ends of fabric.

PLASTIC RULER: an 18-inch by 2-inch plastic ruler ruled off in inches, eighths, and sixteenths. Used for pattern alterations, squaring the ends of fabric, and measuring.

L-SQUARE: metal, plastic, or wood L-shaped square. Used for squaring ends of fabric and measuring.

T-SQUARE: 4 inch by 9 inch plastic or metal. Used for squaring fabric, altering patterns or measurements.

YARDSTICK: 36-inch ruler of metal or hardwood. Used for general measuring.

SKIRT MARKER: measurement device with pins or chalk to measure and mark hemline.

TAPEMEASURE: fiberglass or non-stretch 60-inch measure. Used for taking figure measurements and checking flat pattern measurements.

DRAPERY WEIGHT TAPE: weights in tape designed for drapery construction. Used to measure around pattern curves—i.e., neck, armscye, pants crotch. Ideal for taking body crotch measurement as it drapes better than a tape measure.

SEWING GAUGE: a 6-inch metal or plastic ruler with a sliding indicator. Used for measuring and marking buttonholes, hems, and pleats.

HAND TOOLS:

PINS: *ballpoint pins,* or *silk pins* which are sharp, work well for lightweight and medium-weight knits. *Colored plastic heads* are easy to find when pinning knits and *T-pins* are ideal for bulky knits.

HAND-SEWING NEEDLES: for hand sewing, *ballpoint* needles push the yarns apart rather than pierce them. *Sharps* in sizes 7, 8, 9, or *millinery* in 7 or 8 may also be used.

LOOP TURNER: a tool with a latch-hook device at one end which is used to turn cording or tubing.

BODKIN: a small metal device with hook-and-latch end used

Fig. 3-1. Knit fixer.
See page 106.

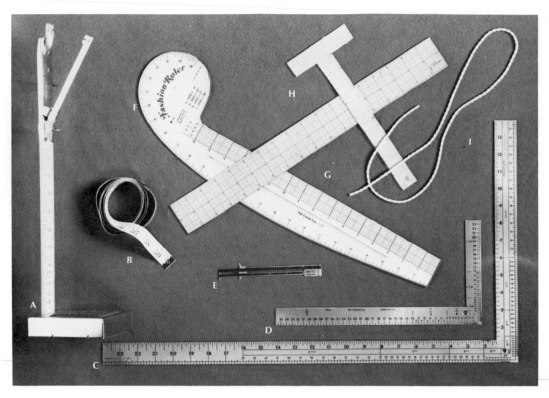

Fig. 3-2. *A*, hem marker; *B*, tape measure; *C*, L square; *D*, L square (small); *E*, measuring gauge; *F*, combination curve ruler; *G*, plastic ruler (2 in. x 8 in.); *H*, T square; *I*, drapery weight tape (measuring curves).

Fig. 3-3. *A*, ballpoint pins; *B*, magnetic wrist pincushion; *C*, tailor's thimble; *D*, dressmaker clips; *E*, magnetic pin holder; *F*, ballpoint handsewing needles; *G*, lingerie-weight thread; *H*, cotton-covered polyester core thread; *I*, loop turner; *J*, bodkin; *K*, bodkin; *L*, pinch n' pull bodkin.

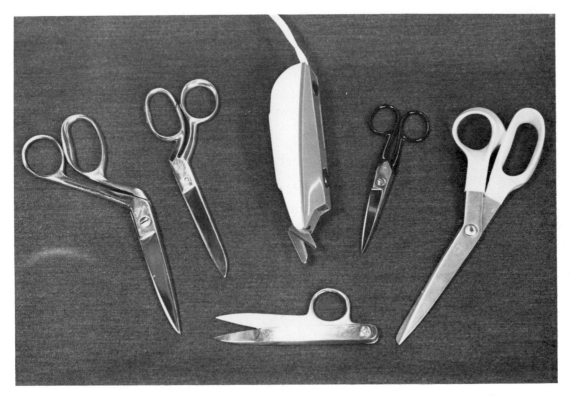

Fig. 3-4. *A*, high bent-handle shears; *B*, bent-handle shears; *C*, electric scissors; *D*, tailor's points; *E*, surgical steel scissors; *F*, clip scissors.

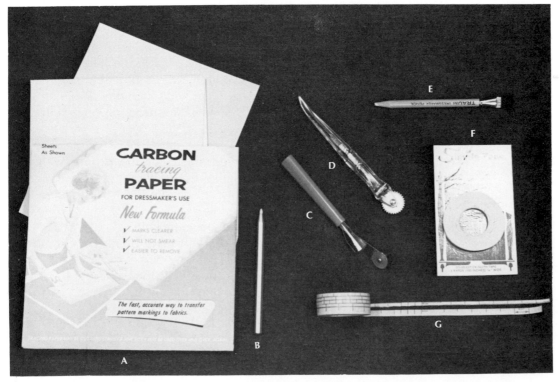

Fig. 3-5. *A*, tracing paper; *B*, Teflon-pointed marker; *C*, smooth tracing wheel; *D*, combination serrated tracing wheel and seam ripper; *E*, marking pencil; *F*, double-stitch cloth tape; *G*, sewing tape.

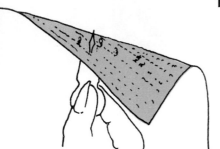

Fig. 3-6. Needle threader for repairing snags.

to draw elastic through a casing or to turn tubing. One type has a ballpoint end for turning tubing with a closed end.

THIMBLE: fits snugly on middle finger when hand sewing. Made of plastic, metal—yes, even silver or gold.

WRIST PINCUSHION: pincushion attached to elastic or bracelet and worn on the wrist for pins which are always handy when sewing or fitting.

THREAD:

Choose a thread in a color which is a shade darker than the fashion-knit fabric. Thread must perform well on your machine and must be functional for garment seam—not pucker, pop, fade, or deteriorate during the life of the garment.

POLYESTER THREAD: is strong and elastic and long wearing. Used on synthetic fabric but can be used on wool. Sensitive to very high temperature or pressing. Cut, do not break, this thread.

SILK THREAD: stretches and recovers, thus is good for wool knits and wool blends if the garment is to be dry-cleaned. Size A is used for seams. *Silk buttonhole twist* is used for topstitching and hand-pick stitching. If used on polyesters which are machine washed, the thread may shrink and pucker. Use size 16 machine needle for buttonhole twist.

COTTON-COVERED POLYESTER THREAD: has characteristics of both the cotton and the polyester. It is excellent for seam strength and higher ironing temperatures. It consists of a high-strength-filament polyester core around which is spun a covering of high quality cotton. The cotton gives the thread excellent sewing characteristics, while the polyester core gives the high strength.

MERCERIZED COTTON: cotton is not as strong as polyester nor does it possess as much stretch; however, if stretch is built into the seam in the machine stitching, it is a satisfactory thread.

THREAD TIPS: if having problems with synthetic thread, store in refrigerator for a few hours to provide humidity. Place an empty bobbin on top of plastic spools of thread to keep them from jumping off the spool pin.

CUTTING:

SHEARS: sharp, bent-handled shears of the proper weight for the knit fabric. Shears designed especially for knits with serrated blades are available. A high, bent-handle shears is designed to cut without lifting the fabric.

ELECTRIC SHEARS: work well on some knits.

SMALL TRIMMING SCISSORS: with sharp points for clipping and trimming.

THREAD CLIPS: for cutting threads at the machine and making small clips for marking. Has one ring and is operated by squeezing clips in palm of hand.

CUTTING BOARD OR CUTTING TABLE: a cardboard board which

opens to 40 inches x 72 inches. Marked with inches (some with bias lines) to which fabric can be pinned.

BLOCKING BOARD: can be constructed at home. It consists of a piece of plywood 30 inches x 48 inches (or as long as desired). Cover with several layers of wool. Add a firm cotton cover which has an even square design. Sew twill tape on outer edge and tack to board. Used for fabric squaring, layout, and pressing and blocking.

PATTERN PAPER: *brown wrapping paper* may be used for corrected pattern or for cutting an extended pattern (whole pattern piece for patterns which are placed on fold). Special *pattern paper* comes in rolls or sheets which are marked with dots in 1-inch squares or bias lines. A nylon nonwoven which is 36 inches wide and transparent, called "Trace-a-Pattern,"* is also available.

A PATTERN HOLDER: available in spray cans, may be applied to pattern to hold it temporarily in place during cutting. Pattern may be repositioned easily and spray does not harm knit fabric.

MARKING:

TRACING PAPER AND TRACING WHEEL: use smooth or serrated tracing wheel with tracing paper for smooth knits or to mark linings or underlinings.

TAPES: *Scotch Magic Transparent Tape* is used to stay areas for machine stitching, to mark notches and dart lines, and to label the right or wrong side of fabric. *Zipper adhesive tape* (Simple Tape)† is sticky on both sides. Can be used when applying zippers or for "basting" seams.

TAPE-STITCH‡ is used as guide for topstitching, as basting for applying zippers and hems, to mark pivot points, for stay marking, measure for buttons and buttonholes, and as a guide for hand stitching.

MARKING PENCIL: soft, chalk-like pencil in red or blue for marking notches or labeling. The marks will wash out.

PINS OR A SCISSORS CLIP may also be used for marking. Small clips mark ends of darts, notches, gathering points, etc.

PRESSING:

STEAM IRON: for pressing darts, seams, and garment pressing. Use with a press-cloth on right side of garment.

IRONALL§: attachment made of Nomex (high-temperature-resistant nylon) which clips on to the sole plate of the iron. No press-cloth is needed and fabrics will not scorch.

BROWN PAPER STRIPS: are placed under darts and seams when pressing to prevent imprints on right side of garment. Also used

---

* Trace-a-Pattern—a tradename of Stacy Fabrics
† Simple Tape—a tradename of Risdon Mfg. Co.
‡ Tape-Stitch—a tradename of Belding Corticelli
§ Ironall—a tradename of Ultra

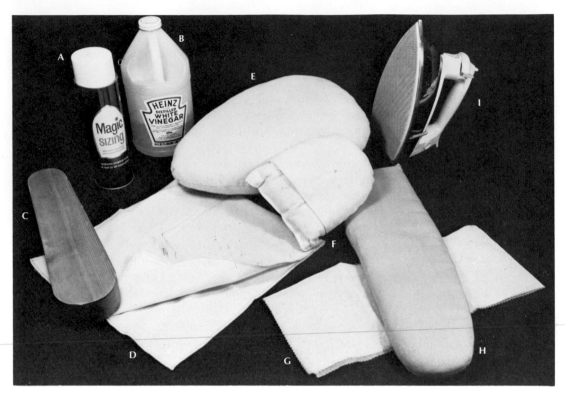

Fig. 3-7. *A,* fabric sizing; *B,* white vinegar; *C,* beater or clapper; *D,* wool/cotton press cloth; *E,* tailor's ham; *F,* press mitt; *G,* see-through press cloth; *H,* sleeve press pad; *I,* steam iron.

Fig. 3-8. *A,* shell hammer foot; *B,* blind hammer; *C,* roller presser foot; *D,* gathering foot.

on top of press-cloth (saturated with vinegar/water) when setting creases.

TAILOR'S HAM: used for pressing curved areas such as princess seams, bust darts, hip curves, etc.

PRESS MITT: fits over the hand for pressing small curved areas.

SEAM ROLL: long tubular cushion used for pressing sleeve seams, and long seams where seam imprint is a problem.

BEATER OR CLAPPER: block of wood used to flatten seam edges, particularly on wool-knit tailored garments.

SPRAY STARCH/FABRIC FINISH: used for spraying edges of knits which tend to curl.

WHITE VINEGAR: used in solution with water on press-cloth covered with brown paper to set creases.

CHEESECLOTH: several layers can be used as a press-cloth.

MACHINE ATTACHMENTS:

ROLLER-PRESSER FOOT: consists of two rollers on a hinge which roll over the fabric, allowing it to pass under needle without dragging. Excellent for spongy, loopy knits. The *Even-feed Foot* is an attachment designed by the Singer Company to feed the fabric through evenly.

BLIND HEMMER: the blind stitch may be built into the machine. The attachment assists in guiding the hems through the machine in a quick, even manner.

GATHERING FOOT: has a single hole and a slot to be used when gathering one piece of fabric and attaching it to another. The longer the stitch, the tighter the gathering. Used to make ruffles or for gathering edges.

SHELL HEMMER FOOT: rolls and hems the fabric in a shell-like pattern when using the zigzag stitch at 4 and the stitch length at 2.5–3. Used for sheer knits and tricots.

4

KNIT TRIMMINGS

SHAPINGS

Test all linings, underlinings, and interfacings with the fashion knit by holding them together over your arm. Check to see that they relate well to each other in color, texture, and care. There are many commercial products available at your fabric store—i.e., woven cotton/polyester, woven all-polyester, woven cottons, and organdy; *and*, nonwovens in various weights of polyester, bias or regular; fusibles in wovens and nonwovens; as well as canvas, either washable or dry-cleanable.

UNDERLININGS: when underlinings are used, knits lose their "give." Used for yokes or shaping areas which need to be stabilized. Also provide a backing for lacy or loose, bulky knits. Choose a product which is compatible with the fiber content of the fashion knit. Markings may be transferred to the underlining. Preshrink fabric.

INTERFACINGS: such areas as collars, cuffs, garment fronts, buttonholes, and edges are often interfaced. Interfacing adds stability, strength, body, and crispness. Used in hems to prevent ridges from showing. Available in either woven or nonwoven, fusible or nonfusible, and all-bias nonwoven. Hair canvas is used for coats and suits of wool, or garments which will be dry-cleaned. Washable woven cotton-polyester, or nonwoven all-bias featherweight or lightweight polyester, are suitable for washable polyester knits. There are fusibles in wovens or nonwovens for crisp areas like flaps, stand-up collars. A nonwoven fusible with crosswise stretch has been developed for coats and suits. One needs to check carefully that ridges do not show through on the right side of the fashion garment.

LININGS: some tailored coats, vests, and jackets are lined. If stretch is desired, choose a lightweight knit such as a tricot or a stabilized tricot for lining. A polyester crepe is also suitable. When using wovens as linings, allow a generous pleat (1½ inches at CB of garment). Preshrink washable linings.

STAYS: preshrink linen or cotton twill tape which is used for stays for seams. *Organdy* serves as a stay for bound buttonholes, gussets, etc.

POLYESTER FLEECE: polyester which resembles lamb's wool. Used for trapunto in hems and seam edges, shoulder shapes, and for sleeve pads or heading.

FASTENERS

SNAPS: available in metal, nylon (transparent or in colors), or silk-covered. Come in sizes 00–4. Larger sizes for coats, 2–4. May cover with lining fabric.

HOOKS AND EYES: metal in sizes 00–5. May work over fasteners with buttonhole twist. Large, flat, metal hook-and-eye closures are available to sew on, or there is a no-sewing variety with clamp in back. The latter is used for slacks, skirt waistbands, and men's pants.

BONNIE CLASP*: flat nylon closure which is sewn on by hand or machine. One side slips into the other and locks. Can be dyed, machine dried, and takes up to 40 lbs. of strain.

---

*   Bonnie clasp—a tradename of E-Z-Buckle, Inc.

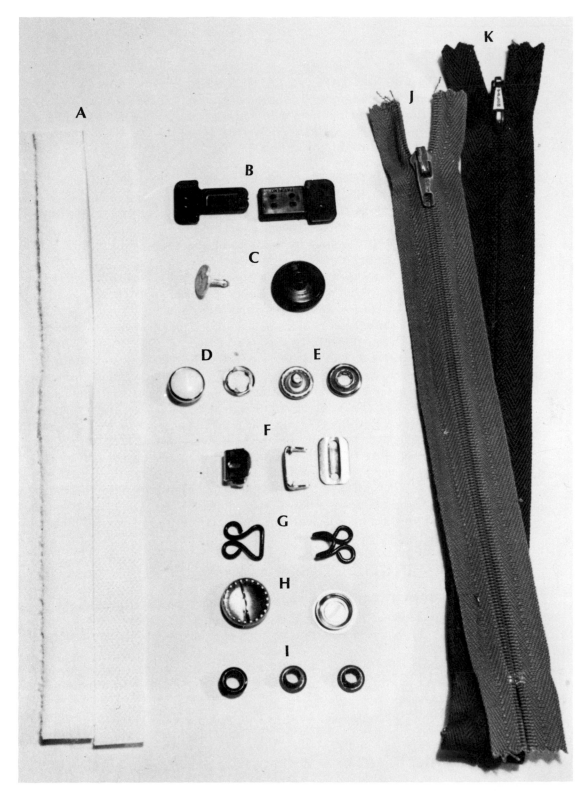

Fig. 4-1. *A*, iron-on self-closing hook and loop nylon tape; *B*, Bonnie Clasp; *C*, detachable button; *D*, gripper pearl snap fastener (*left*, pearl button; *right,* stud); *E*, gripper pearl snap fastener (*left*, pearl button; *right,* stud); *F*, hook and eye closure (no sewing); *G*, coat hook and eye; *H*, buttons to cover; *I*, eyelets; *J*, Eflon coil zipper; *K*, invisible zipper.

NYLON CLOSURE TAPE (VELCRO*): consists of two strips. On one side there are minute hooks and the other side has a pile or loops. Used for adjustable and wraparound closures; for removable collars; cuffs and trims; for maternity wear; to hold belts in place. The "hook" tape side is placed away from body. Available in type which is sewn on or ironed on.

DOT SNAP FASTENERS: may be hammered or attached with pliers. Are strong and durable and applied after garment is completed.

DOT SNAPPER BUTTONS: button attached to a dot snapper. No button-holes needed. Use for sportswear.

BUTTONSNAPP†: a cover-with-fabric button shell which is attached to a snap. No buttonholes are needed.

ZIPPERS: are available with flexible *nylon or polyester coil* in most fashion colors. Also come in lightweight or heavier metal. *Invisible* zippers have tape at the top with teeth or coils underneath. *Decorative* zippers come in colors, have coarse teeth and a decorative pull. The kind of zipper to choose depends on the use:

SKIRT OR NECKLINE: opens at one end with a bottom stop. Skirt zippers are 6 inches to 9 inches while neckline zippers run from 4 inches to 36 inches. *Invisible* zippers vary from 7 inches to 24 inches while *decorative* zippers come in a variety of lengths.

TROUSER ZIPPERS: open at waistline and are heavy duty. Range in length from 6 inches to 11 inches. Tapes are usually wider.

SEPARATING ZIPPER: opens at both ends. Usually 10–24 inches in length. Also available in reversible version.

ZIPPER MEDALLIONS: available in various designs to attach to zipper slider as a decorative feature.

EYELET: metal ring attached to garment. Used for prong of a buckle or for a lacing effect closure.

FINISHING SUPPLIES

STRETCH SEAM LACE: flexible narrow laces used for finishing hems.

SEAM TAPE: a new, soft rayon seam tape, guaranteed not to shrink, offers flexibility. It may be used for hems in stable knits and for staying seams.

TRIMS: braids, ribbing, knit polyester ribbons, laces in polyester, orlon, cotton, or wool. Choose color and fiber which will relate to fabric. Pre-shrink.

BELTING: stiffening available in different widths which is covered with self-knit. For length, encircle your waist with the belting and add 7–9 inches extra for finishing and extension.

ELASTIC: skirt elastic in ¾ to 1 inch widths is used for waistbands. May substitute ¾-inch swimsuit elastic. *Wide decorative elastic trim,* available

---

* Velcro—a tradename of Scovill Manufacturing Company.
† Buttonsnapp—a tradename of William Pryn, Inc.

for waistbands, may also be used for sweater ribbing, belts, cuffs, and for knickers.

WEIGHTS: assist in the draping of knit fabric. Round lead weights are covered with a square of fabric and tacked inside the neckline or hemline, wherever needed. Lead strips are encased in fabric and sold by the yard. Chain weights are attached along the facing or hemline of jackets.

5

PREPARING TO SEW

PREPARATION OF THE KNIT FABRIC

POINTS TO REMEMBER ABOUT KNITS:
- Knits have a lengthwise rib, or wales, and crosswise courses.
- Knits have more *crosswise "give"* than lengthwise. The diagonal does not necessarily possess the greatest stretch.
- *A thread cannot be pulled to straighten*—as with woven fabrics— as knits do not have warp and filling yarns interlaced.

STRAIGHTENING KNIT FABRICS:
WOOL DOUBLE KNITS AND JERSEYS:
- Can be straightened by steaming and pulling. Polyester knits are "fixed" permanently during finishing, so cannot be squared by pulling on diagonal.

TUBULAR KNITS:
- Run a hand basting on a lengthwise rib.
- Cut along a lengthwise rib.
- Some patterns are designed for tubular knits, so fabric is used in "tube" form.

FLAT KNITS:
- Run a hand basting on lengthwise rib.
- Fold right side out on lengthwise rib. Square ends and baste ends together for preshrinking.

BONDED KNITS:
- Straighten by running a hand basting on rib on "face" fabric.

SQUARING THE ENDS:
- Square ends by running lengthwise rib on side of table and "square" the end of fabric on the end of the table.

or
- "L"-square may be used by running the long arm on lengthwise rib and the other arm at the end of the fabric for squaring.

or
- Cutting board may be used by pinning knit to vertical and horizontal line markings on board.

PRESHRINKING:

Read the label on the bolt or included with the purchase of the knit fabric. If it doesn't state that fabric is preshrunk and it is washable, wash it.

100 PERCENT POLYESTER:
- Launder in gentle wash cycle with warm water and mild detergent.
- Dry on low or warm temperature in dryer. May spray dryer drum, before loading, with anti-static fabric softener to prevent static build-up.
- Usually need not press.

100 PERCENT WOOL:
- Have preshrunk by dry cleaner.

or
- London-shrink (roll in damp towel or sheet).

COTTON KNITS:
- Have a tendency to shrink so machine wash and dry. May desire to wash twice.
- Wash unless labels indicate less than one percent shrinkage.

OTHER WASHABLE KNITS:
- Wash unless labels indicate less than one percent shrinkage.
- Generally *rib* trims are not preshrunk before cutting as they become relaxed and difficult to handle. It is also hard to determine stretchability.

PREPARING KNIT FOR PATTERN LAYOUT:
- Steam press if necessary. Test press fold line. If the creases cannot be removed, refold fabric.
- Allow the fabric to "relax" flat on the cutting table for 24 hours to regain normal dimension. Knits may be stretched slightly on the bolts.

LAYOUT OF PATTERN ON FABRIC

It is as important in knits as it is in woven fabrics that the pattern be cut "on the grain" or on the lengthwise rib. Secondly, the most "give" is usually placed crosswise on the garment, except for active sports wear such as ski pants and jumpsuits where lengthwise stretch is important.
- Check to see that you have chosen the *correct pattern pieces* for the garment you are making.
- Check to see that you have chosen the *correct layout* for *type of knit fabric* you are using. Some patterns include views for both stable and stretchable knits.

Introducing...the NEW PICK-A-KNIT Rule™

on SIZED FOR STRETCH KNITS ONLY Patterns

A PICK-A-KNIT Rule™ on the back of the pattern envelope shows you how much stretch is needed for that particular pattern.

TEST STRETCH HERE

Simplicity groups unbonded knits into three general degrees of stretchability. Each "SIZED FOR STRETCH KNITS ONLY" pattern is based on knit fabrics that fall into one of these groups. A PICK-A-KNIT Rule™ on the back of the pattern envelope shows you how much stretch is needed for that pattern.

| PICK-A-KNIT RULE ™ | FOR THIS PATTERN—4″ OF KNIT FABRIC MUST STRETCH CROSSWISE FROM HERE ➤ | ▲ AT LEAST TO HERE |

LIMITED STRETCH
— 4″ stretches to 4¾″ (approximately 18% stretch) Garments made from this least amount of stretch will have zipper or button openings. The stretch is sufficient only for wearing comfort and closer fit.

| PICK-A-KNIT RULE ™ | FOR THIS PATTERN—4″ OF KNIT FABRIC MUST STRETCH CROSSWISE FROM HERE ➤ | ▲ AT LEAST TO HERE |

MODERATE STRETCH
— 4″ stretches to 5″ (approximately 25% stretch) This type of knit can be used for pull-on, or pull-over, styles and will be more closely fitted to the body.

| PICK-A-KNIT RULE ™ | FOR THIS PATTERN—4″ OF KNIT FABRIC MUST STRETCH CROSSWISE FROM HERE ➤ | AT LEAST TO HERE ➤ |

VERY STRETCHY
— 4″ stretches to 6″ (approximately 50% stretch) These knits are used for garments that have "body fit" — skinny "sweater" fashions, all-in-one bodysuits and swimsuits.

The New Revised Simplicity Sewing Book tells you all about the new PICK-A-KNIT Rule™ —and all about sewing knits.

How to Use Simplicity's PICK-A-KNIT Rule™

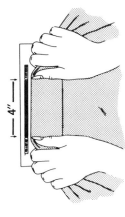

1 Place crosswise grain of knit fabric below the PICK-A-KNIT Rule™, away from the cut edge of fabric, as shown.

2 Hold fabric with thumbs at each end of the 4″ area.

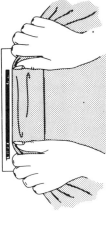

3 Keeping left thumb anchored firmly, stretch fabric gently with right hand to end of rule.

4 If fabric stretches to at least the end of the rule, your knit is suitable for the pattern. Your knit may stretch slightly beyond the rule and still be suitable.

(Courtesy of Simplicity Pattern Co., Inc.)

- Fold fabric *right side out.*
- If *fabric curls,* such as stretch terry, jersey, and tricot, lay pattern on *wrong side* of knit fabric.
- Place fabric on a *flat surface.* Do not allow the fabric to hang off the end of the table. Roll or fold on end to avoid stretching. Fold fabric as you proceed with the layout. Unfold as you cut. Cutting boards, table pads, or an old sheet taped to a table may serve as suitable surfaces for pattern and fabric layout.
- If fabric is *lightweight and smooth,* pin fabric to *tissue paper* before pinning on pattern pieces, then cut through fabric and tissue paper.
- Check carefully for *nap* or one-way reflection on knit. Most knits, including novelty knits, plaids or checks, should be cut with all pieces in one direction.
- Panne and velour should be cut "with nap" layout. When the nap runs down, the fabric appears shiny; when the nap runs up, the color is "richer."
- Check to see if knit fabric will *run or "ladder"* by pulling gently on crosswise-cut edge. If it does, place "laddering" edge at bottom of garment.
- Check *"grain"* line carefully, measuring from basting on lengthwise rib, *not the selvages,* as the selvages are not always even.
- *Pin with sharp pins* to avoid snagging. *Ballpoint pins* or fine dressmaker pins are a must. T-pins are handy for bulky or lacy open knits. May use *pattern holder* spray on pattern.
- *Pin* within dart or seam line. To prevent knit fabric from curling, place pins at right angles to seams.
- On *tubular knits* which have stripes or patterns, place pattern so fabric looks straight in the front. It will be "slightly off" in the back.
- If the fabric stretches about the *same amount in both directions,* place on either crosswise or lengthwise rib.
- For special effects, place fabric on bias.
- When *matching plaids or stripes,* it may be necessary to open fabric to a single layer for layout and cutting. Pattern pieces designed to be placed on the fold often comprise only half a garment section. To facilitate matching during layout, cut entire pattern section out of brown or tissue paper. On *side seams,* match from the bottom up as seams will not match from dart to armscye.

CUTTING KNIT FABRICS

Use *sharp shears* which are heavy enough for the type of knit. A sharp, dressmaker bent-handle shears is satisfactory. Some companies are manufacturing special blades on shears with serrated edges for cutting knits. One company has designed new shears with a high bent handle which cuts without lifting the fabric. Some electric scissors are very satisfactory for cutting knits.

Cut the seam edges straight and even, cutting the notches outward. Some seamstresses prefer to cut all the edges straight and mark notches afterwards with chalk or transparent tape, or by a small clip into the seamline. *Do not cut with pinking shears.*

To save time in trimming and grading seams, may cut all seam edges which will be faced ¼ inch, i.e., neckline and armscye. If a sleeve is to be set into armscye, cut regular seam allowance.

[Note: Run blades frequently between fingers to remove lint.

The oil from fingers will aid in preventing static.]

MARKING KNIT FABRICS

Transparent adhesive tape is a must for the knit seamstress. Mark the right side of the fabric pieces. You can write on the tape with a ballpoint pen. It may be removed easily without damaging the fabric. Place along dart-stitching lines and mark notches, circles, X's, and V's on a square of the tape.

Chalk or pins may also be used for marking. Avoid wax chalk, except on wool knits, as stains may be left on fabric when pressing.

Tracing paper and tracing wheels may be used on some smooth, flat knits. If the garment is underlined, place markings on underlining using the tracing wheel and tracing paper.

For textured knits, *tailor's tacks* work well.

STAY-STITCHING KNITS

The use of stay-stitching for knits should not be overdone. Stay-stitch necklines, waistline seams, and the armscye for sleeveless garments. Stay-stitch at about 12 stitches per inch, usually from seamline to CF or CB.

On sleeveless armscyes, stitch from the shoulder down and on "V"-necklines or deep scoop necklines, stitch from center front toward shoulder.

Transparent adhesive tape may be used to "stay-stitch" or stay corners or "V's" instead of machine stay-stitching.

[Note: Advocates of trade or speed sewing of knits, who have experience in "cutting to fit" and handling knits, rarely do any stay-stitching or basting. They have learned how to feed the fabric into the machine. You, too, can do this with a little practice!]

BASTING UP KNIT GARMENTS

For most sportswear, basting is not necessary; however, on your "better" dresses and slacks of double-knit polyester or wool, you may wish to baste to check fit.

Place garment flat on table. Place pins horizontal to seam at ends and center of seam, then pin at intervals inbetween. Fasten basting with small stitches, basting from top down. Allow thread to remain a little loose for "give." Speed basting by machine may also be used.

HANDLING SPECIFIC FABRICS

Some knits, because of their nature or personality, require a degree of special handling.

SWEATER KNITS:
- Stretch freely in both directions, so the knit clings to the body.
- Choose a pattern designed "for knits only"—i.e., turtlenecks, long sleeveless vests, cardigan sweaters, and flared pants. May underline for a couture look. Avoid bound buttonholes and circular skirts. Elastic casing is usually better than a waistband.
- When fitting the pattern, allow pattern to equal only the body measurements—the ease will come from the knit fabric.
- Stay-stitch ¼ inch from seam edge using 12 stitches per inch (s.p.i.). May stitch over paper the quality of newsprint. Tear away after stitching.
- Machine-stitch with a zigzag stitch .5–1 stitch width and a stitch length of 20 s.p.i. using ballpoint needle. If using straight stitch, stitch 15 s.p.i. Overlock or overedge stitch may also be used.
- Seams may be supported by stitching a matching yarn in the seam or a ⅛-inch soft elastic or a tape. Yarn may be used to finish pressed-open plain seams also.
- Taffeta facings help eliminate bulk.
- Loops, zippers, or machine buttonholes are desirable closures.
- Press over terry-cloth towel with a soft press-cloth to avoid flattening. Allow to dry before handling.

WET-LOOK NYLON TRICOT:
- Fit and alter pattern carefully as seams cannot be ripped because needle marks remain in the fabric.
- Preshrink fabric.
- When cutting, fold fabric with right sides together. Use weights, or pin in the seam allowance.
- Mark with chalk on wrong side.
- Machine stitch 12 s.p.i., applying slight tension. Stitch with shiny side down.
- Does not ravel, so plain or welt seams may be used.
- Press with warm, dry iron.

SINGLE-KNIT JERSEY:
- Avoid circular skirts. Wool and cotton jerseys drape well, but synthetic jerseys may pucker at the seams.
- Edges may roll and fabric is slippery. Cover cutting table with sheet of tissue paper. Pin fabric to it.
- Stitch with a fine ballpoint needle with 12 s.p.i. Use a small, round-hole throat plate if using straight stitch. Stitch ⅛ inch from cut edge to prevent curling or use a knit seam.

- Stay waistline, shoulder, and elbows of long sleeves with pre-shrunk tape.
- On synthetic jerseys, use machine-worked buttonholes rather than bound buttonholes.
- Hems may be catch stitched or fused.

STRETCH KNITS:

- Use lengthwise stretch for slacks; crosswise for blouses, skirts, or dresses, and two-way stretch for bathing suits and ski pants.
- Choose a pattern with slim, simple lines and according to specific type of stretch.
- Relax fabric 24 hours before cutting.
- In layout, be sure stretch is going in correct direction.
- Use medium pressure for stitching. Reinforce seams with second row of stitching unless a stretch stitch is used.
- Stabilize neck, shoulder, and waistline areas.
- Stay buttonhole area. Do not stretch while applying zippers.

TUBULAR KNITS:

- Available in rib, puckered, and popcorn stitches of cotton, nylon, rayon, or blends with polyester or acrylics.
- Use a roller-presser foot or wide-presser foot and a sharp, fine, ballpoint needle.
- Special patterns are available for 10-inch or 11-inch tubular knits, thus eliminating side seams.
- When cutting, allow fabric to relax, and "stick" with pins to cutting board.
- Use zigzag on seams. Stretch a little in front and back of needle.
- Stabilize shoulder seams except in tank tops.
- Clean-finish with a "quickie" edge finish (Chapter 11, p. 71) the armscye and neck edge of tank tops. Gently stretch from shoulder to about one inch above underarm. Stretch in underarm area. Do not stretch in finishing the scoop neck.
- May finish neck and armscye with ribbing, or finish the neck as a turtleneck.

STRETCH TERRY:

- Be sure to launder before cutting.
- Use heavier shears for cutting.
- Wrap presser toes with magic transparent tape or stitch with roller-presser foot.
- Stitched overedged seams or flat-felled seams are appropriate.
- Handle like sweater knits.

FAKE-FUR KNITS:

- Select pattern designated for deep pile or buy a size larger pattern.
- Cut with nap, with fur running downward. Cut pieces singly. Cut facings onto garment, eliminating seams. Use heavy shears or razor blade cutter to cut through backing.
- Use size 14 or 16 needle and cotton/polyester-core thread.

- Adjust pressure on machine to about 10 s.p.i. Do test stitching.
- Press open plain seams. (Low temperature, please!) May catch stitch seam flat on inside and shear off pile (fur).
- Some fake-fur knits have a design on the knit backing which is used for the right side, with the fur on the inside. Use welt seams for these garments.
- Tape shoulder and neckline seams.
- Hair canvas or medium-weight canvas may be used as interfacing.
- Hems may be faced with a bias piece of lining fabric or satin, as in fur coats.
- Loops, toggles, or leather fasteners are popular closures although buttonholes can be made.

BONDED KNITS:

- Usually a single knit stabilized with acetate or tricot backing. Most of natural stretch is eliminated.
- Be sure to check if knit is bonded "on grain."
- Treat as a firm double knit in sewing.

6

KNITS AND THE SEWING MACHINE

The home-sewing industry in America has grown into a booming business. Partly responsible—at least for the success of sewing with knits— has been the import of foreign home-sewing machines allowed after World War II. The new, improved machines make it possible to stitch knits without skipped stitches and "thread jams." There has been a trend, also, in sewing with knits to really "use" the home-sewing machine for something more than a straight stitch; the use of the blind machine hem, monograms, zigzag and stretch stitches, overlock and serge stitches, speed basting, presser-foot gathering, and shell edging will be referred to in this book. It is important, then, to learn how to use your sewing machine to take advantage of its new, improved flexibility.

One reason there have been problems in sewing knits on some machines is that knits contain more yarns than wovens and therefore possess more fabric density. Also, some knits "give" more than others while other knits follow the needle, holding so closely to it, that they prevent the top thread from forming the loop necessary for the bottom thread to hook into, in order to form a stitch. Another problem is that some knits resist the penetration of the needle and the needle pushes the fabric into the needle hole, forming a bubble and thread jam. Even after preshrinking or laundering a knit, some finishes may remain to coat the needle and keep the thread from feeding evenly. Knowing and understanding these problems can help you overcome them so that knits can be sewn successfully on almost any home-sewing machine.

CARE OF YOUR SEWING MACHINE

Clean and oil sewing machine often as knits will drop more lint and granules into the machine than wovens. Use a brush for cleaning. Oil lightly and wipe machine clean with cheesecloth or soft cloth. *Run machine to work in the oil.* Wipe off thread guides. Clean feed dog, bobbin case, and presser bar thoroughly. Check with your sewing-machine instruction book for points to oil.

Some brands of machines need no oiling, merely cleaning.

SELECTION AND CARE OF SEWING MACHINE NEEDLES

Choose the needle size that is compatible to the thickness of the fabric (consider also seams to be crossed) and the diameter of the thread to be used. Fine-knit fabrics use fine needles and heavier knit fabrics use heavier needles.

The U.S. sizes of needles are size 15 x 1:

9
11 } tricots, synthetic jerseys

14   cotton jersey, double knits

16
18 } power net, heavy knits, swimsuit fabrics

The European sizes of needles are size 705:

60
70 } comparable to U.S. 9

80   "   11

90   "   14

100   "   16

110   "   18

See "Guide to Needle Selection"—White Sewing Machine Company, and "Needle, Thread, Fabric Stitching Guide"—White Sewing Machine Company, page 34.

Sharp-pointed needles may pierce and cut the yarns. A ballpoint needle tends to separate the yarns when stitching. A golden ballpoint is safer for delicate fabrics. The elongated scarf of the needle eliminates skipped stitches.

For sewing knit-backed vinyl, use a 15 x 2 wedge-point needle.

The coarser the fabric, the more rounded the ballpoints should be.

A GUIDE TO NEEDLE SELECTION

The correct selection of needle to suit the thread and fabric being sewn results in more satisfactory stitching. Fine fabrics should be sewn with fine needles, heavier fabrics with heavier needles. For best results, sewing machine needles should be replaced when they become even slightly dull or bent or at the completion of every other garment.

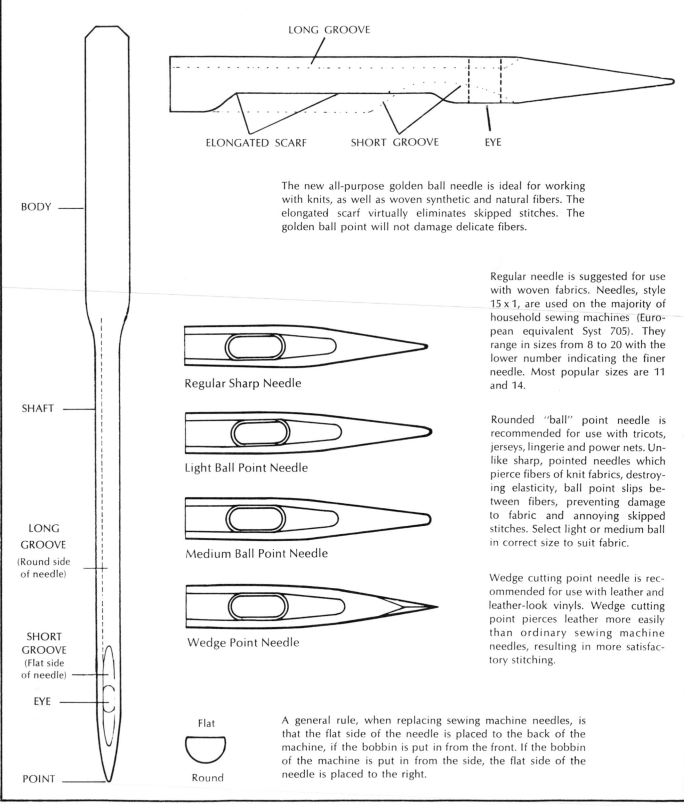

The new all-purpose golden ball needle is ideal for working with knits, as well as woven synthetic and natural fibers. The elongated scarf virtually eliminates skipped stitches. The golden ball point will not damage delicate fibers.

Regular needle is suggested for use with woven fabrics. Needles, style 15 x 1, are used on the majority of household sewing machines (European equivalent Syst 705). They range in sizes from 8 to 20 with the lower number indicating the finer needle. Most popular sizes are 11 and 14.

Rounded "ball" point needle is recommended for use with tricots, jerseys, lingerie and power nets. Unlike sharp, pointed needles which pierce fibers of knit fabrics, destroying elasticity, ball point slips between fibers, preventing damage to fabric and annoying skipped stitches. Select light or medium ball in correct size to suit fabric.

Wedge cutting point needle is recommended for use with leather and leather-look vinyls. Wedge cutting point pierces leather more easily than ordinary sewing machine needles, resulting in more satisfactory stitching.

A general rule, when replacing sewing machine needles, is that the flat side of the needle is placed to the back of the machine, if the bobbin is put in from the front. If the bobbin of the machine is put in from the side, the flat side of the needle is placed to the right.

(Courtesy of White Sewing Machine Company)

One company has designed a special needle for knits for their machine to prevent skipped stitches.

MACHINE NEEDLE PROBLEMS

BENT NEEDLE: can be caused by hitting a pin, the presser foot, or a hard-to-penetrate seam; pulling on fabric; or by changing stitch setting when the needle is down in the fabric. This causes skipped stitches or makes the fabric pull sideways during stitching.

BLUNT NEEDLE: caused from penetrating firm, closely knit synthetic of polyester or nylon. The point becomes burred which causes snags and breaks the yarns.

OUT-OF-SET NEEDLE: caused by hard-to-penetrate seams or by using too fine a needle for the weight of the fabric. To test for an out-of-set needle, place flat side of body of needle on a flat surface. The shaft of the needle should be parallel to flat surface. Out-of-set needles will cause skipped stitches.

COATED NEEDLES: caused by heat generated from stitching or by finishing solution applied to the knits for permanent press or stabilizing. Results in skipped stitches. Clean by running the needle through an emery, or wiping with a clean cloth moistened with sewing machine oil. Wipe out long groove carefully.

or

Run a commercially prepared needle conditioner pad under the needle several times to clean shaft and improve needlepoint.

MACHINE-STITCHING KNITS

TEST STITCH on a scrap of fashion fabric to check for balanced stitch.

FOR STRAIGHT STITCHING: use a straight-stitch presser foot and throat plate (small hole).

TEST STITCH FOR TENSION: stitch diagonally using 12 stitches per inch on two layers of knit. Check the stitches which should be balanced (alike on both sides). If the stitches appear puckered, shorten the stitch length. If not balanced, give a quick pull on the stitching line. If the thread on top of fabric appears straight and tight and the needle thread breaks, *loosen* needle-thread tension. If the thread on underside appears straight and tight, *tighten* the needle-thread tension. Test again. Many machines need no tension adjustment for any type of knit.

TEST PRESSURE: Usually a normal or regular setting is correct. To test for pressure, stitch without thread on two layers of 12-inch lengthwise strips. If the layers come out uneven, lessen the pressure.

WHEN BEGINNING TO SEW: pull the bobbin-needle threads parallel to each other, and to the right and slightly to the back of the presser foot.

• Place the needle into the fabric about ⅜–½ inch from the end of the fabric, then lower the presser foot. Hold the thread ends for a couple of stitches. Continue to support the seam by holding the

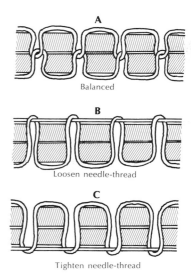

A

Balanced

B

Loosen needle-thread

C

Tighten needle-thread

Fig. 6-1. Test stitch for tension.

NEEDLE · THREAD

Consult this chart whenever a different type of fabric is to be stitched.

The correct selection of needle and thread to suit the fabric will result in more satisfactory stitching. Fine fabrics should be stitched with fine needles, fine thread and short stitches.

TYPE OF FABRIC	MACHINE NEEDLES			
	Size		Point Style	
	U.S. 15x1	Eur. 705	Ball	Leather 15x2NTW
Very Sheer—lace, net, chiffon, batiste, organdy.	09	60		
Nylon tricot, tulle.			Light 10	
Sheer—lawn, blouse and silk crepe, taffeta, voile.	9-11	60-70		
Dress Weight—crepe, velvet, brocades.	11	70		
Sheer wool.	11	70		
Cotton jersey, polyester, double knit.	11	70	Light 12	
Dress leatherette.				16
Medium—wool and silk suitings, shantung, linen, piqué, faille.	14	80		
Knits.			Med. 10	
Medium Heavy—draperies, terrycloth, velveteens, corduroy, felt.	16	90		
Leather, suedes.				18
Heavy—denim, oilcloth, sailcloth.	18	100		
Velours, fake fur.	18	100		
Extremely Heavy—heavy duck, canvas, awning, upholstery.	21	110		
Heavy leather.				18
Elastic Fabric—power net—light swim suits.			Med. 10-12	
Corset, girdle fabric.			Med. 12	
Decorative.	11-14	70-80		
	16	90		
	09	60		
	14	80		

FABRIC · STITCHING GUIDE

For good results on heavier fabrics, use coarser needles, heavier threads and longer stitches. Replace the machine needle when it becomes even slightly dull or bent.

Thread and needle sizes for various kinds and weights of fabrics.

APPROX. MACHINE STITCHES PER INCH	HAND NEEEDLES	THREAD				ATTACHMENTS
		Cotton	Mercerized	Synthetic	Silk	
16-18	10	120	50-60		A	
16-18	10		50-60	Yes		Roller Foot
14	10	100-120	50			
12	9		50			
12	9		50		A	
12	9			Yes		
14	8		Heavy-duty			Roller Foot
12	7-8		50		A	
12-14	8		50	Yes		Roller Foot
10	6-7		Heavy-duty			Roller Foot
8	3-4		Heavy-duty			Roller Foot
10	4-5	30-40	Heavy-duty			
10	4-5		Heavy-duty			Roller Foot
8	3-4	10-30	Heavy-duty			
6-8	3		Heavy-duty	Yes		Roller Foot
12-14	9			Yes		Roller Foot
8-10	5-6		Heavy-duty	Yes		Roller Foot
			Embroidery Thread 50-70			
			Buttonhole Twist		D	
			Darning Thread			
			Metallic Thread			

(Courtesy of White Sewing Machine Company)

left hand in the back and the right hand in front of the needle, applying slight tension or firmness.
- Stitch at a moderately even speed.
- On some knit fabric and some machines, a piece of tissue paper may be placed between the feed dog and the knit. This protects the fabric from snagging and moves it under the feed dog more smoothly. Tear away tissue after stitching.

MACHINE STITCHES FOR KNITS should provide a seam that will elongate or give with the fabric unless it is a stable seam which is stayed. Smaller stitches build more thread into the knit per inch, therefore more stretch.

A GUIDE FOR INTERPRETING THE METRIC SYSTEM MACHINE STITCH LENGTHS:

    1—18–20 stitches per inch
    2—12–16 '' '' ''
    3— 8–10 '' '' ''
    4— 5–6   '' '' ''

There are a wide *variety of stitches* appropriate for knit seams:
 STRAIGHT STITCH: used for plain seams and knit seams.
 NARROW ZIGZAG: used for plain seams and knit seams.
 WIDER ZIGZAG: used for finishing seams.
 OVEREDGE or OVERLOCK: used for finishing, or for a seam which is stitched and finished in one operation.
 BLIND STITCH: used for finishing, applying zippers, and when guided to the left, is used as an overedge or imitation serge.
 STRETCH STITCHES: variety of stretch stitches on different machines—i.e., straight stretch, three-step zigzag, multistretch, feather stitch, etc.
 CHAIN STITCH: used for basting and stay-stitching.

MACHINE ACCESSORIES

A roller-presser foot works well on loosely constructed knits such as sweater knits, raschel, and novelty-yarn knits.
- A piece of magic transparent tape wound around the toes of a regular presser foot may serve as a substitute for a roller foot.
- Some machines have an attachment called a "Dual Feed," an "Even Feed," or a "Match-Maker" foot which substitutes for the roller-pressure foot. These attachments perform a hold-and-lift action, eliminating skipped stitches, and feed fabric evenly with proper tension.
- Do not use a zigzag attachment as it has a tendency to "grab" lightweight knits or jerseys and tricots.
- Some of the presser feet which are handy for machine sewing on knits are: gathering-presser foot, shell hemmer, button-presser foot, zipper foot, buttonhole foot, and blind stitch foot.

Study your machine manual; be creative and learn to use your machine to the utmost for your knit sewing!

7

STITCHING
SEAMS AND DARTS; PRESSING

Knits possess resiliency and stretch—some more than others. To avoid "popped" seams, stretch must be built into the seams. This may be accomplished in several ways: by using a thread which possesses elasticity such as polyester, nylon, or cotton-covered polyester or silk; by stretching the fabric slightly and thereby building thread into the stitch; or by using an automatic stretch stitch on the sewing machine. A *smooth, non-puckered seam, before and after laundering a knit garment,* is essential.

Before stitching seams on the machine, test on a scrap of fashion fabric. Check to see that you have a balanced tension. Looser knits require about 8 or 9 stitches per inch and firmer knits 10 to 12 stitches per inch.

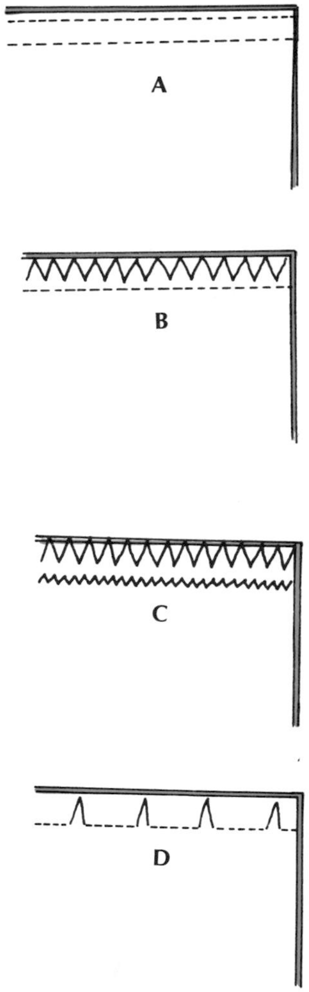

STITCHES FOR SEAMS

A "knit seam" is constructed using two rows of straight stitch approximately ¼ inch apart, stretching the fabric as it is sewn. Trim seam allowance close to second row of stitching. (See Fig. 7-1, A.)

Stitch a row of straight stitch, stretching fabric slightly as sewn. Trim to ¼ inch and zigzag or overedge the two raw edges together. (See Fig. 7-1, B.)

A narrow zigzag with a stitch length of 12–16 stitches per inch provides a stretch seam. May overcast raw edges with a large zigzag or overedge. (See Fig. 7-1, C.)

Many machines offer an automatic stretch stitch. Some have an overedge, overlock, or serge stitch which stitches the seam and finishes the edge in one operation. (See Fig. 7-1, D.)

REGULAR SEAM: on double knits, particularly on skirt and pant seams, a ⅝-inch seam allowance may be used. Stitch with a regular stitch while stretching. Press seams open. The seams need not be finished.

NARROW SEAM: is suitable for children's clothes, sportswear, hand knits, and raschel open knits, or when seams are to be pressed in one direction. Also on jerseys, tricots, and fabrics which curl.

STITCHED AND PULLED SEAM: used on lightweight knits as tricots and jerseys. The tension is looser. Allow 4 inches of thread at end of seam. With fingers, ease excess thread into seam, stretching small distances at a time.

GRADING SEAMS: enclosed seams on collars, cuffs, and facings are graded or layered. This refers to trimming off the seams leaving the seam

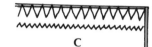

Fig. 7-1. Stitches for knit seams.

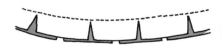

Fig. 7-2. Grading and clipping seams.

Fig. 7-3. Taping seam.

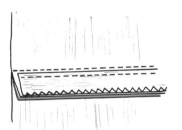

Fig. 7-4. Taping seam after construction.

which is uppermost the widest—i.e., in a front facing, the garment seam is wider than the facing seam.

CLIPPING SEAMS: enclosed curves are clipped to prevent a "pulled" appearance. Clipping at various intervals gives more strength to seamline.

STAYING SEAMS: preshrunk linen tape, cotton tape, or seam binding may be stitched into the seam, catching one edge on the seam allowance, with the bulk of the tape toward the garment. To apply tape after the seam has been constructed, stitch one edge close to the seam allowance and the outer edge with a zigzag stitch. The back of neck or shoulder seams on cotton and tricot knits may be stayed with self-fabric strip. (See p. 136.)

SKIVING SEAMS: to remove bulk on seam, cut edge of heavy knits; hold shears as flat as possible to cut edge and trim off very close to edge. This bevels the edge on an angle and is called "skiving."

SEAM TID-BITS: when stitching *shoulder seam,* place the back shoulder seam against the feed dog to ease onto seam. When a ⅝-inch seam allowance is used, trim *armscye-sleeve seam* to ⅜ inch on top half, ¼ inch on lower half, finishing edges if desired with overedge or zigzag stitch. Control *bias seams* with tape—i.e., neckline, shoulder, waistline.

DARTS

Stitch from *widest to narrowest* part using a straight stitch. Stitch along the fold on just a couple of threads at end of dart, allowing machine to run off and chain. Cut thread about 2–2½ inches long and tie in a loop knot. Cut end, leaving ½ inch.

- Slash darts to about ¼ inch from point and press open for heavy double knits.
- In medium-weight knits, *slash dart on fold line.* Remove some fabric from top of dart by "layering" and "skiving."
- Clip contour waistline darts to prevent "pulled" look.
- On some garments the fabric allowed for the *dart* may be *eased* onto the other seam allowance—i.e., elbow dart, bust dart, back shoulder dart. Stitch a stay of seam tape on the straight seam allowance in the dart area. Pin-ease the dart fullness in the marked dart area. Stitch seam as usual.

PRESSING

The fiber content of the knit fabric determines the temperature of the setting on the steam iron for pressing. Always press, not "iron," fabric so as not to distort the fabric. Press lightly in *lengthwise* direction with lifting and lowering motion. Handle carefully to avoid stretching.

- Place strips of brown paper under seam allowances and darts to *prevent imprints* on the fashion fabrics.
- Use moist cheesecloth, if *additional steam* is needed. Use synthetic setting for synthetics.

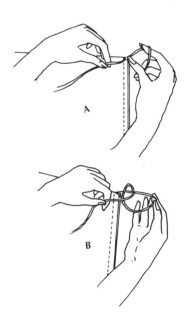

Fig. 7-5. Tying a loop knot.

- When pressing on the right side, use a press cloth to *prevent iron-shine or flattening* the surface texture.
- If knit *fabric shines,* allow steam to penetrate only on seams and finger press.
- On *soft knits with cashmere,* allow the iron to barely touch the fabric. Steam and pat into shape so as not to flatten texture. Allow to dry thoroughly before handling.
- An aid to *pressing* is an *attachment* the shape of the bottom of the iron, constructed of a material developed by the aerospace industry. No press-cloth is needed and the heat is spread evenly, using a temperature setting between cotton and wool for most fabrics.
- *Press* seams flat after stitching *along the stitching line* with the steam iron and/or damp press-cloth. Then press seam open or to one side if the seam is narrow.
- If *seams curl*—i.e., cotton knit—spray with spray starch or a fabric finish. Then press in one direction and machine-stitch the two raw edges together.
- *Press darts* along stitching line first. Then press open or in the proper direction. Shape by pressing over a press mitt or tailor's ham.
- Press *narrow seams* to one side, away from front of garment.
- To remove *imprint of hems,* run tip of iron under hem on wrong side of garment since stitches are set back ¼ inch from cut edge of hem.
- Remember to *press as you sew.* Always press before crossing with another seam. However, to save time, do as much sewing as possible before going to the ironing board.
- To *set a crease,* saturate and wring out a press-cloth in a solution of vinegar and water. Place saturated press-cloth on knit with brown paper on top. Press, applying pressure. This technique may also be used for removing creases. (Not permanent-press finishes.)

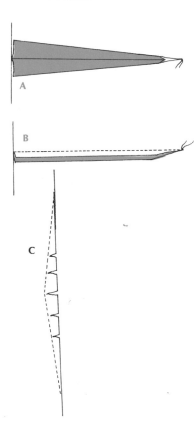

Fig. 7-6. Constructing darts.

8

POCKETS

Most of the traditional methods used for pocket making—such as the welt, patch, bound, and flap pockets—may be used for knits. However, there are some unique methods adapted from the trade which are usable for home sewing on knits.

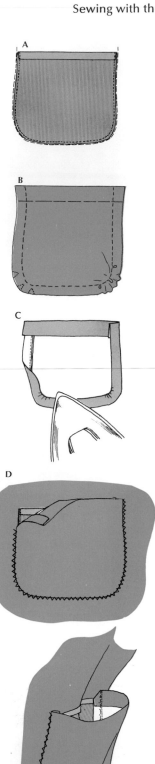

First, do familiarize yourself with the terms used by professionals in pocket making. The *mouthline* is the opening of the pocket. A *stay* is a piece of fabric placed on the wrong side of the garment to strengthen the mouthline. The *upper-pocket pouch (lining)* is the portion of the finished pocket which lies against the garment. The *underpocket pouch (lining)* is the portion which lies against the lining or the wearer of the garment. A pocket *facing* is a piece of garment fabric attached to the pocket lining so that the garment fabric shows when the pocket is used, rather than the lining.

If one is certain of the pocket location, it is much easier to complete the pocket while the garment is flat.

LINED PATCH POCKET

This patch pocket is attached with the stitching on the inside, a common method used in the trade. If desired, topstitching may be added. *Topstitching* is particularly desirable to cover the raw edges if the pocket is *unlined.* The lined pocket is used for jackets and sports coats, and the unlined for knit sportswear.

MARK POCKET LOCATION:

- Mark accurately with a basting the exact location of the pocket on the garment.

ATTACH LINING TO GARMENT:

- Cut the lining the size of the finished pocket from tricot or a stabilized nylon—i.e., Underknit.* Use the pocket pattern piece minus seam allowances.
- Turn back ½–¾ inch across the top of the pocket lining toward the wrong side of the lining.
- Place the right side of the lining on the right side of the garment, easing the outer edge slightly (⅟₁₆–⅛ inch) *inside* of the finished pocket marking on the garment. (See Fig. 8-1, A.)
- Stitch with a regular machine stitch close to the raw edge of the lining. The stitching will be *inside* the pocket marking. Because the stitching is close to the raw edge, lining fabrics which ravel easily are not suitable.

ATTACH POCKET: METHOD A

- Turn back the hem on the pocket toward the wrong side of the garment.
- Machine baste around the pocket at a little less than ⅝ inch. The heavier the fabric, the less the seam allowance. (See Fig. 8-1, B.)
- Using a pin, pull a stitch in a couple of places around the curve of the pocket, causing the seam allowance to curl under.

or

- Turn back the seam allowance, hand baste into position.

or

- Press over cardboard shape. (See Fig. 8-1, C.)
- Place the pocket over the lining with right side up and ease the

---

* Tradename for knit lining.

outer edges inside the marked pocket lines. The pocket should appear "eased."

- Baste the pocket onto the garment using the longest zigzag stitch on the machine and a stitch length of 2–3. Be sure the zigzag stitch barely catches the edge of the pocket. (See Fig. 8-1, D.)
- Remove the hand-basting stitch.
- Opening the pocket, stitch by machine with a regular machine stitch around the pocket from the inside of the pocket on the seam-stitched line or a thread's width toward the inside of the pocket, using a regular presser foot. (See Fig. 8-1, E.)
- Remove the zigzag basting stitch.
- Miter the corners of the pocket and hand stitch to the pocket facing. (See Fig. 8-1, F.)
- Slip-stitch the lining to the facing.

ATTACH POCKET: METHOD B (Pocket-facing seam enclosed)

- When attaching the pocket, allow the pocket facing to remain loose. Stitch only to the fold line. (See Fig. 8-2, A.)
- Turn the pocket seam allowance and pocket-facing seam allowance toward the pocket. Turn down pocket facing on fold line. (See Fig. 8-2, B.)
- Slip-stitch facing into position on the inside along the stitching line.
- Slip stitch lining to the facing.
  [Note: For the unlined pocket, omit steps referring to lining.]

LINED PATCH POCKET: Quickie Technique

This is a simple trade method of constructing a lined pocket with the seams enclosed. Tricot, stabilized nylon, or self-knit fabric may be used for the lining. It is a quickie method used for children's garments and sportswear.

- Place the right side of lining against the right side of the pocket. Extend the lining ⅟₁₆ inch beyond the cut edge of the pocket.
- Stitch around the entire pocket on the designated seam allowance.
- Grade seams and clip curves. (See pp. 39–40.)
- Slash *only the lining* for about 1 inch near the bottom. (See Fig. 8-3.)
- Turn pocket inside out through the slash.
- Optional: may hand stitch the opening closed.
- Baste and/or press around the outer edge of the pocket, rolling the lining under slightly.
- Attach pocket to the garment by hand or by topstitching.

FLAP PATCH POCKET

This is a patch pocket with one side sewn in the side seam. The flap is a continuation of the pocket. Attach pocket before joining side seams of garment.

- Cut the knit fabric the desired length of pocket + two times the finished width of the flap + ½ inch (¼ inch for roll + ¼-inch seam allowance).

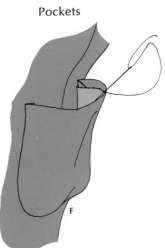

Fig. 8-1. Attaching patch pocket, Method A.

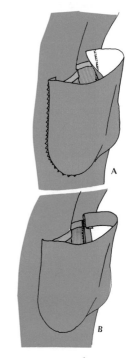

Fig. 8-2. Attaching patch pocket, Method B.

Fig. 8-3. Lined patch pocket ("quickie" technique).

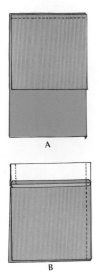

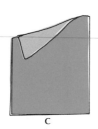

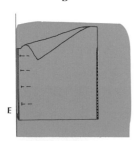

Fig. 8-4. Flap patch
pocket in side seam.

- Cut the lining the length of the pocket + two ¼-inch seam allowances. Cut the width, allowing a ¼-inch seam allowance + ⅝-inch side-seam allowance.
- Place right side of lining against right side of knit fabric. Stitch a ¼-inch seam. Press open. (See Fig. 8-4, A.)
- Fold, right sides together, on fold line of flap. Stitch down width of flap on one side, using garment seam allowance of ⅝ inch. Stop at seamline. On the other side, stitch the entire lengthwise seam ¼ inch. Trim corners of flap at an angle. Turn pocket to the right side. Press. (See Fig. 8-4, B.)
- Position bottom of pocket on garment. (See Fig. 8-4, C.) Stitch ¼-inch seam at bottom by placing right side of pocket on right side of garment. (See Fig. 8-4, D.)
- Roll finished edge of pocket side back, exposing ¹⁄₁₆ inch of lining. Stitch to within ¼ inch of bottom and to seamline on top. Finish top and lower ¼ inch by hand. (See Fig. 8-4, E.)
- Roll pocket back over seam. Press.
- Pin pocket to garment front-seam allowance. Baste-stitch into position.
- Attach pocket permanently in garment side seam.

WELT POCKET

METHOD A

This simplified method uses one strip of self-fabric for welt and lining pouch when making welt pockets. The depth of the pocket can be changed by cutting the lining longer and the width of the welt can be altered by changing the spacing of the marking lines. It is adaptable for men's wear, sport shirts, sweaters, and knit jackets.

CUT POCKET AND STAY:
- Cut a fabric stay about 3½ x 7 inches of lightweight preshrunk cotton or organdy, or a featherweight bias nonwoven polyester.
- Cut knit fabric for the welt and lining 7 x 8 inches. This makes a finished pocket about 3½ inches deep. Cut longer for a deeper pocket.

MARK THE FABRIC STAY:
- Mark the mouthline of the pocket with a basting.
- Draw a line ½ inch above and below the mouthline. This measurement results in a finished ½-inch welt.

ATTACH FABRIC STAY TO THE GARMENT:
- Place mouthline marking of stay over pocket marking on the wrong side of the garment.
- Using a machine-basting stitch and contrasting thread, machine-baste the marking drawn on the stay. (See Fig. 8-5, A.)

ATTACH POCKET LINING:
- Place the *right* side of the pocket lining upward against the right side of the garment along the mouthline.

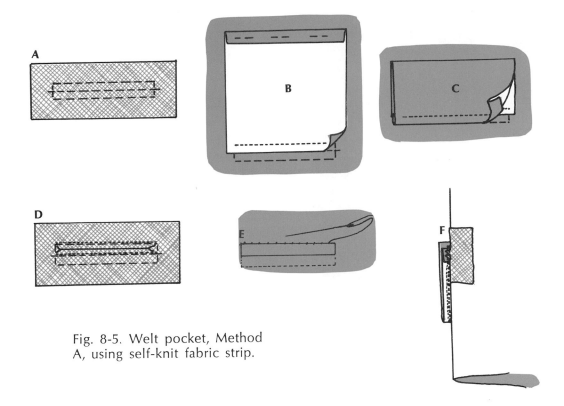

Fig. 8-5. Welt pocket, Method
A, using self-knit fabric strip.

- From the wrong side, stitch along the top marked line of the rectangle using 12 stitches per inch and matching thread. Reinforce the ends by retracing. (See Fig. 8-5, B.)
- Turn to the right side. Fold under the loose end of the pocket lining 1 inch to the wrong side. Pin.
- Align folded edge with the marked line *below* the mouthline.
- Turn to wrong side of garment and stitch along mouthline marking, retracing at ends. (See Fig. 8-5, C.)

CUT OPENING:
- From the wrong side, cut garment fabric between rectangles with a ⅜-inch triangle at each end. Cut only the fabric and stay. (See Fig. 8-5, D.)

COMPLETE POCKET:
- Pull the pocket lining through to the wrong side.
- Baste the welt into position, closing the pocket. (See Fig. 8-5, E.)
- Fold the garment and stay back over the pocket, exposing the triangles. Stitch the ends of the pocket from the top of the pocket lining, across the base of the triangle to the fold line of the pocket lining. Do a second row of stitching to make it more secure. (See Fig. 8-5, F.)
- Repeat on other side of pocket.
- Remove the basting, closing the pocket.

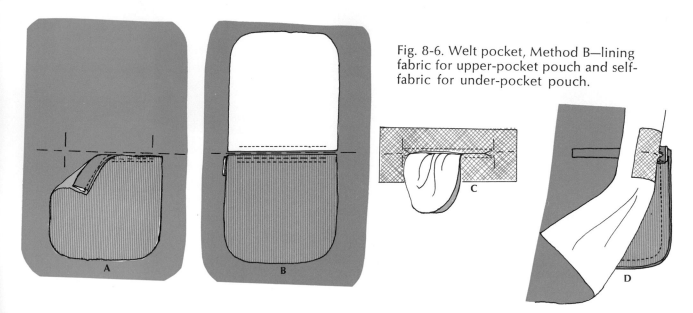

Fig. 8-6. Welt pocket, Method B—lining fabric for upper-pocket pouch and self-fabric for under-pocket pouch.

WELT POCKET

METHOD B

This method uses *lining fabric for the upper-pocket pouch and self-fabric for the under-pocket pouch.* The directions for this welt pocket will be ¾ inch x 5 inches; however, measurements may be varied to construct the size of pocket desired.

- *Mark mouthline placement* of pocket with basting. Mark ends.
- *Cut a fabric stay* of organdy 3½ x 7 inches. Center, and baste under the mouthline on the wrong side of garment.
- *Cut a strip of self-fabric* on lengthwise for the welt, 2½ x 7 inches.
- *Cut a piece of lining fabric* (stabilized nylon or tricot) for the upper-pocket pouch, 6 x 6½ inches. Cut a piece of self-fabric 6 x 7 inches for the under-pocket pouch.
- Press welt in half lengthwise. Attach raw edge to right side of upper pocket, aligning raw edges. Baste-stitch together close to edge. (See Fig. 8-6, A.)
- *Chalk mark* the mouth opening on the welt (5 inches long).
- *Place wrong side of upper-pocket pouch of lining* (welt down) on right side of garment. Align welt pouch with mouthline markings. Stitch between marks ½ inch from cut edge. Retrace at ends. (See Fig. 8-6, A.)
- *Place right side of self-fabric* under pocket pouch on right side of garment, aligning raw edge with welt-pouch raw edges. Chalk mark ends of pocket. (See Fig. 8-6, B.)
- *Stitch ¼ inch* from raw edge between markings. Retrace at ends.

The distance between the two rows of stitching will be ¾ inch (width of welt).

- *Turn to right side of garment.* Slash between stitching lines, leaving ½-inch triangles at end. Cut through garment fabric *only.* (See Fig. 8-6, C.)
- *Pull pocket pouches through* to wrong side of garment. Press.
- *Fold garment back at end of pockets.* Stitch and retrace triangle to pouch at end of pocket and stitch around the pocket pouches, seaming them together. (See Fig. 8-6, D.)

SELF-FABRIC FLAP

To eliminate bulk at the ends of the flap on a self-fabric flap, try this method:

- Cut flap twice the desired length of flap + two seam allowances and the desired width + two seam allowances.
- Seam ends of strip, forming a circle with right sides together. Press seams open.
- Stitch seam on bottom of flap, shaping at corners as desired.
- Turn right side out.
- Apply to garment as false-flap pocket or use for a flap pocket.

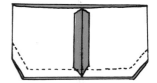

Fig. 8-7. Self-fabric flap.

FLAP POCKET

Design a flap any size or shape and make the pocket pouch as deep as desired. The directions below are for a 2¼-inch-wide flap and a mouth-line 5¼ inches long.

MARK MOUTHLINE:
- Mark mouthline with a basting 5¼ inches long. Mark ends.

CUT AND ATTACH STAY:
- Cut stay of organdy or nonwoven bias interfacing 1½ x 6½ inches.
- Center on mouthline on wrong side of garment. Baste.

CONSTRUCT FLAP:
- Cut knit flap 3 x 5¾ inches. Shape corners as desired.
- Lay piece of lining (stabilized nylon, tricot, or woven fabric) right side up. Baste flap, right side down, on lining on bias on top of lining. Cut around flap. Seam with ¼-inch seam allowance on three sides, extending lining seams very slightly over knit flap. Turn inside out. Press. Baste around edges. Topstitch if desired.

CUT AND CONSTRUCT POUCH:
- Cut a pouch of lining fabric 6½ x 12 inches.
- Cut two facings 2¼ x 6½ inches. Cut one of knit and one of *lining.*
- Lap one edge of facing ¼ inch over one end of pocket-pouch lining. Zigzag stitch raw edge of knit facing to pouch lining. Divide strip in half. The half just stitched becomes the *upper pocket.*

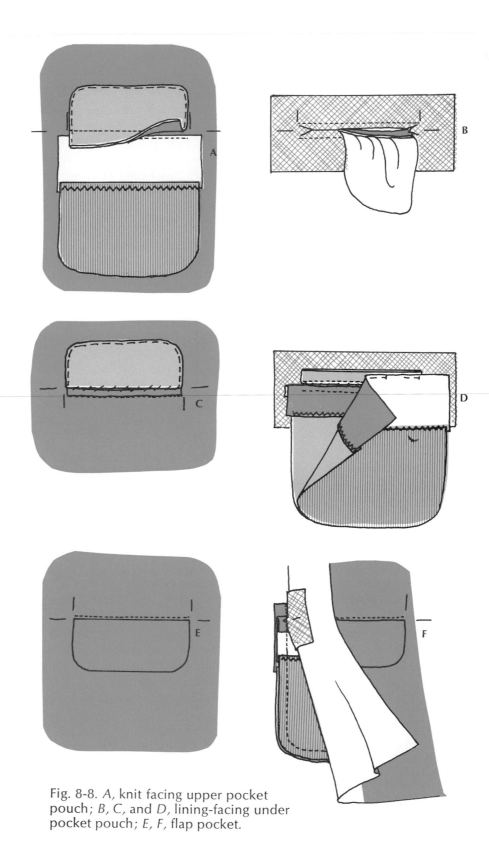

Fig. 8-8. *A*, knit facing upper pocket pouch; *B*, *C*, and *D*, lining-facing under pocket pouch; *E*, *F*, flap pocket.

- Place wrong side of remaining lining facing on right side of under-pocket pouch, aligning raw edges. Turn under lining-facing and straight stitch the two together at lower edge.

ATTACH FLAP:

- To establish roll line on flap, turn seam allowance over fingers. Pin and baste-roll fold line.
- Measure for a 2½-inch flap (finished width) and draw a chalk line or baste.
- Place flap, lining side up on garment, matching marked line to coat mouthline marking. Stitch. Retrace on ends. Pin flap seam up onto flap.

ATTACH UPPER POCKET:

- Baste upper pocket, right side against right side of garment, with raw edge under flap seam.
- Stitch ¼ inch from previous line of stitching on wrong side of garment. Retrace ends. The two rows of stitching will be parallel and a ¼ inch apart.
- Cut garment only between stitching lines forming triangles at end.
- Push pocket pouch through slash to wrong side forming a ¼-inch piping over the seam allowance.
- Stitch in the seam well.
- Baste mouthline of pocket in position.

ATTACH UNDERPOCKET POUCH:

- From *wrong side* of garment, place right side of underpocket face down against right side of upper pocket, aligning raw facing-underpocket edge with raw edge of flap. Pin across top.
- Topstitch from *right side* above flap seamline, attaching top of underpocket.

COMPLETE POCKET:

- Fold garment back at end of pocket. Sew around entire pocket, catching triangles at end of pocket. Make pockets desired length. Trim off if pocket is uneven at bottom.

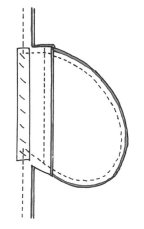

Fig. 8-9. Taping pocket in a seam.

POCKETS IN A SEAM

Pockets in a seam are frequently used on knit garments. To keep the pockets from sagging, attach seam tape or linen tape along the seamline. (See Fig. 8-9.) Another method is to cut the two pockets in one.

- Cut two pockets the width of the front panel of garment and desired depth.
- With right sides together, stitch one upper-pocket piece to front-seam allowance, ending at ⅝-inch seam allowance. Repeat for other side. Clip to stitching. Turn pocket to inside of garment (like turning a pillowcase).
- Attach underpocket piece to upper pocket at top and bottom, ending at ⅝-inch seam allowance. Stitch through center, dividing pockets.

- Stitch seams joining center panel to side panel of garment, leaving pocket-seam allowance open. Clip side-panel seam allowance above and below pocket.
- Stitch ends of underpocket pouch to side-panel seam allowance at ends of pocket. Press.

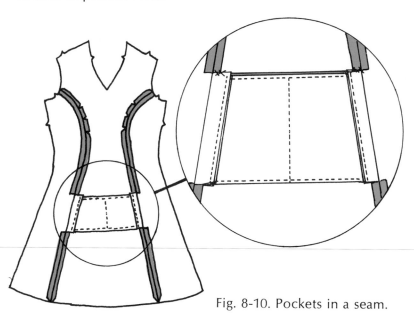

Fig. 8-10. Pockets in a seam.

9

CLOSURES

Most of the popular closures used for woven fabrics are applicable for knits—i.e., buttons, buttonholes, loops, eyelets, and zippers. The Chinese ball-button and frogs, nylon tape (Velcro), or concealed covered snaps, or hooks and eyes, or hanging snaps are other suggested fasteners. It is important not to stretch the fashion knit when applying the appropriate closure and to stabilize the area when needed.

BUTTONHOLES

Bound buttonholes may be used on stable knits and moderately stretchy knits. Interface the button and buttonhole area. *Hand-worked* buttonholes may be made on a man's sports coat, a tailored or a couture garment. *Machine-made* buttonholes are used for sportswear and children's garments. Always make a test sample buttonhole before working them

Fig. 9-1. Fashion drawing showing buttonhole in a seam.

on the garment. Attach facing before making the machine-worked buttonholes as machine buttonholes are made through the facing. On sweater knits, a strip of magic transparent tape will keep the knit fabric from buckling and catching on the presser foot. Place where buttonholes are to be made and make pencil markings on the tape. Paper under the knit adds firmness for some knits while machine working buttonholes.

BUTTONHOLE-IN-A-SEAM

This buttonhole is constructed by omitting the stitching on the seam at intervals when applying the band.

GARMENT FRONT:
- Allow a seam allowance beyond the center front.

BAND:
- Determine the width of the band by the diameter of the button to be used. A rule of thumb to follow is to use the diameter of the button plus 1 inch plus two ⅝-inch seam allowances.

  EXAMPLE: ⅝ inch button

  ⅝ inch + 1 inch + ⅝ + ⅝ = 2⅞ inch strip

  seam allowance

[Note: Buttonholes may be made on a garment with or without a facing.]

WITHOUT A FACING:
JOINING BAND TO GARMENT:
- Place right side of band to right side of garment at CF.
- Mark position of buttonholes.
- Stitch, retracing at beginning and end of each buttonhole marking. (See Fig. 9-2, A.)
- Press seams open.

FINISHING BAND:
- Fold band toward the wrong side of the garment extending the raw cut edge ⅝ inch beyond the CF.
- Slash the ⅝-inch seam allowance at the top and bottom of each buttonhole through the loose length of band only. (See Fig. 9-2, B.)
- Tuck the seam allowance under the band in the buttonhole location.
- Repeat the procedure for each buttonhole.
- Pin band into position.
- Machine "stitch in the ditch" from the right side between the buttonholes. (See Fig. 9-2, C.)
- Attach the "tucked under" edge of the buttonhole by hand using a slip stitch.

WITH A FACING (Cut the garment and band seam as above):
ATTACH BAND TO GARMENT:
- Stitch the right side of the band to the right side of the garment, leaving openings at intervals for the buttonholes. (See Fig. 9-3, A.)

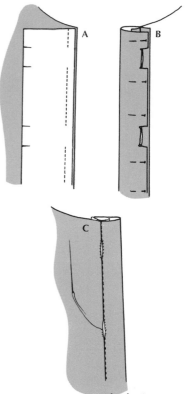

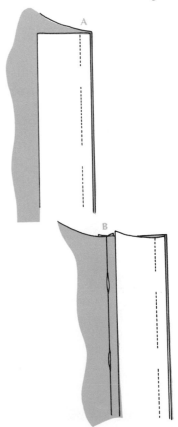

Fig. 9-2. Buttonhole in a seam without a facing.

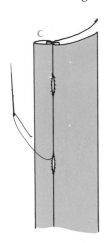

Fig. 9-3. Buttonhole in a seam with a facing.

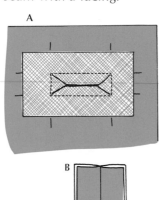

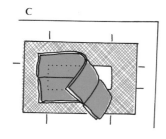

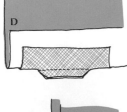

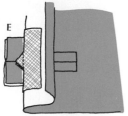

ATTACH BAND TO THE FACING:
- Stitch the other side of the band, right sides together, to the facing. Also leave openings at intervals for the buttonholes.

PRESS BOTH SEAMS OPEN

COMPLETE BUTTONHOLES:
- Turn facing and band to the inside of right garment front.
- Align the buttonholes from both seams.
- Slip-stitch openings of buttonholes together.
- Press.

OPTIONAL: If you desire to make the band more secure, the following may be done:
- Stitch in the "ditch" between the buttonholes aligning two seam allowances,

or

- Turn to the inside and stitch extended seam allowances together between the buttonholes, close to the previous stitching line.

BOUND BUTTONHOLE

Make a test sample buttonhole before working on your garment. There are many methods for making buttonholes and you may have your favorite method. If you don't, try this one.

PATCH/WINDOW METHOD:
- Determine length of buttonhole by adding the measurement of the diameter of the button to the thickness of the button.
- Cut a patch of organdy or organza for each buttonhole 1 inch longer than the buttonhole and 2 inches wide. Select color that matches as closely as possible to fashion knit.
- For each buttonhole, cut two pieces of fashion knit 1½ inches longer than the buttonhole and 2 inches wide.
- Center organdy patch over buttonhole, marking on right side of knit garment.
- Using 20 stitches per inch, stitch a rectangle beginning at middle, pivot at corners, counting stitches at end, and overlap stitches when ending. Rectangle will be ¼ inch in width (⅛ inch on each side of marked line).
- Cut in the middle, forming triangles at end. Cut *to* stitching at corners, but not *through*. (See Fig. 9-4, A.)
- Turn patch to the wrong side forming a window. Press seam allowances toward garment.
- Machine-baste two strips of fashion knit in the center, right sides together. Press open, forming the lips. (See Fig. 9-4, B.)
- Place the lips in position, centering in the window from the right side. Pin/tape/or slip-baste into position. (See Fig. 9-4, C.)
- On the wrong side, stitch the lengthwise seam allowances to lips just outside the previous stitching so the organdy patch does

Fig. 9-4. Patch/Window bound buttonholes.

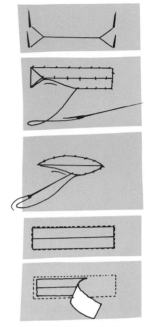

not show from the right side. Extend stitching about ⅜ inch beyond end of buttonhole through organdy patch and buttonhole lips. (See Fig. 9-4, D.)

- Cord buttonhole, if desired, by running a cord or yarn through the lips.
- Secure ends by folding garment back and by stitching across the triangle on each end of buttonhole. (See Fig. 9-4, E.)

COMPLETING BOUND BUTTONHOLE IN FACING:

Stick a pin through both ends of buttonhole to mark location on facing. (See Fig. 9-5, A.)

PATCH/WINDOW METHOD: Apply a patch to right side of facing. Stitch a rectangle about 1/16 inch larger than buttonhole rectangle. Turn to·wrong side. Slip-stitch to wrong side of buttonhole. (See Fig. 9-5, B.)

SLASH METHOD: Cut slash to within ¼ inch of end of buttonhole and cut diagonally into each corner. Turn under a rectangle. Slip-stitch to wrong side of buttonhole.

FISH EYE OR ELLIPTICAL: Slash length of buttonhole. Turn under and slip-stitch knit facing to buttonhole, forming a fish eye or elliptical shape. (See Fig. 9-5, C.)

QUICKIE KNIT METHOD: Machine-stitch rectangle around buttonhole from the right side. From facing side, trim away facing close to line of stitching, leaving a raw edge. Since knits do not ravel, this is a quick flat method. (See Fig. 9-5, D and E.)

or

Fuse facing to garment in buttonhole area. Slit an opening.

Fig. 9-5. Completing bound buttonhole in facing.

SEWING ON BUTTONS

Reinforce fashion knit in area where buttons are attached with a folded square of nonwoven interfacing. The reinforcement may be placed on inside of garment or between facing and garment. On tailored garments, use a stay button. Make a thread shank when attaching button.

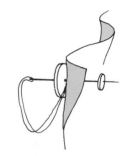

Fig. 9-6. Sewing on buttons with a stay button.

LOOPS

Loops and buttons are an attractive closure for the shoulder or front of a garment. Prepare loop of lengthwise of knit about 1 to 1½ inches wide. Stitch and turn as directed for belts on page 105. Plan location and size of loops carefully. Tape and stitch loops to garment before applying facing.

ZIPPERS

Zippers are a common closure for knits. For dresses, the invisible zipper with polyester coil or metal teeth, or a hand-picked lapped zipper are popular. On shells or pullovers, an exposed or decorative zipper, or a zipper in a shoulder seam, are fashionable.

Fig. 9-7. Loops.

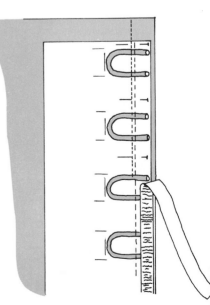

TIPS FOR ZIPPERS

Always *preshrink* zipper tape by placing in hot water. Pat in towel and allow to dry flat. Press.

- With *coil invisible zipper, press back* the sides of the coils on both sides to flatten before inserting.
- When applying zippers, may *baste-stitch* the outer edge of tape to the seam allowance with a regular presser foot *first,* then stitch with a regular machine stitch and *zipper foot* close to the zipper teeth.
- *Ease* knit fabric into the zipper slightly to keep zipper from rippling.
- Before applying a lapped zipper with neckline facings or bindings, *finish the ends of the neckline trim* before applying the zipper. (See "Edge Finishes," Chapter 11, p. 68.)

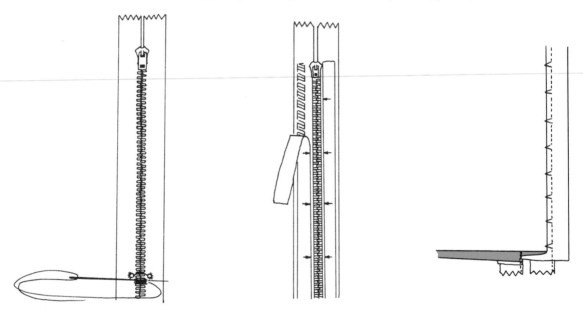

Fig. 9-8. Shortening a zipper.

Fig. 9-9. Zipper adhesive.

Fig. 9-10. Blindstitching a zipper.

- To *shorten a zipper,* take several whipstitches over the teeth ¼ inch below end of zipper. Sew a straight eye (from hook and eye) just above the whipstitches. Cut off excess tape ½ inch below eye, right through zipper and tape.
- A *zipper adhesive* is available which *holds zipper* in place while stitching. The adhesive strip is pressed with fingers to zipper tape next to the zipper teeth. A wax paper is removed and then the garment will adhere to the adhesive.
- Use *special foot attachment* for applying invisible zipper. Use *zipper foot* for regular zipper.

- A *quickie method* for completing the overlap on a lapped zipper is to use the blind stitch on the machine.

INVISIBLE ZIPPER

Press zipper coil flat. Do not stitch seam below zipper before inserting zipper.

- Open zipper. Place face down on right side of fabric on right back of garment. Allow about ¾ inch from top of teeth to top of garment. Align the teeth ⅝ inch from center back. Stitch, using the special invisible zipper foot attachment, from top down until foot touches the slide pull.
- Close the zipper. Pin other side of tape to right side of left back of garment, beginning same distance from top and aligning teeth on ⅝-inch seam allowance. Open zipper.
- Stitch tape from top down until foot touches the slide pull. Backstitch.
- Close zipper. Fold garment so right sides of zipper are together. Begin ¼ inch above stitching at bottom of zipper and ¹⁄₁₆ inch toward the garment from the seam line and stitch the remainder of the garment seam.
- Stitch the bottom of the zipper tape which extends inside of the garment to the seam allowances on both sides.

Fig. 9-11. Invisible zipper.

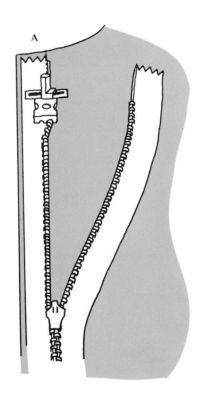

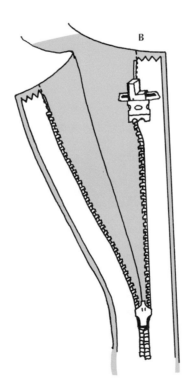

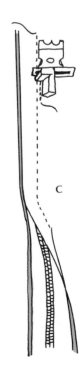

Fig. 9-12. Zipper
underlap.

ZIPPER UNDERLAP

If a zipper down the center back of the garment irritates sensitive skin,
apply an underlap. On the inside of garment, stitch a preshrunk piece of
grosgrain ribbon or self-fabric to the right-side garment-seam allowance.
Hem the ribbon at the top and apply a small snap.

EXPOSED ZIPPER WITHOUT A SEAM

Cut a stay of woven cloth the length of the zipper + 2 inches and 4
inches wide. May use organdy, lightweight cotton lining, or a crisp
interfacing.

- Position and pin the stay on the right side of the garment and
  draw a line in the center of the stay to mark the designated zipper line.
- Stitch a rectangle around the designated zipper line. Most zipper
  teeth measure about ¼ inch in width so the rectangle will be
  ¼ inch wide, and the zipper length plus seam allowance at top
  for the length.
- Cut down center of rectangle to about ¼ inch from the bottom
  and clip to each corner, forming a triangle.

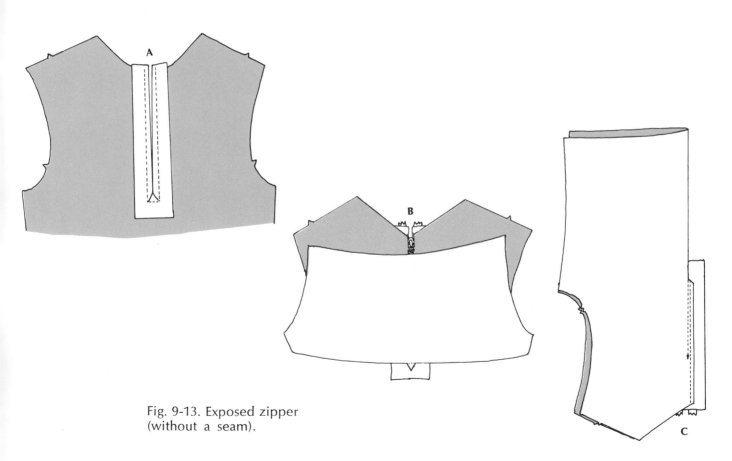

Fig. 9-13. Exposed zipper
(without a seam).

- Turn the stay to the wrong side. Press.
- Position zipper in the opening so the teeth are exposed. Pin zipper at bottom at the end of the finished rectangle.
- Fold garment bottom up so the triangle at the bottom of the rectangle is exposed. Stitch across the end attaching the stay, triangle, and zipper.
- Stitch up the sides, from the bottom up, from the wrong side of the garment, stitching on the seam allowance of the garment and on the woven edge of the zipper next to the teeth.

[Note: May use transparent tape or machine stitching to stay cut opening, placing it a scant ½ inch from each side opening.]

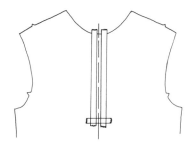

Fig. 9-14. Tape as stay for zipper opening.

ZIPPER IN A SHOULDER SEAM

A zipper in a shoulder seam is used when the neck opening should be quite small and yet large enough to go over the head comfortably. Used in children's garments and men's too.

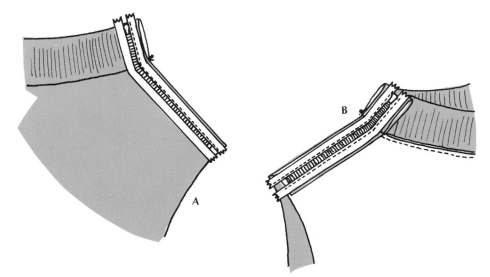

Fig. 9-15. Zipper in a shoulder seam.

- Sew the right shoulder seam.
- Divide the neckline and ribbing into four equal parts. Match the markings and apply to the neck edge with a ¼-inch seam, leaving the left shoulder open. (See p. 80.)
- Press and topstitch seam allowance from the right side.
- Place the zipper right side down on the right side of the shoulder seam, with the top of the zipper even with the neck edge or finished edge of the trim. The end of the zipper can extend beyond the seam allowance for the sleeve because after the sleeve is in, the zipper can be cut off. Stitch from the wrong side of the zipper along the edge of the teeth.

- Stitch the other side of the zipper in the same manner. Fold back the ends of tape to the wrong side at neck edge and fasten by hand.
- Attach the sleeve, cutting off the excess zipper if it is too long.

EXPOSED ZIPPER FOR A TURTLENECK

This method for applying a coil zipper in a turtleneck collar may be used on a left shoulder seam as well as for a center opening without a seam. The zipper extends to the roll "fold-over" of the collar. Extend the zipper just *to the fold* for *turnover* and *stand-up collars.*
APPLICATION OF TURTLENECK COLLAR TO GARMENT:
- Pin and stitch the turtleneck collar with the two right sides together to the neck edge, stretching the collar to fit the opening. If a knit seam is used, press seam allowance upward; if a plain seam is used, press seam allowance open, clipping *garment* seam allowance where necessary for smoothness.

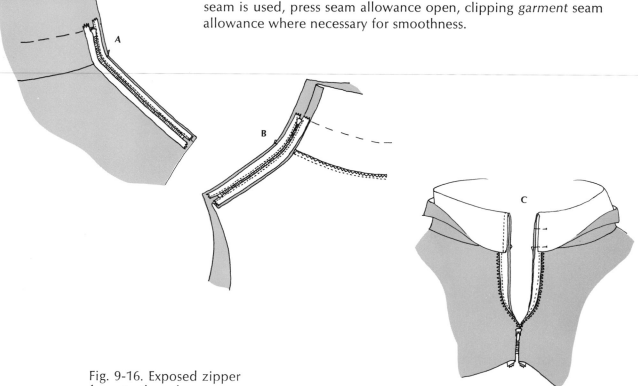

Fig. 9-16. Exposed zipper for a turtleneck.

- Mark the roll line of the turtleneck collar by folding the collar wrong sides together, matching the seam allowances at the neck edge on the inside of the garment. Pin. Then roll the collar toward the right side as it will be worn. Mark the roll line with a pin on both ends of collar. Remove pins at neck seam allowance.

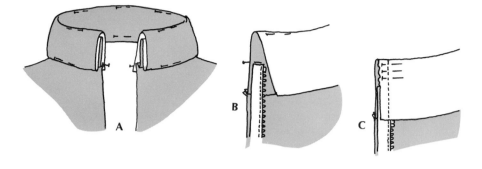

Fig. 9-17. Exposed zipper (coil) for turtleneck, turn-over, or stand-up collar.

APPLICATION OF ZIPPER:

- Pin and stitch the right side of the zipper to the right side of the garment, allowing the teeth at the top to extend *to* the marked roll line.
- Open the zipper. Fold the collar on the marked roll line, right sides together, over the stitched zipper.
- Pin ends of collar from roll line to top of zipper tape, easing in top collar which allows for roll. Pin remainder of collar over stitched zipper tape.
- Turn over so the previous stitching line shows. Stitch ends of collar, beginning at fold line and on down through zipper tape to bottom of collar.
- Repeat for the other end of the collar.
- Turn right side out. Roll collar into position.
- Stitch in the "ditch"—or seam well—around the neckline, attaching the collar to the neck edge, or attach the two seam allowances together with a hand stitch.

LAPPED ZIPPER

This couture method of applying a zipper is more time consuming as the "finishing" is completed with a hand-pick stitch. It is commonly used for a center-back application.

- On the *left back,* fold back a ⅝-inch seam allowance for the overlap. Machine baste ⅜ inch from the fold through both thicknesses. Press.
- On the *right back,* place closed right side of zipper to right side of fabric on the placket seam allowance. Align edge of zipper teeth *away* from the cut edge on the marked seam allowance. This will allow for a pleat and sufficient overlap on the finished zipper.
- Machine-baste the zipper tape to the seam allowance at the *outer* edge, stitching from the bottom to the top. After 1 inch, open the zipper.
- Close zipper. Machine-stitch the zipper tape close to the teeth, using a zipper foot and regular length stitch. After 1 inch, open the zipper.

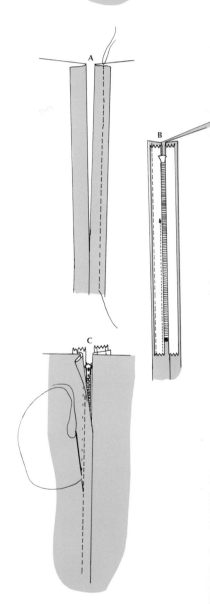

Fig. 9-18. Lapped zipper.

- Close zipper. Turn zipper into position, folding seam allowance to inside of garment. Press.
- Pin overlap in position so overlap meets designated seam allowance. Note a pleat at bottom of underlap.
- Hand-pick stitch the overlap through garment and zipper tape using the machine basting as a guide.
- Remove machine basting. Press.

DECORATIVE TRIM ON ZIPPER

Ribbon or braid may be used to trim the zipper as well as other portions of the garment. The zipper may be colored for contrast or match the trim.

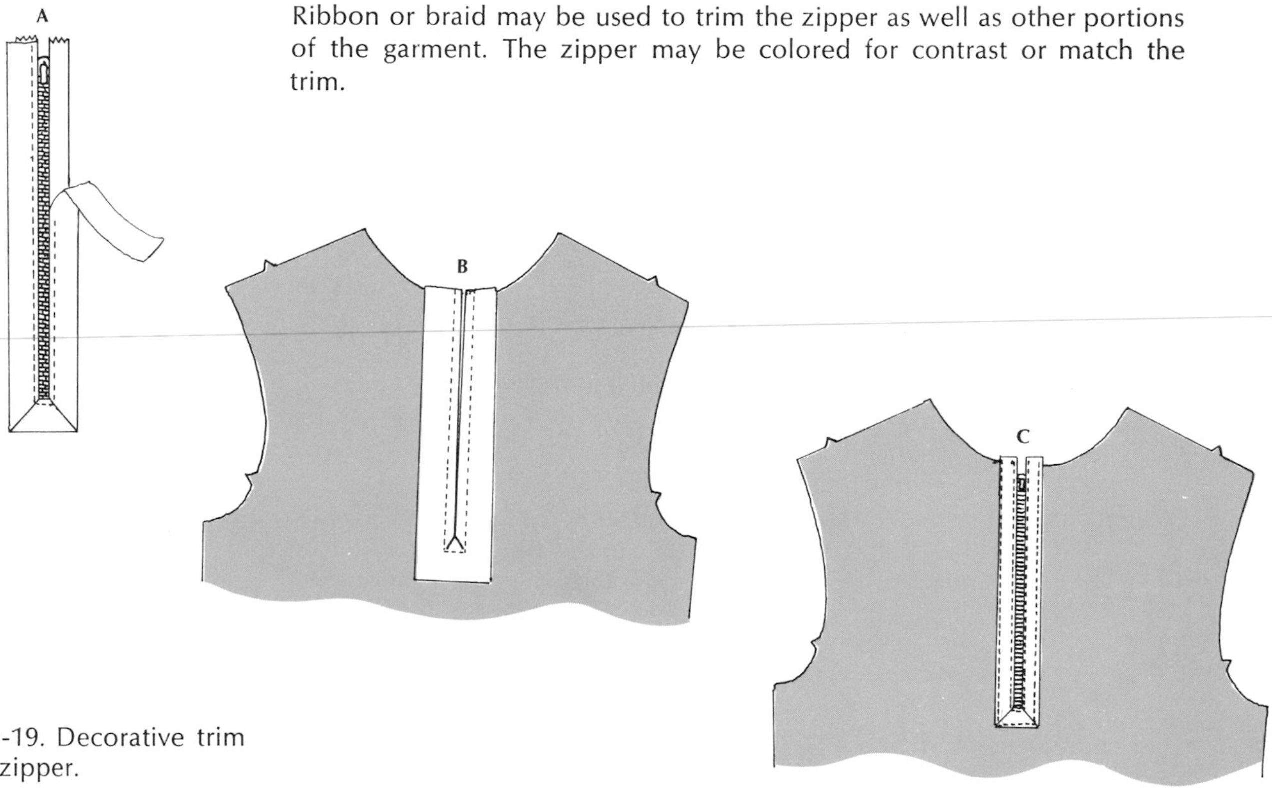

Fig. 9-19. Decorative trim on a zipper.

- Topstitch the braid to the zipper tape. Miter at corners.
- Apply a stay to the opening. Stitch a rectangle ½ inch in width (¼ inch on each side of seam allowance). Slash, turn to the wrong side. Press.
- Place the zipper on the right side of garment. Turn to the inside of the garment and slip-stitch the facing-garment seam edge to the zipper tape.
- Turn to the right side of garment. Machine-stitch the outer edge of the braid trim to the garment.

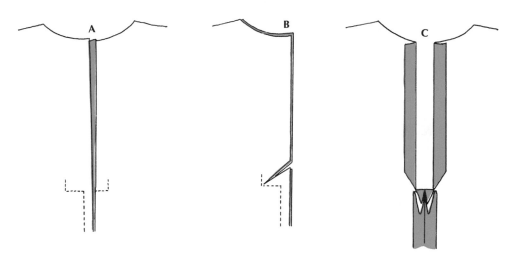

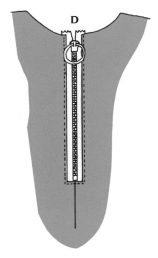

Fig. 9-20. Exposed decorative over-sized zipper.

EXPOSED DECORATIVE OVER-SIZED ZIPPER

The over-sized decorative zipper usually has an attractive pull and is available in a variety of colors.

- Stitch the regular ⅝-inch garment seam allowance to the end of zipper. Fasten threads.
- Stay-stitch on each side of opening 16–20 stitches per inch from seam line for ⅜ inch, pivot, and stitch up 1 inch.
- Slash the seam allowance on each side to the corner.
- Press back 1-inch seam allowance for zipper. Press down at the bottom.
- Center zipper in the opening, right side up. Pin and baste. Machine-topstitch close to the fold around the zipper.
- Remove bastings. Press.

10

SHAPINGS

Shaping is used sparingly with knit fabrics as it is the comfort from the stretch of knit that makes knits so bright on the fashion horizon. Shapings include *linings, underlinings,* and *interfacings. Stays* are important also in retaining the shape in certain areas of knit garments—i.e., behind buttonholes, pockets, and in seams.

To refresh your memory: *linings* are constructed separately from the garment; *underlinings* are attached separately to each piece of fashion fabric knit before constructing the garment; and *interfacings* are placed between the fashion garment and a facing. *Stays* stabilize areas to keep them from stretching.

INTERFACINGS

SELECTION AND USE

Interfacings are more often used with the more stable knits rather than with the stretch knits. The selection of the interfacing depends on the reason for using it:

- To support and reinforce for strength (buttons and buttonholes on a dress or jacket front, yokes).
- To add padded look for trapunto, quilting, or rolled look (hems, belts, seams).
- To retain shape and prevent stretch (faced edges, buttonholes, pockets, waistbands, collars, flaps, belts).

Remember that an interfacing should be lighter in weight than the fashion-knit fabric. Be sure that it is washable if the knit fashion fabric is washable. Woven permanent-press cotton/polyester fabrics, bias featherweight and lightweight nonwoven fabrics, synthetic taffeta, iron-on interfacings (woven and nonwoven), and firmer woven interfacings (washable ad dry-cleanable) are possible choices for knits. For tailored knit suits and men's sports coats, a hair canvas may be used for the collar and coat front.

On jerseys you might use the lightweight cotton-and-dacron blend fabric or bias featherweight nonwoven fabric. Cut woven fabric on the bias for rolled collars and also for cuffs. For a firmer appearance on collars and cuffs, use medium-weight bias nonwoven or a more crisp woven interfacing. Iron-on interfacing (woven or nonwoven) may add the desired crispness and stiffness to flaps, stand-up collars or for faced edges. Polyester fleece is desirable as an interfacing for trapunto or for padded seams and hems.

DRESSMAKING TECHNIQUE FOR INTERFACINGS

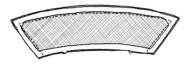

Fig. 10-1. Dressmaking technique for applying interfacing to collar.

Interfacings may be applied according to methods used for dressmaking whereby the interfacing is applied to the wrong side of the garment. The interfacing is caught in the seams, then trimmed close to the line of stitching. Trim away interfacing at corners of collars, cuffs, and lapels before applying.

COUTURE TECHNIQUE FOR INTERFACINGS

This method is more time consuming, but eliminates seams and produces a flat edge.

Remove slightly more than seam allowances from interfacing. The interfacing is attached with loose catch stitches picking up just a thread on the fashion knit.

On *shaped* collars, attach the interfacing to the undercollar. For *shirt collar* with a band for a stand, interface the band which attaches to the undercollar. *Bias turnover* collars may have the entire collar interfaced or the outer half of collar extending beyond the fold. Run a permanent basting on the fold line.

For a *band or sweater cuff* or *lapped cuff*, interface the outer side of the cuff extending ¼ inch beyond fold line.

FUSING TECHNIQUES FOR INTERFACINGS

There are basically two methods of fusing used in knit sewing. In one method, a fusible web or bonding film is applied to the interfacing or garment to adhere the two separate pieces of fabric together. In the other method, the interfacing is either a one-sided or two-sided fusible on which the adherent is already applied to the interfacing. These interfacings are either woven or nonwoven.

When using either fusing technique, follow the manufacturer's directions carefully for best results. Test on fashion fabric.

FUSING WEB OR BONDING FILM:
  Apply the fusing adherent to the desired area. *Interfacings* may be fused to the fashion fabric before applying. Check on a sample to be sure that a "ridge" will not show on the right side of the garment. *Armscye facings* may be fused to the garment *around outer edges only.* See page 73. *Interfacings may be fused* to the entire armscye, neck, or jacket-front *facing.* This adds firmness and eliminates the ridge which may result from the former technique.
  Two-sided fusible nonwoven web may be stitched into collars as an interfacing. Complete collar. Do not press. Apply collar to garment. Then fuse collar and undercollar together by proper pressing according to directions. There is no problem with undercollar "peeking" out, because you now have "one" collar—the two layers are treated as one. This is ideal for tailored men's and women's shirt collars, cuffs, belts, and flaps.

FUSIBLE INTERFACING:
  The one-sided fusible nonwoven interfacing with crosswise stretch only is designed especially for tailoring knits. It provides

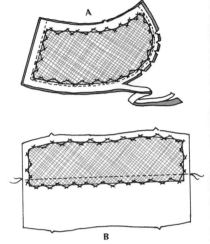

Fig. 10-2. Couture technique for applying interfacing to collar.

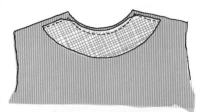

Fig. 10-3. Attaching inter-facing to underlining.

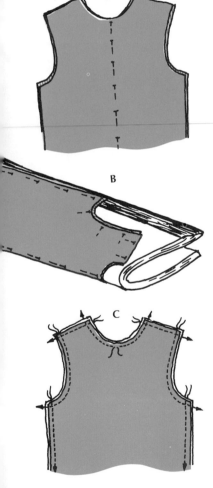

Fig. 10-4. Applying underlining.

a firm, tailored appearance when applied to the front of a man's sports coat, yet provides crosswise stretch.

The one-sided fusible woven interfacing which is washable and dry-cleanable is fused to the wrong side of the fashion fabric. It extends ⅛ inch into seam allowance. It may be used for collars, cuffs, flaps, and for jacket front and back canvases in tailoring knits.

UNDERLININGS

A stretchy knit is never underlined as the natural "give" of the knit would be lost.

Knits are underlined when the knit fabric is very lacy and open so that the underlining prevents the fabric from stretching or sagging and also adds opaqueness. Yokes or sections of a garment may be underlined when rigid tailored lines are desired. Sometimes a knit garment is underlined in the shoulder area for more wearing comfort—polyester-and-wool knits are uncomfortable for sensitive skin.

APPLICATION:

If a stable double knit is underlined, one needs to remove some of the underlining so it will not bubble inside the fashion garment.

[Note: May attach interfacing to underlining before attaching to garment.]

- Pin center front of underlining to center front of garment. Baste.
- Fold garment toward one side from the center, smoothing underlining with hand so the excess moves into side-seam allowance. May fold over a flat fabric board or thick magazine.
- Pin along edge.
- Trim away excess underlining.
- Stay-stitch the two layers together, using 10 stitches per inch, with the underlining uppermost. Stitch in the same direction on both sides. Stitch all the way out to the end of the seams rather than pivoting at the corners. This prevents a "bubble."
- On darts, stay-stitch through center first—through both layers—before stitching from the widest portion to the point of the dart.

When a somewhat stretchy knit is underlined, it may be desirable to hand baste the underlining and fashion knit together in the *center* and around *side* and *top edges*. Hang for 24 hours. After fabric has relaxed and slack has sagged, remove bastings, realign upper edges and center line, smooth out, and rebaste.

LININGS

SELECTION AND USE:

Double knits of wool or polyester are not usually lined. However, there are several reasons to use a lining: for support of design of garment; for comfort in wearing; for finished appearance; or for opaqueness on an open, lacy knit. Linings also give the couture touch to fine garments. Linings may void the use of a slip. Some prefer a taffeta slip (stabilized nylon or polyester) to achieve the results of lining.

A polyester woven lining in satin, surah, or crepe, or a knit lining are available for lining knits. Or select a tricot knit used for lingerie. China silk or voile or batiste is suitable for some slip linings.

APPLICATION:

For a *dress,* construct the lining separately and attach at neckline, armscye, and zipper tape. Another method is to attach the lining to the garment, wrong sides together, at the armscye and neckline, then apply the facings. Attach lining to zipper tape. Hem lining and garment separately.

Skirt linings are attached at waist and zipper only. Jackets and coats are lined for comfort and for finished appearance. If an unstructured appearance is desired, do not line.

Line *pants* at the knees. Cut a piece of lining 12 inches long and the width of knee area of pants. Overedge the top and bottom of lining pieces. Center over knee, attaching to front-seam allowance. Use an *invisible* hand stitch to attach and lower edge of lining to fashion-knit fabric.

Vests (long or short) may be lined or unlined. However, a vest may be completely lined with a flip lining, avoiding the use of facings.

Fig. 10-5. Facings on a lined garment.

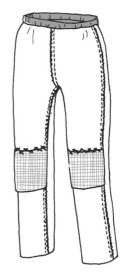

Fig. 10-6. Lining pants at knees.

FLAP LINING TECHNIQUE

This lining can be used on a vest, dress, or jumper which has a center-front or center-back seam, has two side seams, and shoulder seams at least two inches wide.

- Cut lining the same as the garment. Omit facings.
- Stitch in darts and shoulder seams of lining and garment. Press.

Fig. 10-7. Flap lining.

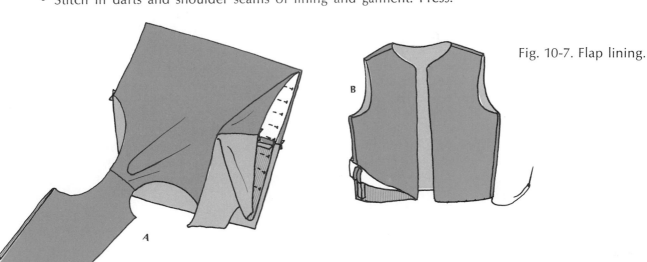

- Place lining and garment, right sides together. Pin around armscye, neck, and front or back opening. (Omit center opening if zipper is to be used.) Extend lining seam allowance 1/16 inch beyond fashion-knit fabric.
- Stitch neck, armscye, and front or back seams. Trim, grade, and clip seams.
- Turn right side out by reaching between the front of the garment and the lining, grasping the back lining and pulling through shoulder seam.
- Press seams.
- Place side seams, right sides together, lining to lining, garment to garment, matching armscye seams. Stitch from armscye side seam. Press seams open.
- Hand stitch bottom of garment.

[Note: If zipper is inserted in back, insert before hemming.]

11

EDGE FINISHES

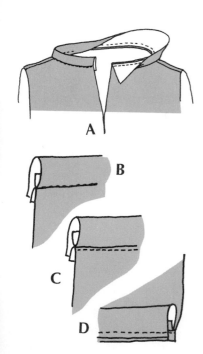

Fig. 11-1. Self-fabric trim as binding.

The couture or home sewer may finish edges of *necklines, armscyes, hems, patch pockets, flaps,* and *front* and *neck edges* of *Chanel jackets* using self-fabric, commercial braid, commercial ribbed banding (see Collars, Chapter 12), or the commercial rolled edging used in trade sewing. A "quickie" method involves turning back the raw-seam-allowance edges and machine finishing. Also, facings of self-fabric or a compatible fabric may be used.

BINDINGS OR TRIMS

SELF-FABRIC TRIM AS BINDING

Self-fabric trim is used on high fashion garments and inexpensive garments—the difference in the cost of the garment is often related to the technique used in application. Knit-fabric trim may be the same fabric as the garment or a contrasting color or texture in a knit fabric or a rib knit.

Here are some general pointers which will be helpful in cutting and applying self-fabric as binding.

PREPARING THE GARMENT:

- Remove the *seam allowances* or *hem allowances* from the edges to be bound—i.e., armscye, neck edge, or front and bottom of jackets.

OPTIONAL: in trade, the edges to be bound are not stay-stitched. Some home dressmakers prefer to stay-stitch the edges ⅟₁₆ inch less than the finished width of the completed trim.

CUTTING THE BINDING:

- Cut the binding trim on the *crosswise* of knit fabric to obtain stretch and "give." (This is similar to the bias or diagonal on a woven fabric.)
- Cut binding strips *four times* the *desired width* of the *finished binding.*

OPTIONAL: overedge on edge of binding trim.

APPLYING THE BINDING (open flat method):

- Place the right side of binding trim to the *right* side of the garment (unfinished edge if one edge was overedged). Stitch by machine, using the *same seam allowance as the desired width of the completed trim.*
- Press the seam allowances open on the stitched seam. Clip on curved seam when necessary to make the seams lie smoothly.
- Trim by skiving (holding shears at an angle) ⅟₁₆ to ⅛ inch off the *binding seam allowance only* to allow for bulk when the binding rolls back on the desired fold line.
- Fold binding trim over the seam allowances to the wrong side of the garment. Pin or baste into position.
- *Machine-stitch in the "ditch"*—or seam well—from the right side, or stitch from the right side close to the seam well. An *alternate method* is to stitch the binding and garment seam allowance together from the wrong side close to the first line of stitching; or stitch by hand using a running catch stitch (tailor's hemming stitch).
- When applying binding, *ease* the trim slightly around *outside curves.* This will allow the trim to fit smoothly on the outer edge which is longer. *Examples:* around collars, patch pockets, flaps, and lower curve of jacket fronts.
- On *inside curves,* stretch binding slightly so the trim will fit the shorter inward curve when the trim is turned back.
- The *wider the bindings,* the *more* stretching is necessary.

FINISHING THE ENDS:

- Measure the binding to fit the *armscye.* Seam with right sides together, forming a circle before applying.

or

- Use the common trade method of binding the armscye before stitching the underarm seam.

or

- Fold under the beginning of the binding trim at the underarm seam. Continue around armscye bringing the raw edge over the folded edge.

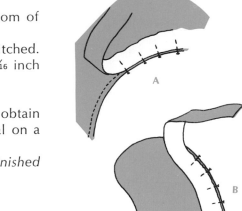

Fig. 11-2. Binding curves. *A,* inside curve; *B,* outside curve.

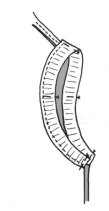

Fig. 11-3. Trade method for applying ribbing on armscye.

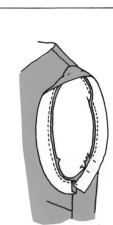

Fig. 11-4. Finishing ends of binding.

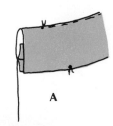

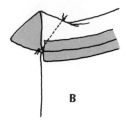

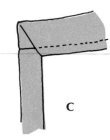

Fig. 11-5. Mitering self-fabric trim at end on neckline.

NECKLINES:

- Traditional dressmaking methods may be used for *finishing the ends of the binding trim on tricots, jerseys, and lightweight knits.* The raw edges at the end of the trim may be turned under *before* the first row of stitching.

or

- The raw edge may be turned under before stitching in the "ditch" —or seam well—which is the second row of stitching.

MITERING

Mitering is recommended to remove bulk for double and bulky knits. If *lapped* zipper application method is used, miter the *overlap* side. If *center* application is used, *miter both sides.*

MITERING ENDS OF SELF-FABRIC TRIM:

- Apply right side of trim to the right side of the garment. Press seam allowances open and trim binding seam allowance as mentioned above. Fold trim into position on the fold line.
- Thread-mark point **a** on the fold line ⅝ inch from the cut edge. (Width of zipper seam allowance.)
- At raw edge of trim, thread-mark point **b** 1¼ inches from cut edge. (Two times width of seam allowance.)
- Fold binding on the fold line with right sides together.
- Holding finger at point **a,** pivot binding trim so that point **b** meets cut edge.
- Machine stitch trim between **a** and **b.**
- Press seam open. Trim to ⅛ inch. Turn to the right side. Press.

MITERING CORNERS OF SELF-FABRIC TRIM:

When applying binding trim around corners of *collars, vents,* and *jacket fronts,* the corners are mitered. In lighter weight fabric or commercial trim the fabric may not be removed, but in heavier fabrics such as double knits and textured knits, the fabric in the miter is stitched from the inside and the excess fabric is removed.

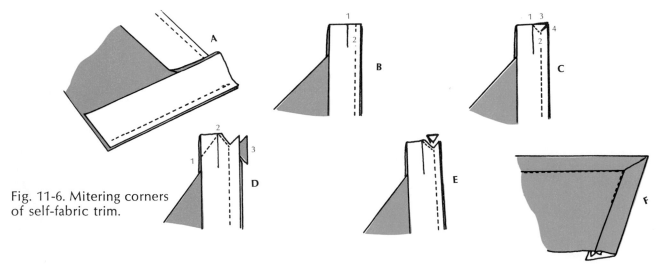

Fig. 11-6. Mitering corners of self-fabric trim.

MITERING AFTER APPLYING BINDING:

- Apply right side of trim to the right side of garment as described above. Stop the stitching ½ inch from the corner (or the width of the designated seam allowance). Retrace a couple of stitches. (See Fig. 11-6, A.)
- Turn the binding around the corner, forming a triangle and again matching the raw edges. Stitch to the corner, using the ½-inch seam allowance (or designated seam allowance). *Stitching lines must meet at the corner.* Retrace again. (See Fig. 11-6, A.)
- Fold the garment extending the corner of the binding out flat. (See Fig. 11-6, B.)
- Measure the width of the seam allowance to the left of the stitching. Draw a line from the fold down about 1 inch. *Illus. B—1–2.* Join the end of the stitching to the marked line at the fold by stitching. (See Fig. 11-6, C, 1-2.)
- Miter the trim on the inner side of the jacket by marking a line on fold of trim *parallel to fold* of garment ending at previous stitching line. (See Fig. 11-6, D, 1-2.)
- Remove triangle as shown in Figure 11-6, E if fabric is firm. If fabric is sleazy, slash on darkened lines and press open. (See Fig. 11-6, C, 3-4.) Trim off binding seam allowances on inner side to ⅛ inch. Trim off triangle at top of seam allowance. (See Fig. 11-6, D.)
- Complete applying trim as suggested above. (See Fig. 11-6, F.)

PREPRESSING AND STITCHING MITER BEFORE APPLYING BINDING:

OUTSIDE CORNER:

- This method is desirable for trims which can be prepressed, providing creases which act as stitching guidelines.
- Fold and press self-fabric trim or binding trim in half. May press seam allowances.
- Place binding trim on garment edge as it will be sewn.
- Press miter around corner. (See Fig. 11-7, A, 1.)
- Open trim to the wrong side. Crease lines will appear as shown in Figure 11-7, B.
- Fold binding crosswise, right sides together on folded line. (See Fig. 11-7, B, 1-2.)
- Stitch on diagonal crease lines from 1–2–3. (See Fig. 11-7, C.)
- Trim seam lines to ⅛ inch. (See Fig. 11-7, C.)
- Trim and complete attaching the binding.

INSIDE CORNER:

- Fold and press self-fabric trim or binding trim in half. Press in seam allowances.
- Place binding trim on garment edge as it will be sewn.
- Press mitered corner. (See Fig. 11-7, A, 2.)
- Open trim to expose crease. (See Fig. 11-7, D.)
- Fold binding crosswise, right sides together on folded line. (See Fig. 11-7, D, 1-2.)
- Stitch on folded triangular lines. (See Fig. 11-7, E.)

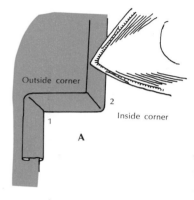

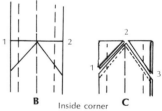

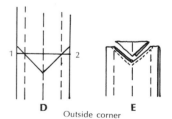

Fig. 11-7. Prepressing and stitching miter before applying binding.

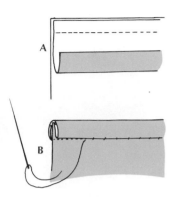

Fig. 11-8. Rolled binding.

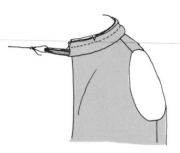

Fig. 11-9. Shaping rolled binding with yarn.

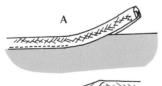

Fig. 11-10. Applying commercial braid.

- Trim off triangle at corner of seam allowance. Remove triangle at center leaving ⅛-inch seams.
- Turn and complete attaching binding.

ROLLED BINDING

To achieve a rolled or "bouffant" effect with a binding, self-knit fabric may be folded into the binding. The French binding is one such method. An edge trim may be inserted into the binding around the neck and sleeve. Rolled binding may be used for *neck edge, hemline,* or as a *cuff on a sleeve.*

Another technique is described below:
- Determine how many layers of fabric are desired in the "roll."
- For four layers of binding, cut the binding three times the desired finished width + the ⅝-inch seam allowance—i.e., for a ¾-inch finished roll, cut the binding 2⅞ inch wide.
- Apply the right side of binding to right side of garment using ⅝-inch seam allowance.
- Fold other end of binding back ¾ inch. Press lightly.
- Bring folded edge over seam allowance *to* stitching line.
- Slip-stitch into position.
If trim is to be added:
- Apply *right* side of binding to *wrong* side of garment.
- Trim may be inserted when slip-stitching finished binding.
[Note: A rolled binding may be shaped by applying the binding, leaving the ends open. Cut 20 to 30 strands of four-ply knitting yarn twice the length of rolled binding. Tie a string in the middle, fold in half, and pull through binding. Add the amount of yarn to achieve the desired roll. Cut yarns ½ inch from end. Turn in ends of binding and fasten by hand.]

COMMERCIAL BRAID

Pre-folded trim may be used to finish the raw edges of a neckline or armscye. Most are pressed slightly off-center with the top side slightly narrower. Flat braid or trim is used on a finished edge as a border, or to outline a pocket, collar, front edge or hem, or to create a design.

ONE-STEP METHODS FOR PRE-FOLDED TRIM:
- Pre-shape braid or trim for curved edges.
- Slip the raw edge of garment into the braid with the narrower side on top (right side of garment).
- Machine-stitch from the right side.

TWO-STEP METHOD:
- Use technique described above for applying self-fabric binding.
- May finish the wrong side by hand.

or

- Fold braid over raw edge.
- Hand stitch on the right side of garment first.

- Machine-stitch from right side close to edge of braid, catching underneath side of braid.

COMMERCIAL ROLLED-EDGE TRIM

The rolled-edge trim is used in the knit garment industry on shells at the neck and armscye. It is now available to the home sewer from ½ inch to 1½ inches in width. The roll remains permanent on the trim. It may be applied with the roll down or up when completed.

NECK EDGE:
- Apply zipper first.
- Begin trim at center back extending the trim ½ inch beyond the zipper teeth. Place flat edge of trim even with cut edge of garment. Stitch close to the roll attaching trim to garment.
- Stretch trim slightly at the back curve of the neck.
- Fold end back over zipper.
- Turn trim to wrong side into finished position. Only the roll will be visible on the right side.
- Tack at several points to hold into position

or

- Topstitch from the right side close to the seam line.

ARMSCYE:
- Apply trim before finishing underarm seam. It is difficult to piece rolled-edge trim successfully.

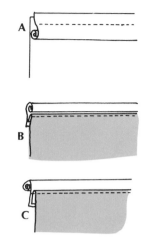

Fig. 11-11. Applying commercial rolled-edge trim.

SEAM ALLOWANCE AS A FINISH

"QUICKIE" METHOD OF EDGE FINISHING USING SEAM ALLOWANCE

This method utilizes the seam allowance to finish the edge of the knit garment. It is a "quickie" method and used for tank tops, knit tops for children, and play clothes.
- Stay-stitch edge on seam allowance (⅝ inch).
- Fold seam allowance to the wrong side of the stitching line. Press. Machine-stitch ⅜ inch from the edge.
- Trim off remainder of seam allowance close to the stitching.
- Stitch another row close to folded edge.

or

- Use a three-step zigzag or fancy stitch through entire ⅜-inch seam.

or

- Overedge the raw edge. Machine-stitch close to the folded edge and catch the inner edge lightly by hand to the garment.

or

- Place a strip of shaped bias tape on neckline; fold seamline over tape and topstitch with two rows of straight stitching.

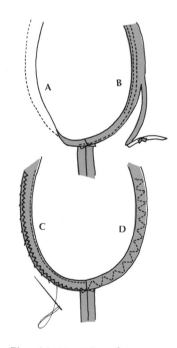

Fig. 11-12. "Quickie" method for edge finish.

Fig. 11-13. "Quickie" edge finish on seam allowance (taped).

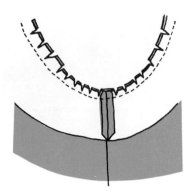

Fig. 11-14. Clipping and grading seams.

FACINGS

Facings are frequently omitted on knit garments to avoid bulk. If used, facings may be constructed of other lighter weight fabrics—e.g., taffeta is sometimes used in the shoulder area on wool knits for added wearing comfort. Facings may be attached with bindings, may be constructed with a straight or crosswise strip of fabric, may be shaped or fitted like a garment, or may be cut as an extension onto the garment.

FACING TIPS

FINISHING EDGES:

The inner edge of facings may be left "raw," except in some cotton or jersey knits which may "curl." Some home sewers prefer to *overedge the raw edge* so it appears more finished or does not curl.

CLIPPING AND GRADING SEAMS:

When clipping facing seams, remember that the more curved the seam, the more clips are necessary for the garment to lie smoothly. When grading seams, the garment seam is left longer.

UNDERSTITCHING:

Understitching by hand or machine holds the facing in position. After applying facing, grade seams, clip where necessary, and press *both* seam allowances toward the facing. Stitch by machine or hand *through* the facing and both seam allowances.

ANCHORING:

Never attach free edge of facing around the entire edge of the garment. The tacking must not show on the right side of the garment.

Use an over-and-over stitch to tack facing to garment at seams and darts.

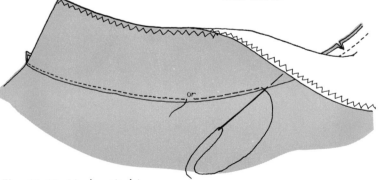

Fig. 11-15. Understitching.

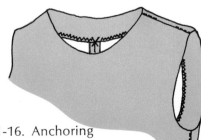

Fig. 11-16. Anchoring facings.

On spongy knit fabrics, stitch in seam well (or by hand) for about 1 inch with matching thread. This may also be done on facings of hip-hugger pants or skirts at the dart and seamline to hold waistline facing in position.

FUSING:

In textured and heavy polyester knits, facings may be fused to the garment. Cut a piece of fusing material about ½ inch to ⅝ inch wide to fit the outer edge of the facing. Press on the wrong side of the facing. Attach facing to garment.

Clip and grade seams. Turn facing to the inside of garment and press fused edge (remove paper first) onto garment. For two-sided web, fuse two together in one operation.

In some cases, one may fuse *featherweight bias nonwoven fabric* or another interfacing to the wrong side of the entire facing before applying the facing to the garment. This provides a firm facing.

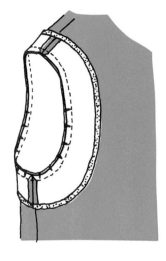

Fig. 11-17. Fusing facing.

ONE-PIECE NECK AND ARMSCYE FACING (NARROW SHOULDER)

This method works well when the shoulder seam length is narrow—less than 2½ inches. It is not necessary for the garment to have a center back seam.

- Stitch facing to garment with right sides together at the *neck* and at the *armscye,* leaving 2 inches free below the shoulder.
- Grade and clip seams. Turn facing to the inside of garment.
- Open facing at shoulder and stitch garment and facing seam in one seam.
- Turn in seam allowances on top of armscye and slip-stitch.

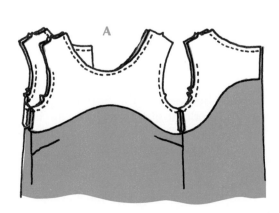

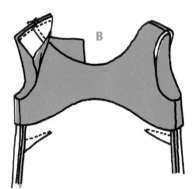

Fig. 11-18. One-piece neck and armscye facing (narrow shoulder).

ONE-PIECE NECK AND ARMSCYE FACING (WIDER SHOULDER WITH CENTER-FRONT OR CENTER-BACK OPENING—"TUNNEL METHOD")

Stitch garment shoulder seams with right sides together. Stitch facing seams at shoulder. Press open. Allow side seams and center front or center back to remain open.

- Placing right sides together, stitch facing to garment around neck edge and armscye.
- Grade and clip seam allowances.
- Turn garment to the right side by placing hand between the facing and garment and pull the·back of the garment through the "tunnel" at the shoulder.
- Open facing and stitch facing and garment seam in one continuous seam.

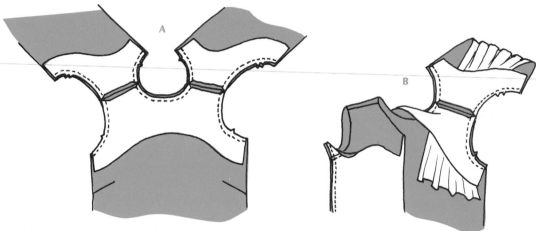

Fig. 11-19. Facing—wider shoulder with CF or CB opening —"tunnel method."

SHAPED ARMSCYE FACING

This method of applying an armscye facing is designed for *bulky or heavy knits.* It eliminates some of the extra bulk at the tip of the shoulder where the shoulder seam folds back on itself.

- On the garment armscye, stay-stitch a *little less than* ⅜ *inch* from the cut edge, beginning at the shoulder, to the notch on front. Continue from the notch to the underarm seam by stay-stitching a *little less than* ⅝ *inch* from the cut edge. Repeat the same procedure on the back armscye of the garment bodice.
- Stitch the shoulder seams and underarm seams of the garment. Stitch the seams of the armscye facings.
- Press the seams open. Trim seam allowances diagonally at end of shoulder, facing, and underarm seams.

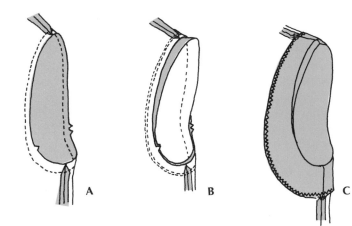

Fig. 11-20. Shaped arm-scye facing.

- Place a mark or pin ⅞ *inch* from the armscye edge of the facing at the highest point of the shoulder.
- Place the right side of the facing to the right side of garment. Matching the notches, pin from notch to notch on the underarm seam allowance.
- At the high point of the shoulder, key the ⅜-*inch* stay-stitching line on the garment bodice to the ⅞-*inch* mark on the facing. Pin to the notches, gradually tapering the seam allowances to ⅝ inch at the notches. Stitch the entire armscye.
- Press the seam open over the top half of the armscye. On the lower half of the armscye, press the facing with the seamline slightly to the inside. Clip and grade seams to about ¼ inch.
- Fold the facing to the inside of the garment on the regular ⅝-inch designated seamline of the garment. The seamline will be about ¼ inch from the armscye at the point of the shoulder, tapering to the notches on the front and back. This eliminates seam bulk at the high point of the shoulder—where the shoulder seam intersects with the facing seam.
- Tack the interfacings on the seamlines at the shoulder and underarm.

BINDING TRIM AS FACING

Use a *binding trim as a facing for armscye* (bulky fabrics). This method places the seam allowance inside the garment, rather than at the garment edge over the top half of the armscye. This technique may be used for armscye facings, ends of collars, and for neck facings at top of zipper. The directions are given for a ⅝-inch seam allowance.

- Stay-stitch the upper half of the armscye from notch to notch, ⅜ inch from cut edge.
- Stay-stitch the lower half of the armscye from notch to notch, ½ inch from cut edge.
- Trim seam allowances to ⅛-inch width. Remove ¼ inch around top half of armscye seam and ⅜ inch from lower half.

- Pin ¾ to 1 inch crosswise strip with right side toward the right side of the garment around armscye. Stitch ¼ inch seam.
- Press seam open.
- Clip through seam allowance at notches. On lower half of sleeve, press binding-facing to the inside of the garment so that the seamline is on the edge.
- On upper half of sleeve, press binding-facing to inside of garment so that the seam line is ⅛ inch plus from the edge.
- Complete by stitching in the "ditch"—or seam—well by machine.

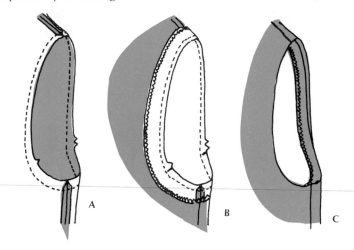

Fig. 11-21. Binding trim as facing.

BINDING USED AS PIPING WITH A FACING

This is designed for suits or vests or other edges using a facing and a ¼-inch finished piping on the edge.

- Remove ⅝-inch seam allowances from garment and facing.
- Stitch 1-inch piping strip, right sides together, to edge of facing.
- Stitch other edge of piping strip with right sides together to garment edge.
- Press seams open. Skive ¹⁄₁₆ inch from seam lines on the piping *only*.
- Fold facing back into position matching seam lines.
- Attach seam lines together by hand or machine.

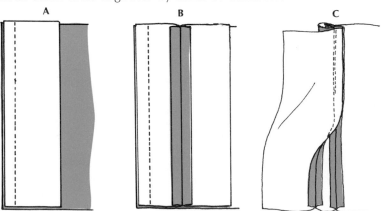

Fig. 11-22. Binding used as piping with a facing.

FINISH FOR END OF NECK FACING FOR INVISIBLE ZIPPER

In this method the seam does not fall on the edge of the zipper which eliminates bulk. The directions are designed for a ⅝-inch seam allowance.

- Join shoulder seams of the neck facing. Finish outer edge of facing if desired.
- Install zipper. (See *Zippers,* Chapter 9, p. 55.)
- Trim ⅝ inch from the center back of *both ends of facing.*
- Pin facing on the garment right sides together, matching raw edge of facing to raw edge of garment at CB. Stitch a ⅜-inch seam catching the facing, zipper tape, and garment seam allowance.
- Reposition facing matching notches and shoulder seams. Note that a fold will be formed at center back. Stitch a ⅝-inch seam allowance around neck edge, attaching the facing to the garment.
- Grade, clip, and turn facing to the inside of the garment. Understitch if desired.

Fig. 11-23. Finish for end of neck facing for invisible zipper.

FINISH FOR END OF NECK FACING FOR LAPPED ZIPPER

This finish for the end of the neck facing for a lapped zipper eliminates bulk and the edges lie smoothly and flat. This may also be used for a slot application finishing both sides.

- Finish the raw, outer edge of facing if desired.
- Pin the right side of the facing to the right side of the neck edge.
- Turn back 1 inch of facing at left side of garment facing (lapped side of zipper placket). Trim off ½ inch of facing.
- Machine-stitch facing to garment on designated seam allowance. Grade and clip seam except at the 1-inch extension at the end of facing.
- Understitch. Turn facing to inside of garment.
- Machine-baste zipper-placket opening on seamline, keeping facing out of the way.
- Apply zipper. (See p. 59.)
- Turn facing into position on the inside of the garment. Press.
- Hand stitch ends of facings next to zipper teeth and the extension fold at the neckline.
- Apply a closure.

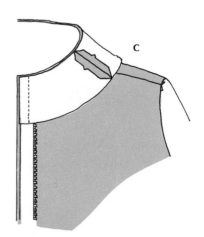

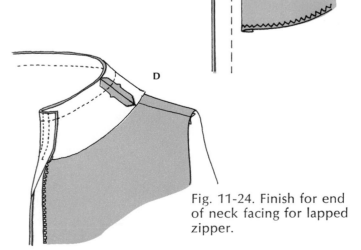

Fig. 11-24. Finish for end of neck facing for lapped zipper.

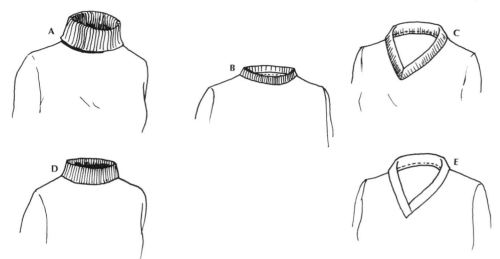

Fig. 12-1. Neckline finishes. *A*, turtle; *B*, crew; *C*, V-neck; *D*, mock turtle; *E*, self-fabric.

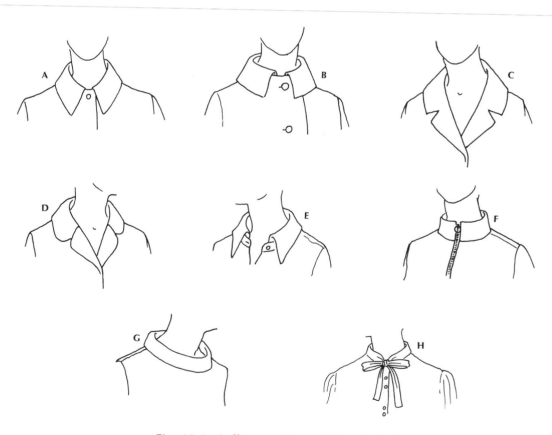

Fig. 12-2. Collars. *A*, shaped; *B*, rolled; *C*, shawl; *D*, notched; *E*, collar with stand; *F*, standing; *G*, bias turnover; *H*, tie.

12

NECKLINE FINISHES, COLLARS, AND PLACKETS

Ribbing may be applied to the neckline making a turtleneck, mock turtle, or a crew neck.

A V-neck may be finished with binding of self-fabric or a facing. (See Edge Finishes.) Ribbing or self-fabric may trim a V-neck which is finished at the V with a miter or with a lap.

Shaped, rolled, notched, standing, tie, shawl, stand, and crosscut turnover collars may all be made in knits. Most dressmaking books give instructions for the various types of collars. However, there are a few shortcuts and methods for removing bulk which are especially appropriate for knits.

Fig. 12-3. Measuring ribbing around head.

CREW NECK, TURTLENECK, AND MOCK TURTLE

SET-IN METHOD

CUT NECK RIBBING:

Cut ribbing across width of fabric. Self fabric can be substituted if it stretches approximately one-half its length, i.e., 8 inches stretches to 12 inches. If it does not stretch sufficiently, you may apply it and add a zipper.
SUGGESTED WIDTHS:
CREW NECK: 3 inches wide (½ inch smaller for child).
TURTLENECK: 9 inches wide (1 inch smaller for child).
MOCK TURTLE: 4½ inches wide (1 inch smaller for child).
LENGTH OF RIBBING:
Measure length by stretching strip around the largest part of the head. Add a ¼-inch seam allowance to each end.

or

Use a 3:4 ratio—3 inches of neckband for every 4 inches of neck seam; i.e., 16-inch neck-seam measurement would require a 12-inch band.

STITCH END OF RIBBING:

- Place right sides together. Stitch a ¼-inch seam allowance.
- Press seam open and fold in half lengthwise with the wrong sides together.

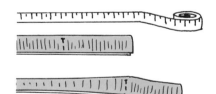

Fig. 12-4. Measuring neck ribbing.

Fig. 12-5. Stitching end of ribbing.

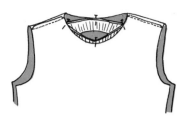

Fig. 12-6. Marking and attaching ribbing at neck.

MARK RIBBING AND NECKLINE:

- Divide ribbing into quarters. Mark with pins. Seam will be placed in center back.
- Fold garment in center back and center front and mark with pins. Place CF and CB together and pin in quarters. Note that the quarter marks do not fall on the shoulder seams.

STITCH NECKBAND ON GARMENT:

- Turn garment inside out. Pin right side of ribbing to the right side of the garment, matching quarter markings. Place ribbing seam at CB.
- Stitch with garment down and ribbing up, doing a quarter of the neckline at a time.
  CREW NECK: stretch ribbing to fit neckline and stitch.
  TURTLENECK: stretch ribbing and also neck edges while sewing, as neck edge is smaller than the crew neckline.

TOPSTITCH BACK NECKLINE:

- On a crew neck, may topstitch back-seam allowance. Do not stretch.

"QUICKIE" SEAMLINE METHOD

Stitch tape into left-shoulder seam.

- Prepare and mark ribbing and garment neckline as directed above.
- Pin ribbing to garment with right sides together, folding back about 1¼ inches on each end at right open shoulder.
- Stitch, using a ¼-inch seam allowance, beginning at right shoulder through a single layer for 1¼ inches. Continue through double layer of ribbing to the opposite side, ending with 1¼ inches in a single layer. (See Fig. 12-7, A.)
- *Pin right-shoulder seam. Stitch beginning at edge of neck ribbing, continuing to tip of shoulder. (See Fig. 12-7, B.)
- Stitch in "ditch"—or seam well—around neck edge.

or

- Stitch opening at right-shoulder seam to seam allowance on the inside.

Fig. 12-7. "Quickie" seam-line method for applying ribbing.

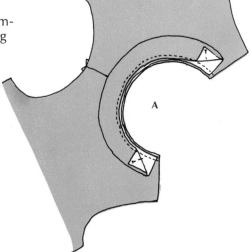

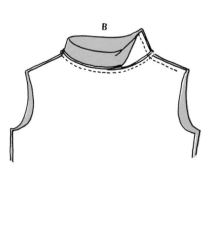

PREFINISHED KNIT TURTLENECK BAND

When a commercial prefinished knit turtleneck band is used, it is turned to the right side and applied in a single layer.

- Complete steps as in "Quickie Method" above as far as the *asterisk,* with the exception of stitching a single edge (rather than double edge) of wrong side of band to right side of garment.
- Begin stitching right shoulder seam *slightly less* than half of the turtleneck ribbing and continue to armscye edge of shoulder seam.
- Turn garment to right side. Clip at end of stitching on turtleneck. Complete stitching seam to end of ribbing with the right sides of ribbing together.

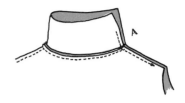

V-NECK BAND

METHOD A: TWO-STITCH METHOD

CUT TRIM:
- Use crosscut fabric or knitted ribbing.
- Measure back neck seam and from shoulder to V on each side. Cut trim that length and 2½–3 inches wide. Easing band at back neck will provide seam allowance.
- Seam banding with right sides together, using ½-inch seam.
- Pin right side of banding to right side of garment with the seam allowance at center back, or slightly toward band near shoulder seam. Ease about 1 inch of garment onto banding across back neck by stretching the banding.
- Begin stitching at V. Continue around, leaving needle in V.
- Stitch miter from pivot at V (1) to (2) to (3). (The angle equals half of folded ribbing—i.e., 1 to 2 = 2 to 3 = 3 to 4 = 4 to 2.) (See Fig. 12-9, C.)
- Slash along lengthwise fold of ribbing to stitching from 4 to 2. Slash along bottom fold to mitered stitches at seam allowances— 1 to 4, and continuing from 4 to 3. Press open.
- Fold neckband in half to wrong side of garment.
- Attach unfinished edge by hand *or* with overedge stitch *or* by stitching to seam about ⅛ inch from edge.

Fig. 12-8. Applying prefinished band for turtleneck.

Fig. 12-9. Applying band for V-neck–two-stitch method.

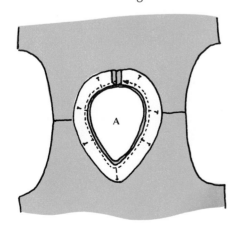
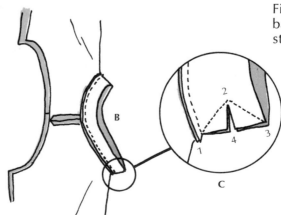

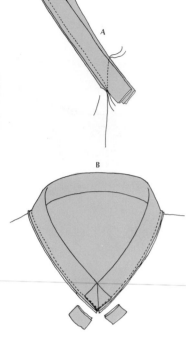

METHOD B: ONE-STITCH METHOD

Cut the ribbing or banding about 2 inches longer than the neckline measurement.

- Fold band in half lengthwise. Beginning at V with 1 inch extending, pin raw edges of ribbing to garment, right sides together. Stretch across back of neck (about 1 inch on garment).
- Stitch beginning at V and continue to about ¾ to 1 inch from V. Retrace. Cut thread. Pin first end out of the way. Turn to inside of garment and complete stitching, matching stitches exactly to V.
- Clip *garment only* at V.
- Pull banding out flat and stitch angle through both ends of binding forming a miter.
- Press seam open. Trim off excess and fasten edges of miter to seam allowance with a few hand stitches.

METHOD C: OVERLAP METHOD

The directions are for a man's garment neckline. Reverse for ladies.

- Cut a strip of self-knit fabric, crosscut at least 2½ inches wide and 2 inches longer than the neckline measure.
- Fold in half lengthwise. Press.
- Place two pieces of transparent tape at the center-front V with one edge on the marked seamline. This stays the fabric and acts as a seam guide. Optional: May stay-stitch V. If piping is desired, apply to neckline before the V-neckline band.
- Pin the band to the right side of the garment at the neckline, matching the raw edges. Be certain the raw ends of the band extend at least 1 inch beyond center front of V. Stretch the band across the back of the neck using 3:4 ratio.
- Begin stitching 2 inches from the right-center-front V. Continue stitching ending at the left-center-front V. Reinforce the stitching.
- Clip the seam allowance just to the stitching or tape at the center-front V.

Fig. 12-10. Applying band for V-neck—one-stitch method.

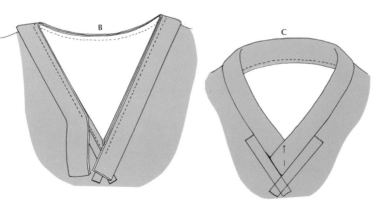

Fig. 12-11. V-neck—overlap method.

- Turn the band toward the neckline so the seam allowances will be on the wrong side of the garment. Push the ends of the insert through the 2-inch opening so that they are on the wrong side.
- From the wrong side of the garment, pin the ends of the band to the seam allowance of the 2-inch unstitched area. Check the right side of the garment to be sure the band lies correctly.
- From the wrong side of the garment, stitch the 2-inch area, backstitching at the center-front V.
- Remove the tape from the right side of the garment. Trim the neckline seam to ¼ inch and finish the seam.
- Optional: Topstitch ⅛ inch from the seamline on the right side of the garment.

COLLARS

TURNOVER COLLAR

This is a very popular collar for knit garments and is in high fashion too! It is sometimes misnamed a rolled collar.
- Cut the collar on the crosscut or bias.
- Usually an interfacing is not necessary, but with some soft jerseys, a lightweight bias nonwoven may be used. If one is used, cut the same as the collar. Place on wrong side of collar. Baste with long, loose, permanent basting stitching ¼ inch from the fold *on* the *undercollar*.
- Overedge the neck edge of the upper collar.
- Pin wrong sides of collar together, neck edges even. Run a basting along the fold line.

Ease may be built into the upper collar, so that when it turns over there is sufficient fabric to roll. The amount of ease depends on the weight of the fabric. The directions given will allow for a ⅜-inch ease:
- Fold collar wrong side out on the basted fold line. Pin on fold line on ends.
- Place upper-collar neck edges back ⅜ inch from undercollar neck edge. Pin and baste-ease into seams at end of collar.
- Stitch ends of collar. Trim corner, grade and press open seams. Turn to the right side.
- Shape collar on seam press or collar roll.

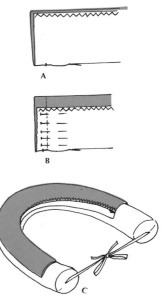

Fig. 12-12. Turnover collar.

SHAPED COLLAR (REMOVING BULK FROM SEAM ON OUTER EDGE OF COLLAR)

CONSTRUCTING THE COLLAR:
Undercollar may be constructed of self-fabric or matching nylon or polyester taffeta. Interface if desired, although usually not necessary.
- Mark dot at seam allowance on point of upper and undercollar.
- Run a basting at ¾ inch from cut edge on undercollar.

- Place right side of outer edge of upper collar ½ inch down from right side of outer edge of undercollar between dots A and B.
- From the undercollar side, stitch on ¾-inch marked basting seam-line across the entire outer edge of collar, ending in line with dots A and B.

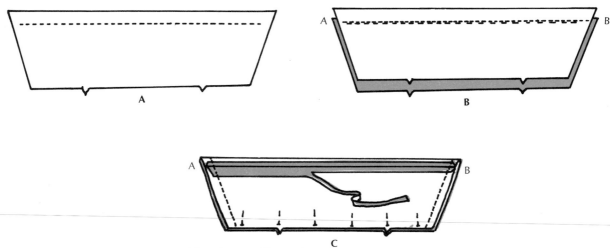

Fig. 12-13. Shaped collar.

- Trim upper-collar seam to a scant ¼ inch and the undercollar seam to ⅜ inch. Press seams open on edge presser.
- Match neck edge of upper and undercollar at outside seam and the dots of upper and undercollar. Stitch a ⅝-inch seam from neck edge to fold of collar. A fold will be formed at dot A and B. Tie threads. Repeat on other end.
- *Fusing web* may be stitched into a shaped collar if a firm, tailored collar is desired. The upper and undercollar is fused together after the collar is applied to the garment. The collars become "one."
- *A collar stay,* Rollex,* which may be cut with ordinary shears and sewn into any collar with width up to 6 inches, holds and controls the roll of collar at opening.

APPLYING THE COLLAR (front facing and back-neck facing):

- Pin collar to neckline, matching properly.
- Machine-stitch from center back to center front first on one side, then the other.
- Seam back-neckline facing to front facing at shoulder, with right sides together. Press seams open.
- Turn facing back over collar. Stitch facing over the collar.
- Clip, grade, and trim seam allowance. Press open.

  * Rollex—Curless Corp.

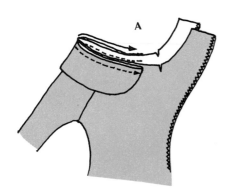

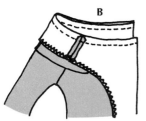

Fig. 12-14. Applying collar with front facing and back neck facing.

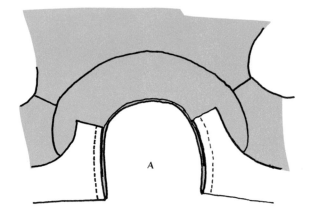

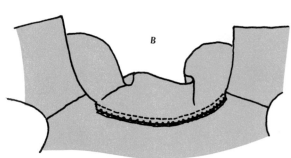

Fig. 12-15. Applying shaped collar—trade technique.

APPLYING SHAPED COLLAR (trade technique, front facing—no back facing):

This method is excellent for lightweight knits, children's clothes, tricot robes, etc.

- Pin collar to position at neckline, right side of undercollar to right side of the garment.
- Fold the facing back over the right side of collar.
- Stitch, beginning at the center front, just to the shoulder seams on both sides.
- Clip the collar and neckline seam at the shoulder seams.
- Pull seam through to right side of garment on the undercollar side.
- *From the undercollar side,* stitch the two layers of collar and the back neckline seam together. Trim to ¼ inch and overedge seam. The seam will lie under the collar.
- Attach the facings to the shoulder seam allowance.

STANDING COLLAR

Shape standing collar before applying to neck edge to prevent collar from standing away from the neck at folded edge.

- Shrink upper-collar edge and stretch seam edge.
- Take in collar at open-end seam edge to compensate for the amount stretched.
- Apply as for binding. See page 67.

PLACKETS

Plackets at the neckline featuring the tailored shirt look are popular for men, women, and children. A collar may be added at the neckline or contrasting trim in self-fabric or commercial trim.

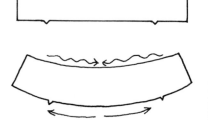

Fig. 12-16. Proper fit of standing collar. *Left,* right; *right,* wrong.

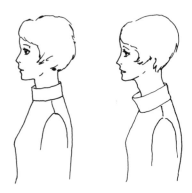

Fig. 12-17. Shaping standing collar.

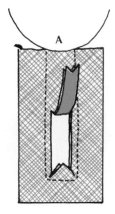

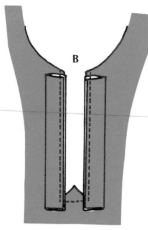

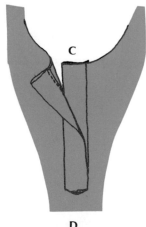

Fig. 12-18. Tab front
placket.

TAB FRONT

The tab can be made of self-fabric or contrasting fabric. Make opening long enough so the top will go over head comfortably.

WITHOUT A FACING

CUT FABRIC STAY AND TAB:
- Cut fabric stay of organdy or featherweight bias nonwoven fabric— 4 inches x 1 inch longer than tab opening.
- Cut two tabs lengthwise of fabric:
  LENGTH—length of opening + 1 inch.
  WIDTH—2 times width of finished placket + two, ¼-inch seam allowances.
- Press center fold lightly on stay.
- Press tabs in half lengthwise, wrong sides together.

MARK GUIDE ON STAY (Example for 1-inch-wide finished placket):
- Mark a rectangle the width of finished tab + two ¼-inch seam allowances and the desired length.
  OPTIONAL: The guidelines could be marked on paper and traced onto garment. The staylines are then stitched on the garment only.

ATTACH STAY TO GARMENT:
- Tape stay to wrong side of garment, matching center front of stay to center front of garment.
- Stitch rectangle lines using 12 stitches per inch.
- Cut along stitching lines leaving a ¼-inch seam allowance on sides. At the base, leave a ¾-inch triangle. Clip at point of triangle to corners.

ATTACH TABS:
- Place the folded tabs on right side of garment, matching cut edges of tab wtih cut edges of garment and stay. Pin.
- Turn to wrong side of garment and stitch along stay-stitching lines to corner. Retrace at bottom.
- Pin tab in position from the right side of garment, pushing free ends through to wrong side.
- Lift up garment. Stitch across the base of the triangle, attaching it to two tab ends.
- *Women—right over left*
- *Men—left over right*

TRIMMING TAB AND NECKLINE

Cut trim 2 inches wide on crosscut of fabric—self-fabric or ribbing.
- Stitch a ½-inch seam with right side of trim to right side of garment, beginning at end of placket and continuing around neck

to end of placket. Remember—stretch around back-neckline curve and ease at front-neck curve.

- Fold trim to wrong side of garment over seam allowance. Pin.
- Stitch in "ditch"—or seam well—from right side.
- Trim away excess seam allowance.
- May add buttons and buttonholes.

VARIATIONS OF TAB FRONT

POINTED V ON TAB:
- The V on the tab extends below the placket opening. Allow 1 inch extra.
- Place right sides of tab together. Stitch a V, allowing ¼-inch seam allowance on cut edge.
- Clip, turn, and press.
- Apply as directed above.

NARROW TAB PLACKET AND V-NECK WITH TRIM:
- Cut V neck on garment.
- Press crease on center front of garment for tab-placket opening.
- Cut trim:
  WIDTH: 1½ inches on crosscut.
  LENGTH: Around neck edge + 2 times length of placket opening + 3 inches.
- Press trim in half lengthwise with wrong sides together.
- Stay-stitch a "box" at bottom of neck opening: ¼ inch on each side of center front and up on sides 1½ inches.
- Pin and stitch trim to neckline, beginning at end of placket, allowing 1½ inches extending beyond placket. Continue around neckline to other end of placket. *Stretch trim* slightly around back of neck. *Ease trim* at point of V.
- Slash down center front to ¾ inch from end, then angle to corners forming a triangle.
- Turn garment to right side, turning placket to proper position whether for man or woman.
- Push free ends of tab through to the wrong side. Pin.
- Lift up garment. Stitch across base of triangle, attaching it to two tab ends.
- Press seam allowances toward garment.
- Stitch near seam from the right side around neck and placket, holding seam allowance in position.
- May trim with buttons.
- Lift up garment front, exposing triangle at base of placket. Stitch across base of triangle on stay guideline, attaching both tabs to triangle.
- Shape top of tab to fit neckline.

Fig. 12-19. Trimming tab and neckline.

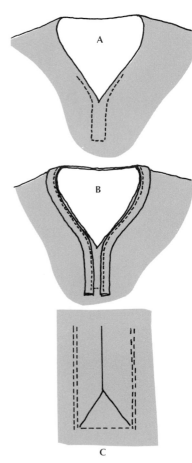

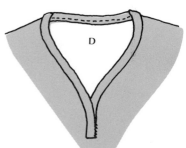

Fig. 12-20. Narrow tab placket and V-neck with trim.

SIMPLIFIED TAB PLACKET

This is a simplified method—foolproof for the beginner—for children, or for men and boys who are novices at fashion knit construction. (Finished tab is 1½ inches wide.)

- Mark placket opening with two pieces of transparent tape on right side of garment, aligning the edge with center front. Place another piece across bottom.
- Cut two tabs 3¼ inches wide and the desired length of opening + 1 inch. Press in half lengthwise with wrong sides together.
- Place cut edges of tab even with edge of transparent tape. Stitch a ¼-inch seam, ending at tops of crosswise tape. Retrace.
- Slash down center front between tape to ¾ inch from bottom. Slash to each corner—to end of stitching. (See p. 86 for directions for men or women.)
- Fold tabs into position. Fold ends of tabs to wrong side.
- Lift up front of garment. Stitch tabs and triangle across base of triangle.
- Remove tape. Wasn't that easy?

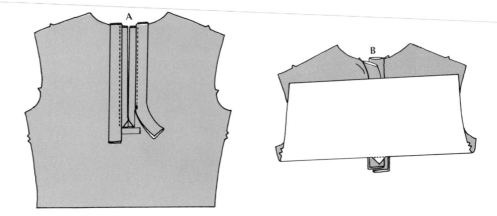

Fig. 12-21. Simplified tab placket.

13

SLEEVES AND SLEEVE FINISHES

Patterns designed specifically for knits present no problems in setting the sleeves, providing you have selected the type of knit suggested by the pattern designer. If there is more than ¾ inch of ease between the notches of a set-in sleeve, you may desire to remove the excess *before* cutting out the knit fabric. Trade techniques or traditional dressmaking techniques may be used in setting sleeves.

SLEEVES

REMOVING EXCESS EASE IN CAP

When the sleeve is already cut, remove a small amount of curve on each side of the cap from the high point of sleeve to the notch. Remove the same amount on the front and back of sleeve.

If the cap is unusually high and pointed you may remove up to ¼ inch on cap, tapering to notches. However, if the upper arm is heavy, a "pulled" look may result if the cap is not high enough.

TRADE TECHNIQUE FOR A SET-IN SLEEVE

Sew shoulder seam of garment. Leave underarm seam open.
- Match top of sleeve to shoulder seam. Match underarm seams. If pattern has notches, match notches.
- Stitch with *sleeve on bottom* and the *garment on top,* stretching armscye to fit sleeve.
- Stitch underarm seam from bottom of garment up to end of sleeve.

DRESSMAKER TECHNIQUE FOR SET-IN SLEEVE

Set sleeve into armscye as for woven fabrics. Trim seam allowance to ⅜ inch over top of sleeve and ¼ inch in lower half. May overedge the raw edges.

[Note: If sleeve is already cut and you have difficulty easing in fullness on a stable knit, machine-baste-ease from notch to shoulder point on front and back removing about ⅛ inch between each point, tapering to notch and shoulder point.]

STAY UNDERARM KIMONO SLEEVE

Cut a piece of seam tape or linen tape 4 inches in length.
- Shape with steam iron. Pin and stitch into seam with a shortened stitch. Clip seam allowance only.
- If curve is sharp, fold tape at curve.
- Press seam open.
  [Note: May desire to stay entire armhole on set-in sleeve of a stretchy knit.]

Fig. 13-1. Removing excess ease in sleeve cap.

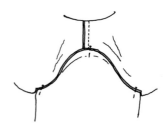

Fig. 13-2. Trade technique for setting sleeves.

Fig. 13-3. Dressmaker technique for set-in sleeve.

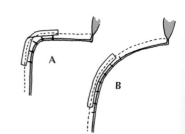

Fig. 13-4. Staying underarm kimono sleeve.

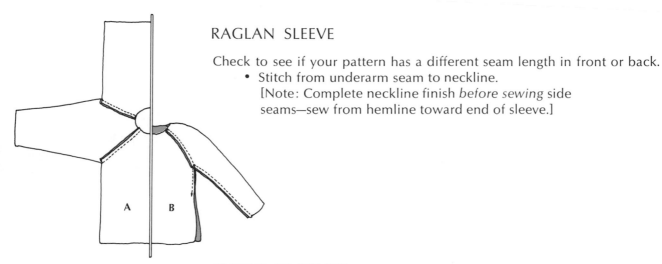

Fig. 13-5. Raglan sleeve.

RAGLAN SLEEVE

Check to see if your pattern has a different seam length in front or back.
- Stitch from underarm seam to neckline.
  [Note: Complete neckline finish *before sewing* side seams—sew from hemline toward end of sleeve.]

SLEEVE FINISHES

FABRIC HEM

- Measure and turn up fabric hem. See hems, page 100.
  [Note: An open-arm machine is ideal for applying cuffs and hem finishes on sleeves.]

FUSED HEM

- Durable and flexible hem. See hems, page 102.

SEAM ALLOWANCE FINISH

- "Quickie" method. See page 71.

Fig. 13-6. Ribbing for sleeves, necklines, and bottom of pullovers— trade cuff technique.

TRADE CUFF (SWEATER CUFF)

Used for sleeve cuffs for long or short sleeves, necklines, and at bottom of pullovers.
- Cut the ribbing or self-fabric knit the desired length, plus two seam allowances; and twice the desired width, plus two seam allowances.
- Stitch the ends of the cuff forming a circle. Press seams open.
- Fold cuff banding with wrong sides together, aligning raw edges. Press.
- *Divide sleeve into quarters and mark with pins. Divide cuff into quarters. Mark with pins.
- Place right side of cuff against right side of sleeve, matching cut edge of sleeve and cuff. Stitch with *garment on bottom,* stretching cuff rim to fit.

Fig. 13-7. Trade cuff. (sweater cuff).

- Trim seam allowance to ⅜ or ¼ inch. Overedge or overcast raw edge.
- Turn cuff down into position with the seam allowance turned toward garment. This gives a slight blouson effect.

MODIFIED TRADE TECHNIQUE FOR SWEATER CUFF (used for stable knits):

- Follow the technique above to the asterisk.
- Stitch two rows of machine gathering at lower edge of sleeve.
- Turn sleeve with the wrong side of the knit out. Place cuff circle inside sleeve, matching raw edges, adjusting sleeve gathers to fit cuff.
- Stitch through two layers of cuff and sleeve.
- Trim seam and overedge or overcast raw edge.
- Turn cuff down into position, pushing seam allowance toward sleeve.

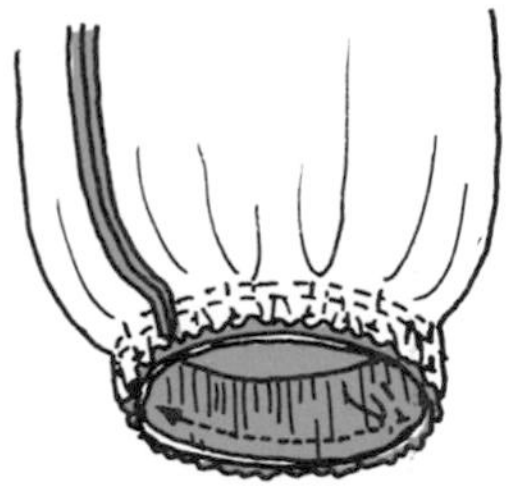

DRESSMAKER TECHNIQUE FOR SWEATER CUFF:

This method is similar to method described for applying binding to sleeve or neck edge.

- Prepare cuff as detailed above.
- Machine gather sleeve with two rows of stitching. Turn sleeve inside out with wrong side out. Place cuff inside sleeve with right sides together. Adjust gathers. Stitch through *one* layer of cuff (finished right side), and the sleeve.
- Turn sleeve right side out. Turn cuff down into position. Press seam allowances into cuff. Grade and trim seams if necessary.
- Fold inner edge of cuff over seam allowance. Do not fold under.
- Stitch in the "ditch"—or seam well—from the right side.

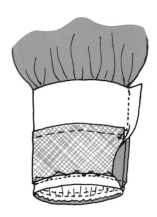

Fig. 13-8. Modified trade technique for sweater cuff.

Fig. 13-9. Dressmaker technique for sweater cuff.

BINDING

Bind with self-fabric ribbing, or trim. See page 66.

- Cut ribbing 2 inches smaller than armscye opening.
- Trim away 1 inch on garment armscye as 1 inch extra will be added in ribbing.

COMMERCIAL BRAID: See Edge Finishes—page 70.
ROLLED EDGE TRIM: See Edge Finishes—page 71.
FACINGS: See Edge Finishes—page 72.
FALSE CUFF: See Hem—page 102.
ROLLED BINDING AS CUFF:

- Cut and prepare length of cuff as described above. Prepare sleeve with machine gathering as described above.
- Cut desired *width* of cuff and proceed in attaching as directed under rolled binding, page 70.

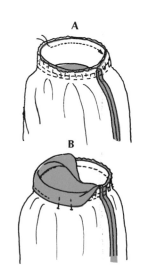

Fig. 13-10. Binding as a cuff.

14

WAISTBANDS AND WAISTLINES

Elastic is preferred by many for knit skirts or pants. The top of the garment may be tapered at the side seams and/or shaped with darts. The elastic is usually ¾–1 inch wide and may be applied with or without a separate waistband. Swimsuit elastic may be substituted for regular "skirt" elastic.

The elastic may be applied inside a casing folded back on top of the garment or with a waistband which is attached separately. If a waistband is used, it should be cut with the stretch, remembering that the garment needs to stretch enough to go over the hips. Cut the elastic 1 to 2 inches shorter than the waist measurement, or try it on around the waist until it fits comfortably and allow for overlap. The fabric band is about ¾–1 inch larger than the waist measurement as it should also stretch enough to go over the hips.

An elastic or stretch machine stitch is desirable to provide flexibility; however, a straight stitch may be used if the fabric is stretched sufficiently during stitching.

Following are several methods for applying elastic waistbands for skirts or slacks. Choose the one best suited to the design of the garment and the fabric.

NO SEPARATE WAISTBAND

METHOD A:
ELASTIC ATTACHED TO GARMENT ("SWIMWEAR TECHNIQUE")

This method is also used for applying elastic to swimwear. It is a simple technique; however, the elastic cannot be replaced easily. (Directions for ¾-inch elastic. See illustration, p. 194.)

ALLOW FOR WAISTBAND FOLD:
- Allow 1½ inches at the top of the skirt for a waistband fold.

CUT AND JOIN THE ELASTIC:
- Cut waistline elastic about 1 inch less than waist measurement, or so it fits comfortably.
- Join the elastic ends by overlapping ½ inch, forming a circle.
- Stitch the ends securely by stitching back and forth or stitch a square.

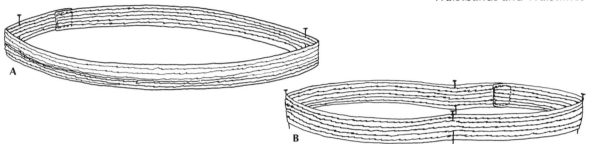

Fig. 14-1. Marking elastic for waistbands.

MARK THE ELASTIC:

- Since the figure is fuller in the front, the garment requires more ease in the front. Approximately 1 inch extra elastic is needed for this ease.
- Fold the circle of elastic in half, with the joining seam located somewhere in the back but not at the side seams or at CB. Mark each side with pins.
- To allow the extra 1-inch ease for the front, move each pin toward the back ½ inch, re-marking the side seams.
- Using these new side-seam marks, divide the front in half and mark the CF, and divide the back in half to mark the CB.

MARK THE TOP OF THE SKIRT:

- Place pins marking the CF, CB, and side seams of the skirt.

JOIN ELASTIC TO THE SKIRT:

- Pin the elastic to the wrong side of the garment, matching corresponding markings at side seams, CF, and CB. Align the raw edge of the skirt and the elastic.
- Place the right side of the garment down on the machine with the elastic up. Use a narrow zigzag stitch stretching the elastic to fit the knit garment, stitching the raw edge of garment and the elastic. If you are using a straight stitch, stretch both the garment and the elastic.
- Turn the garment inside out. Fold the top of the skirt back over the edge of the elastic forming a waistband.
- Use a wider zigzag and stitch on the elastic band edge, stretching the elastic to fit the skirt while stitching. This stitching shows on the right side.

METHOD B: "NO TWIST" METHOD

Same as method described above, up to joining the elastic to the skirt.

JOIN THE ELASTIC TO THE SKIRT:

- Place the elastic on the wrong side of the garment, aligning the raw edges of the fabric and the elastic.
- Zigzag, with the elastic up, the edge of the elastic away from the cut edge.

COMPLETE THE BAND:

- Fold the band down into position on the wrong side of the garment and topstitch with a zigzag attaching the raw edge of the fabric and the other side of the elastic to the garment.

Fig. 14-2. "No twist" method for elastic in casing—Method B.

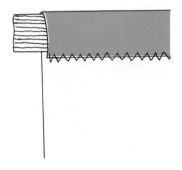

Fig. 14-3. Elastic in casing
—Method C.

METHOD C: ELASTIC IN A CASING

In this method the garment is folded back to form a casing. The elastic may be removed easily if it needs to be replaced or altered.

ALLOW FOR WAISTBAND FOLD:

- See Method A.

CUT AND JOIN THE ELASTIC:

- See Method A.

ATTACH ELASTIC TO FABRIC CASING:

- Fold fabric back to form a casing.
- Place the elastic inside the casing. Hold the casing in position by pinning at quarter points.
- Stitch along the raw edge of the casing with a zigzag stitch pushing the elastic up so that it does not get caught in the stitching.

or

- Stitch the casing first, leaving an opening (about 1 inch) for inserting the elastic.
- Insert the elastic with a bodkin (safety pin may be used). *Do not make a circle of the elastic before threading into the casing.*
- Overlap the ends of the elastic and fasten by hand.
- Close the opening in the casing with hand stitches.

SEPARATE WAISTBAND

METHOD A: DRESSMAKER'S METHOD

This method is adaptable for double knits in skirts and slacks. It could also be used for a garment with a zipper closure by attaching the elastic and finishing both ends of the waistband. May use ¾-inch or 1-inch elastic, as desired. Elastic may be replaced easily.

TOP OF GARMENT:

- Allow ⅝-inch seam allowance. The waistline will extend above.

CUT AND SEW THE WAISTBAND:

- *Width:* Cut the waistband two times the width of the elastic, plus ½-inch drop seam on the inside, plus a ⅝-inch seam allowance. For 1-inch elastic, the waistband will be 3⅛ inches wide.
- *Length:* Cut the waistband 2 inches longer than the waist measurement.
- Sew the ends together forming a circle.

CUT AND JOIN THE ELASTIC:

- Cut the elastic so it fits comfortably around the waistline, plus seam allowances for overlapping.

Fig. 14-4. Dressmaker method waistband.

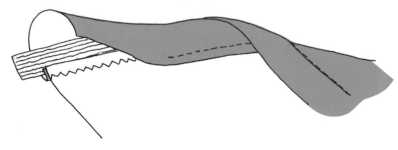

• Overlap the ends forming a circle. Stitch.

MARK THE WAISTBAND, ELASTIC, AND THE GARMENT INTO QUARTERS:

• For better fit, mark elastic and waistband as directed under "Mark the Elastic," pages 92–93.

ATTACH WAISTBAND TO THE GARMENT (FIG. 14-4):

• Slip the waistband circle over the garment with the right sides together. Match markings.
• Stitch a ⅝-inch seam allowance with a stretch stitch.
• Press the seam allowances up into the band.
• Trim the garment seam allowance to ⅜ inch plus and the band seam allowance to ½ inch plus. If fabric is bulky, press seam allowance open.

INSERT THE ELASTIC:

• Insert the elastic into the band toward the front of the waistband, inside the seam allowances. Match markings.

COMPLETE THE BAND (FIG. 14-5, A):

• Fold the waistband down toward the inside of the garment over the elastic. The raw edge of the knit will extend ½ inch beyond the stitching line. Press.
• Machine baste about ¼ inch from the seam line from the wrong side.
• From the right side, stretch and straight machine-stitch in the "well" or "groove." Remove basting stitch. Press.
• Allow the seam allowance to hang free, unfinished on the inside. Optional: Overedge the raw edge.

METHOD B:
SEPARATE WAISTBAND (PROFESSIONAL VARIATION)

This method is flat and professional-looking. It has one seam allowance, extended into the garment with the final stitching a zigzag stitch, which provides for more flexibility. There is no stitching in the "well" on the right side. The elastic may be replaced if necessary.

Follow the previous method up to attaching the waistband—with one exception: Cut the *width* of the waistband *two times the width of the elastic, plus two ⅝-inch seam allowances.*

ATTACH THE WAISTBAND TO THE GARMENT:

• Slip the waistband circle over the garment with the right sides together.
• Stitch a ⅝-inch seam allowance with a stretch stitch.
• Press the seam allowances open.

INSERT THE ELASTIC:

• Insert the elastic into the band toward the front of the waistband, inside the seam allowance pressed into the band. Match markings.

COMPLETE THE BAND (FIG. 14-5, B):

• Fold the waistband down toward the inside of the garment over

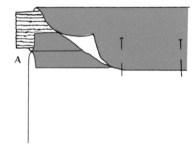

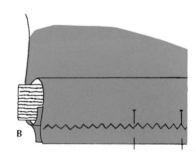

Fig. 14-5. Professional variation of waistband.

the elastic. The raw edge of the knit will extend ⅝ inch beyond the stitching line. Press.
- Place inside of garment down on the machine with the seam allowance to the right. Fold the waistband back onto the right side of the garment, exposing the seam. Stitch the two together close to the line of stitching with a zigzag, stretching if necessary.
- Press.
- Trim garment seam allowance to ½ inch.

METHOD C:
SEPARATE WAISTBAND (NO SEAM OVERLAPPING)

This method of applying a waistband is designed for bulky or heavy fabrics since there are no overlapping seams on the inside.

TOP OF GARMENT:
- Allow ¼ inch for a seam allowance to attach the waistband. Cut, sew, and press the waistband.
- *Width.* Cut the waistband *two times* the width of the elastic plus ½ inch. For a ¾-inch elastic, cut the band 2 inches wide.
- *Length.* Cut the waistband the measurement of the waistline plus 2 inches. This allows for a ⅝-inch seam allowance for joining the ends of the waistband.
- Fold back ¾ inch lengthwise and press.
- Sew the ends together with a ⅝-inch seam allowance forming a circle.

MARK THE ELASTIC AND THE WAISTBAND:
- Divide the elastic and waistband.

ATTACH THE ELASTIC TO THE WAISTBAND:
- Align the edge of the elastic to the edge of the wrong side of the waistband inside the ¾-inch fold-back. The other edge of the elastic will fall into the fold.
- Zigzag or overedge the edge of the elastic to the waistband. Place the elastic side up when stitching.

ATTACH THE ELASTIC WAISTBAND TO THE GARMENT:
- Place the right side of the band (not where the edge of the elastic is attached) to the right side of the garment.
- Match the quarter markings of the band to the garment.
- Stitch a ¼-inch seam allowance, using a small zigzag or stretch stitch. Stretch as needed to fit the garment.
- Press the seam allowance up into the band.

ATTACH THE WAISTBAND SEAM ALLOWANCE TO THE GARMENT:
- Fold the elastic side of the waistband toward the inside of the garment. The band-elastic edge will *just meet* the band-garment seam allowance. (See Fig. 14-6.)
- Pin into position and catch stitch by hand with matching thread.

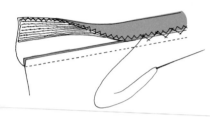

Fig. 14-6. Separate waistband—no seam overlapping.

METHOD D:
SEPARATE WAISTBAND ("QUICKIE" ONE-STITCH METHOD)

This is a simple method—quick and easy to do. It may be bulky on knits which are heavy. (Directions for ¾-inch elastic.)

TOP OF GARMENT:
- Allow ¼ inch for a seam allowance. The waistband will extend above the seamline.

CUT AND SEW WAISTBAND:
- *Width:* Cut waistband two times the width of the elastic, plus two, ¼-inch seam allowances. For ¾-inch elastic, cut the band 2 inches wide.
- *Length:* The length of the finished waistband is ¾–1 inch longer than the waistline measurement. For ⅝-inch seam allowances in the end of the waistband, cut the band the waist measurement plus 2 inches.
- Sew ends together, forming a circle using a ⅝ inch seam allowance. Press.
- Fold band in half lengthwise. Press.

CUT AND JOIN ELASTIC:
- Cut the elastic so it fits comfortably around the waistline, plus seam allowances for overlapping.
- Overlap the ends forming a circle. Stitch.

MARK THE ELASTIC AND THE WAISTBAND:
- Divide elastic and waistband into fourths. Mark with pins. See pages 92–93.

ATTACH WAISTBAND TO GARMENT:
- Place circle of elastic inside the folded waistband circle.
- Place the waistband circle over the garment, right sides together. Align the raw edges of the waistband to the raw edge of the skirt. Match markings of the garment and waistband.
- Stitch the two layers of the band to the garment with a ¼-inch seam allowance, using a zigzag or overlock stitch. Stretch the waistband as needed to fit the garment.
[Note: If the garment seam is ⅝ inch wide, trim to ¼ inch before stitching seam.]

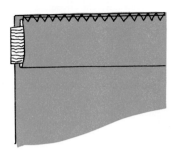

Fig. 14-7. "Quickie" one-stitch method of applying separate waistband.

METHOD E:
SEPARATE WAISTBAND ("NO TWIST" QUICKIE METHOD)

This is a simple, quick method of applying elastic with a separate waistband. The elastic is stitched at the top to provide firmness and, at the bottom, the waistband and the elastic are attached along the waistband-garment seam. The latter stitch limits the stretchability so this method would not be desirable for a figure with large hips and a small waistline.

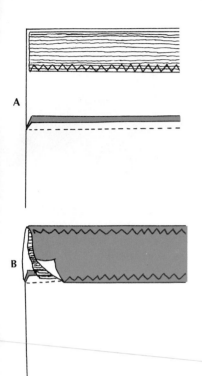

Fig. 14-8. "Quickie" "no-twist" method of applying elastic waistband.

Also, the final stitching shows on the right side. No seam allowances extend into the garment. Cut, mark, and stitch the waistband in a circle.

CUT AND STITCH THE WAISTBAND IN A CIRCLE:
- Cut the width of the waistband *twice the width of the elastic* plus *one* ⅝-inch seam allowance.
- Cut the length of the band the length of the waist measurement plus 2 inches. This allows for a ⅝-inch allowance plus ease.
- Stitch the ends of the waistband, forming a circle using a ⅝-inch seam allowance.

PRESS THE WAISTBAND:
- Press the seams open.
- Press in a ⅝-inch seam allowance along one lengthwise edge.
- Key the folded lengthwise edge and the remaining raw edge and press in half lengthwise.

ATTACH THE ELASTIC TO THE WAISTBAND:
- Place the elastic on the wrong side of the waistband along the fold line.
- Zigzag the edge of the elastic to the *wrong side* of the *inside* of the waistband along the fold line. If a straight stitch is used, stretch both the band and the elastic while stitching.

MARK THE GARMENT AND THE WAISTBAND:
- See pages 92–93.

ATTACH THE WAISTBAND:
- Key markings of waistband to the garment.
- Place and pin the right side of the waistband with the ⅝-inch seam allowance to the right side of the garment (half without the elastic).
- Machine-stitch, stretching slightly (⅝-inch seam allowance).
- Trim the garment seam shorter than the band seam. Press both seams up into the band.
- Turn inside of waistband into position over the seam, so the raw edge of the knit fabric covers the elastic. Zigzag, blind hem, or multiple zigzag, catching the raw edge of the waistband and the elastic to the garment-waistline seam.

WAISTBAND WITH ZIPPER PLACKET

On wool double-knit suits, skirts, tailored slacks, and ski pants, a zipper placket is usually used with the waistband. Elastic may be inserted in a traditional skirt-band technique rather than an interfacing, and the elastic is fastened at each end of the placket. The elastic may be inserted in just the back half of the skirt or slacks. Also, grosgrain or elastic may be used on the inner side of the waistband.

GROSGRAIN OR ELASTIC TECHNIQUE

CUT THE WAISTBAND:
- Cut the waistband length and the waist measure + 1 inch ease + two seam allowances + 1½ inch underlap.

- Cut the width desired + two seam allowances.

PREPARE THE GROSGRAIN:
- Select grosgrain the width of the finished band + ¼ inch.
- Preshrink. Shape with iron to fit contour of waist.

ATTACH THE BAND:
- Overlap one edge of grosgrain on right side of waistband, ⅝ inch from the cut edge. Stitch. Trim seam allowance to ¼ inch.
- Pin right side of band to right side of skirt, allowing one seam allowance to extend on front of placket and 1½ inch underlap + seam allowance on back of placket. Stitch. Trim waistband seam allowance to ⅜ inch and skirt seam allowance slightly less.
- Turn grosgrain ribbon toward inside of garment.
- Machine stitch in the "ditch" or "well" from the right side.
- Finish ends by hand. On the underlap, clip grosgrain at zipper teeth. Turn under and stitch by hand.

APPLY FASTENERS

ELASTIC MAY BE SUBSTITUTED for grosgrain for ski pants. May use a stretch stitch or narrow zigzag, stretching band slightly when stitching.

ELASTIC IN WAISTBAND:
- Cut waistband as directed above.
- Place elastic on fold line on wrong side of waistband on inner side.
- Extend elastic to seam allowances at end of waistband. To prevent elastic from twisting, stitch in the same direction on both sides of elastic.
- Stitch the right side of the waistband to the right side of the garment, stretching somewhat.
- Finish ends of waistband extensions.
- Turn inner side of waistband to wrong side of garment. May overedge edge of waistband. Stitch in "ditch"—or seam well—from right side.

DECORATIVE ELASTIC WEBBING WAISTBAND: Decorative stretch elastic trim is available for waistbands. For methods of application, see Chapter 42, page 228 and page 229.

WAISTLINES

STAYING BODICE-SKIRT SEAM

Cross-grain waistline seams should be stayed on knits, particularly on jerseys. Use seam binding, grosgrain, linen tape, or ½-inch elastic. Attach by hand or by machine to the waistline seam after garment seam is constructed. See page 106 for use of grosgrain.

ELASTIC WAISTLINES (SHIFTS OR SHIRTWAISTS)

On a shift without a zipper or placket, ¾–1-inch elastic may be used at the waistline to provide shape. Measure the elastic to fit the waistline.

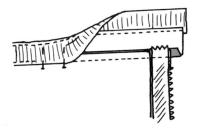

Fig. 14-9. Grosgrain facing for waistband.

Fig. 14-10. Elastic stitched in waistband.

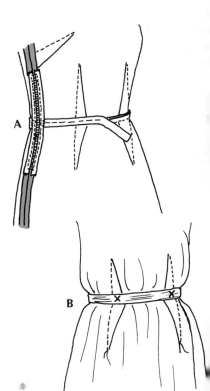

Fig. 14-11. Staying waistlines with A, tape; B, elastic.

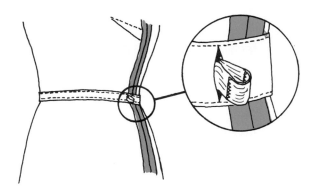

Fig. 14-12. Fabric casing for waistline.

Tack at seams and darts. If a belt is used, the elastic may be stretched and stitched to the garment on the inside.

A strip of fabric (casing) may be stitched to the inside of the garment at the waistline, wide enough for the elastic. The elastic is then inserted. A belt is worn to cover the stitching lines.

15

HEMS

"You have arrived" when it's time to put the hem in the tank top, skirt, dress, or jacket of knit. Remember that the hem in a knit garment should have stretch built into it—compatible with the stretch of the fashion fabric. If all stitches are kept about ¼ inch under the edge of the hem, it is easier to press and avoid hemline marks.

HOW TO MARK THE HEM PLACEMENT

Allow garment to hang 24 hours before measuring for hem so fashion garment can relax and "settle."

- Wear shoes, belt, and undergarments to be worn with the garment when measuring hem.
- The usual hem allowance on skirts, dresses and coats is about 3 inches. It may be less for fuller skirts. Tops are hemmed at about 1 inch.
- Mark dresses, skirts, and coats using a hem marker. Tops are usually just pinned up at desired length.

HEM FINISHES

Turn up hem on marked line. Place pins at right angles to fold line.
INTERFACED HEM:

This hem is desirable for heavier double knits of wool and polyester. It is used on coats, suits, and dresses.

- Trim seam allowance at hemline to remove bulk. (See Fig. 15-1.)
- The hem is interfaced with a bias strip of nonwoven or compatible woven fabric. Cut about 1¼ inch wider than the hem. If the hem is to have a soft, rolled edge, extend interfacing beyond fold line, otherwise, bring interfacing to fold line and fasten

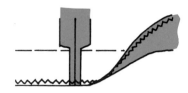

Fig. 15-1. Trimming seam allowance in hem.

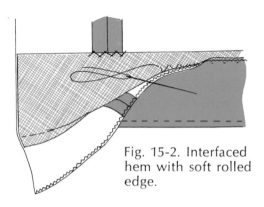

Fig. 15-2. Interfaced hem with soft rolled edge.

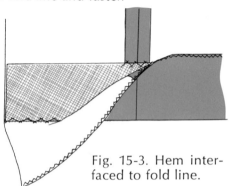

Fig. 15-3. Hem interfaced to fold line.

loosely with a catch stitch. The top of the interfacing may be fastened only at seams or at the entire top edge *if* it doesn't show on the right side. Then attach hem to interfacing using the catch stitch. A *double row of catch stitch* holds the hem more securely.

PLAIN HEM WITH/WITHOUT EDGE FINISH:

Plain hem may be used on medium-weight knits for dresses, coats, and sportswear.

- It is not necessary to finish the raw edge on most knits, but home sewers like the appearance of a finish. The raw edge may be finished with *stretch lace* or *soft tape, pinked,* or *stitched with zigzag, overedge,* or a *straight stitch*. It is not recommended that a clean finish or regular seam tape be used. A *bias Hong Kong finish* is sometimes used on firm knits when couture techniques have been used on the garment.

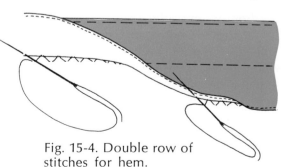

Fig. 15-4. Double row of stitches for hem.

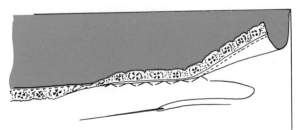

Fig. 15-5. Finishing hem with stretch lace.

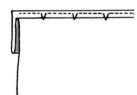

Fig. 15-6. Machine blind hem.

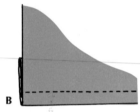

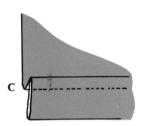

Fig. 15-7. False-cuff hem.

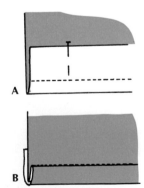

Fig. 15-8. Binding hem finish, "Chanel-trim look."

MACHINE HEM:

For tank tops, pullovers, children's and men's garments, a *machine blind hem* is suitable—flexible and durable and quick to do.

- Turn under hem, leaving ¼ inch of knit fabric extended (top of hem). Machine blind hem, testing the bight first, so that stitches barely catch several threads on the garment.
- May *straight stitch* a hem, stretching slightly as one stitches.

FUSED HEM:

Many home sewers are fusing hem lines on sleeves, skirts, slacks, and pullovers by using one of the fusing materials available on the market today.

- The fusing is applied to the inside edge of the hem, then the hem is ironed into position. Usually the fusing is placed in the top portion of the hem, providing a "rolled" appearance at the fold line. Fusing in the entire hem provides a flat hem.
- This is a flexible and durable hem. The hem may be altered by steam pressing hem, applying new adherent and resetting hem.
- To secure hem, machine-stitch in side seam well through hem and garment.

FALSE CUFF HEM:

This is ideal for a tailored sleeve hem on tops, dresses, and shirts and could even be used for a pants cuff.

- Allow about 2 inches for a pants cuff and 1½ inches for a sleeve cuff.
- Mark hem at ½ inch less than fabric allowed for cuff.
- Fold back hem on marked line with wrong sides together. Fold once more, forming a double hem. Stitch ¼ inch from the folded edge through all thicknesses, holding edge slightly taut. The raw edge will be enclosed.
- Fold hem down and press into position.

BINDING HEM FINISH:

This is a quick method of achieving the "Chanel-trim look," using a hem allowance rather than adding an extra binding trim.

- For a finished ½-inch trim, cut a 2-inch hem allowance.
- Fold up the hem allowance, right sides together. Stitch ½ inch from fold line.
- Fold hem back over stitching line to the inside of the garment. Pin.
- Machine-stitch along or in the seam well from the right side.
- May trim excess seam allowance from wrong side.

TRAPUNTO HEM:

For an elegant appearance on a plain wool double-knit dress, jacket, or coat, interface hem with polyester fleece. Topstitch with several rows of machine stitching, giving the trapunto effect. May stitch designs if desired.

CIRCULAR HEM OR SWEATER KNIT HEMS:
- Zigzag over a yarn or heavy thread on raw edge of knit.
- Turn hem into position by pulling ends of yarn and easing in fullness. Press.
- Catch stitch hem into position.

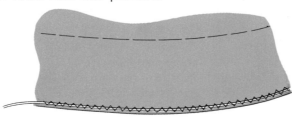

Fig. 15-9. Circular hem or sweater-knit hem.

REMOVING FULLNESS FROM A-LINE HEM (Trade technique):
- To remove excess fullness from A-line hem, fold hem on designated hemline.
- Reshape and restitch side seams at hemline, from fold line down, to correspond to the side seam. The hem will then be shaped to correspond to the garment side seam.
- This technique may be used on sleeve hems also.

Fig. 15-10. Removing fullness from A-line hem.

16

COUTURE TOUCHES AND KNIT CARE

The finishing touches, such as the fasteners at the top of the zipper closure, or at the edge of a front closing under the collar, or a belt loop, are some of the couture touches which will make your garment something "special."

HANGING SNAPS

The hanging snap is used to fasten a stand-up collar or at the top of a zipper. Metal snaps or nylon (Nelly)* transparent snaps may be used.

* Nelly—tradename for snap

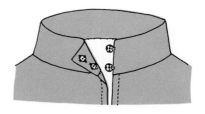

Fig. 16-1. Hanging snap closure.

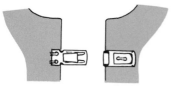

Fig. 16-2. Bonnie Clasp closure.

Fig. 16-3. Covering snaps.

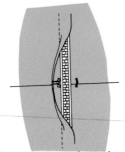

Fig. 16-4. Hook and eye at waistline on lapped zipper closure

Another fastener of nylon, which is flat, very strong, may be ironed and dyed, is a sew-on "Bonnie Clasp."*

COVERED SNAPS

Snaps may be purchased already covered in basic colors. However, it is simple to cover your own. Use an underlining or lining fabric to blend with your fashion-knit fabric. Cut two circles about twice the diameter of the snap. (On heavier fabrics, one layer may be sufficient.) Run a small running stitch with matching thread around the outer edge of the layers. Place snap section face down, working ball gently through knit. Pull up thread securely and fasten. Do the same with the socket section.

HOOK AND EYE

A round, loop, or thread eye, may be used with the hook. It is placed at the top of the zipper; the waistline stay; at waistline on lapped zipper closure; on waistbands; or where there is any strain. Buttonhole twist or two strands of matching thread may be used to *cover the hook and eye* using the blanket stitch.

The thread loop for a hook or button or belt carrier is made in essentially the same manner. Several strands of thread are covered with a blanket stitch.

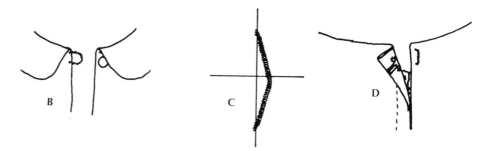

Fig. 16-5. A, C, thread loops for belt carrier; B, button loops; D, "eye" for a hook.

Heavy hooks and eyes are used on pants, shorts, or skirt waistbands. There are some available to the home sewer today which are fastened on the inside with a clip.

BELTS AND CARRIERS

Attractive belts for knit garments may be made from braid trimmings or cord tied with knots (macramé). Metal chain belts or leather belts often add the "extra" touch. Self-fabric belts are simple to construct.

* Bonnie Clasp—E-Z Buckle

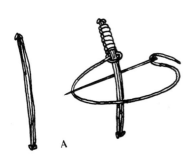

Fig. 16-6. Heavy hook-and-eye closure.

SELF-FABRIC NARROW TIE BELT

This is a "quick" method of constructing and turning a tie belt.
- Cut belt desired length with a point on one end.
- Cut a piece of strong cord (string will work) about 5 inches longer than the belt.
- Attach the string to the pointed end of the belt with a zigzag stitch.
- Fold pointed end of belt to right side of belt, placing cord along the center.
- Fold tie with right sides together and stitch. Be careful not to catch cord.
- Grasp string and pull, turning belt right side out.
- Cut off string. Finish belt ends.

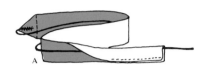

Fig. 16-7. Self-fabric tie belt.

CARRIERS

May work the *blanket stitch* over several layers of thread as described under "hook and eye" above.

A small piece of *nylon tape* (Velcro*), with tiny hooks on one side and a pile on the other side, may be used. Sew by hand, one piece to the belt and the other to the garment. It is also available in iron-on tape.

A *hand-crocheted belt loop* may be made, using a double thread about 20–24 inches long. Fasten the thread. Take a stitch, forming a loop. Place the thread and needle in the left hand. Slip the thumb and forefinger of the right hand through the loop, grasping the needle thread and pulling it through the loop, forming a new loop. Continue making loops to the desired length. Fasten by putting needle through the last loop, forming a knot.

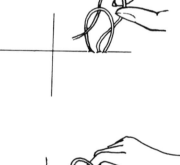

TOPSTITCHING

On some knit fabrics, topstitching flattens an edge holding seams in place, thus creating a crisp edge. On *wool* knits, use silk buttonhole twist on the top and regular thread on the bottom. Use a size 14 or 16 needle. If the bobbin thread becomes the top thread on the garment, thread bobbin with buttonhole twist also. Loosen the top tension. On *polyester* knits, use two spools of polyester or cotton-covered polyester-core thread on the top. If your machine does not have dual spoolholders, wind thread on two bobbins and place one on top of other on spool-holder. A heavy-duty cotton thread may be used on sportswear. Use about 6 to 8 stitches per inch. Allow thread ends to be long enough to be threaded in a needle and worked to the inside and fastened.

If fabric has the *tendency to twist* when topstitching, below are listed some helpful suggestions:

Fig. 16-8. Hand-crocheted belt loop.

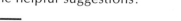

*   Velcro—tradename

- Diagonal baste near the edge.
- Run a basting on each side of the topstitching line.
- Use a roller-presser foot or attachments such as an "Even Feed," "Dual Feed," or "Match-maker."

As a *guide for even stitching* use transparent or masking tape, Tape Stitch,* or the quilting guide. The use of double needles is an effective way of topstitching two rows evenly in one operation.

A *hand-pick stitch* (backstitch) used as topstitching is also attractive. Use two strands of regular thread, buttonhole twist, or three strands of embroidery thread. Run thread through beeswax to keep from tangling. Pinning a strip of graph paper or Tape Stitch next to hand stitching line will help as a guide for even stitches.

For a "puffy" edge finish, place a strip of polyester all-bias fleece along edges of vests or sleeveless coats before topstitching.

SHAPINGS

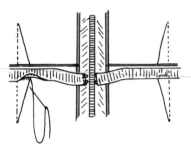

Fig. 16-9. Waistline stay.

Enclose flat circular *weights* in a fabric pouch and attach on the inside of the facing on cowl and draped necklines. Fasten with a French tack.

On the inside of the waist on stretch knits, or when the skirt is heavier than bodice knit, add a *waist stay*. Use ½–¾-inch grosgrain. Cut to waistline measure + 1 inch for finishing the ends. Finish ends and sew on hooks and round eyes (extend over end). Attach waist stay at seams and darts.

To keep a sweater-knit bodice from stretching, or wide slippery necklines or narrow shoulders from slipping off hangers, construct *tape hangers*. Use seam tape or linen tape. Measure from the waist to shoulder at armscye—cut four times this measurement minus about 2 inches. Turn under ends and attach at waistline.

KNIT CARE

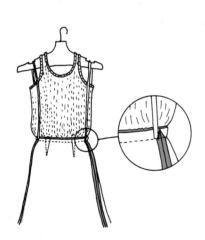

Fig. 16-10. Tape hangers.

Knits are a blessing for the person "on the go" as they are simple to care for—require little time for "Tender Loving Care." Most knit garments you'll make will be both machine washable and machine dryable. Some may be hand washed and line or hanger dried. A few will need to be dry-cleaned.

- *Check the label* with the care instructions which you received when you purchased your fabric. Hopefully, you remembered to include *all* your *findings* with the same "care" qualities.
- Wear *anti-static slips* under nylon and polyesters. *Nonstatic pants liners* may be fashioned to wear with pants.
- Use *tape hangers* to hang garments which have loosely knit bodices and firm, stable, or woven skirts. (See previous section.)
- To repair snags, pull through to the wrong side with a "Knit-fixer" (see Fig. 3-1, p. 15) or a *needle threader* (see Fig. 3-6, p. 18).
- Knits usually only need *"touch-up"* pressing. Use a damp cloth

---

* Trademark for Belding Corticello marked tape

between the fabric and the steam iron when pressing on the right side. If "Iron-all" pressing attachment is used, press-cloth is not needed.

- *Hang knit jackets and coats* on shaped wooden hangers. Hang pants over bar hangers.
- When machine drying, *do not overdry. Remove from dryer immediately* when dryer stops to avoid setting wrinkles.
- *Set creases* with white vinegar-water solution on press-cloth and cover with brown paper while pressing.
- Try rubbing alcohol to *remove ballpoint* pen marks.
- *Cold water detergents,* specifically designed for synthetics or wool knits, are available.
- *Liquid fabric softener,* added to the last rinse, or *anti-static aerosol spray fabric softener,* sprayed onto dryer drum before loading, help reduce static. Thin conductive coating forms on fabrics, which dissipates and prevents build-up of electrical charges.
- *Fabric finish* sprayed on cotton-knit collars or cuffs adds a renewed firmness.
- *Wash white nylon* separately—never with colors—not even pastels. Turn *acrylic knits inside out* when laundering to help prevent abrasion and pilling.
- Be careful of *cigarette burns.* The synthetics fuse and cannot be repaired easily.
- *Pin safety pins over hooks* on knit garments to prevent snags when laundering or dry-cleaning.
- *Pills* can be greatly reduced by brushing small sections of the knit with a semi-stiff brush while holding the garment flat, *or* shave off *pills* on knits with an electric razor.

General washing instructions for machine laundering of synthetic knits:

- Use warm, not hot, water and plain soap or synthetic detergent.
- The addition of a small amount of fabric softener in the final rinse will be helpful.
- Machine dry at synthetic (or low or regular) setting until dry.

GENERAL WASHING INSTRUCTIONS FOR HAND LAUNDERING OF SYNTHETICS OR BLENDS:

- Use warm water and plain soap or synthetic detergent. For wool blends, a cold water detergent may be desirable.
- Rinse well in cool water.
- Add fabric softener, if desired, to final rinse.
- Squeeze out excess water, roll in towel, knead so that towel absorbs excess water.
- Lay knit on a drainable surface, shape it, and allow it to dry thoroughly, *or* hanger dry on a rustproof hanger if the knit is firm and will not stretch out of shape.

The consumer of textiles today receives care information under the Federal Trade Commission Care Labeling Rule.* The Rule requires the

---

* Does not include remnants

fabric supplier to:

> "fully inform the purchaser how to effect such regular care and maintenance as is necessary to the ordinary use and enjoyment of the article, e.g. washing, drying, ironing, bleaching, dry cleaning. . . ."

Consult the *Consumer Care Guide for Apparel* (see p. 13) which was produced by the Consumers Affair Committee, American Apparel Manufacturers Association, Inc. It is based on the Voluntary Guide of the Textile Industry Advisory Committee for Consumer Interests.

The "Triangle System" (see p. 12) is commonly used for o/c sales.

17

WHY SEW LINGERIE?

IT'S EASY: lingerie sewing has probably the highest "satisfaction index" rating of any type of sewing women have invented. The results of one hour's work can bring an immediate sense of gratification. One reason for this quick return on time invested is that nearly everything can be done by machine. The new stretch stitches on so many machines are made to order for sewing lingerie knits. Still, almost all lingerie garments can be made with a straight stitch machine.

Tricot—the leading lingerie knit—is easy to work with once you get over being intimidated by its delicate appearance. It is not all that delicate. It doesn't even ravel.

CREATIVE SATISFACTION: sewing lingerie is one of the great ways to introduce a daughter, a student, or a 4-H Club member to the art of sewing. For a few cents and with a little skill a girl can make pretty and wearable garments of which she will be instantly proud. That feeling of pride will encourage her to go on sewing. How much more gratifying for a young lady of today to make a pretty pair of bikini panties than to make a gingham apron as her starting project!

And among adults, it is amazing to see women who have never taken time to sew—either because they thought it too demanding or too time consuming—suddenly become avid seamstresses. It is not at all unusual for mature women to become absolutely "turned on" by the loveliness of sheers, laces, and the challenges of trimming lingerie with ruffles and roses. They love bringing their lingerie creations to classes where they may share their experiences and take their deserved bows.

As TV seamstress Lucille Rivers puts it, "This is child's play for the woman used to setting in sleeves and making buttonholes."

ECONOMY: Besides being fun, lingerie sewing saves money. Once women realize how simple it is, they resent paying high prices for slips, panties, and nightwear. It need not be regarded as merely one more frivolous feminine hobby. Practical garments can be made as well as frothy ones. Some of the greatest savings may be had from making quilted robes, granny gowns, and pajamas for men and children. Yet we've come a long way from the "homemade" look of yesteryear's flannel nightgown.

COORDINATED COLORS AND INDIVIDUALIZED FIT: Here's a bonus for you. How many women thought matched sets of lingerie were within their financial reach a few short years ago? Some of us have never had the privilege of owning a coordinated lingerie wardrobe before. Nor did we ever have intimate apparel that fitted so well. Just think what it means to be able to make slips that are long enough—or short enough!

COMPARISON WITH OTHER SEWING

TRICOT DOES NOT RAVEL: seams, then, are generally narrower than those used in garments made of woven fabric.

MISTAKES ARE EASILY RECTIFIED: lingerie sewing is not an exacting kind of sewing. Because of the stretchy nature of the fabrics used, a ¼-inch deviation in a seam is not a matter of urgency. When an error is made in stitching, it is usually possible to cut away the seam and start again, rather than spend time ripping seams.

TRADE TECHNIQUES MAY BE USED: from the very way that home sewing of lingerie came into existence, it was inevitable that women should adopt a number of trade techniques which shorten the time spent sewing lingerie. Some of these "short cuts" are methods that may have been formerly frowned on by professionals (home economists and couture seamstresses)—and perhaps still are. But when we women have been willing to wear garments made with these techniques—paid high prices for them, in fact—and been perfectly satisfied with them up until now, why should we suddenly become critical of them because we now have the wherewithal to make our own garments?

To many of us today, time is a primary consideration, so whenever possible we have included in this book trade techniques that will speed sewing time on tricot and related fabrics. For those who adhere strictly to the dressmaker school of thought—we also offer the more time-consuming alternatives. [We find there's a pretty strong resurgence of interest in handwork today . . . perhaps in defiance of the rapidity with which we must do much of our work.]

LONG LIFE OF GARMENTS: all home-sewn lingerie has a surprisingly long life. Tricot—made of nylon or polyester fibers—is exceptionally strong. Used in combination with the better grades of synthetic threads and flexible machine stitching, it creates garments unbeatable for wear resistance. Their complete washability and easy care make them practical as well as long lived.

EASE OF FITTING: last of all, but a major factor in the popularity of lingerie sewing today, is the fact that knit garments are easy to fit.

Aside from bras and girdles—to which a little more attention must be given—fitting is not a crucial matter. Lingerie knits seem to allow for physical imperfection.

Garment lengths may be adjusted easily by lowering and raising hemlines at the time of cutting. Darts and shoulder straps may also be eased up or down to give slips and gowns a better fit. Panties and body suits stretch comfortably to conform with little adjustment to outsized hips or undersized waists. There is very little grief of the kind experienced in fitting garments of wovens.

Much of your success in lingerie sewing will depend on your familiarity with what your machine can do. Get the feel of each new fabric and then go ahead and have fun with it.

18

LINGERIE PATTERNS

CHOOSING LINGERIE PATTERNS FOR KNIT FABRICS

All major pattern companies carry a few lingerie patterns for knit fabrics and are regularly adding more styles and a wider range of sizes. These patterns have a measurement chart on the envelope and are sold by dress sizes.

Fabric shops, mail-order houses, and stores specializing in the knit fabrics are also sources of lingerie patterns. Their patterns may be sold either by dress size or by ready-to-wear lingerie size.

Patterns for pants, petti-pants, and half-slips should be bought to fit hip measurements; full slips and gowns to fit the bust.

Commercial lingerie patterns—those designed by companies specializing in knit patterns—have several sizes printed on one pattern piece. The patterns may be made of stiff paper and have no seamline indicated. (The seam allowance will have been included in the pattern piece.)

These commercial patterns are easier to handle if they are cut apart along the cutting line for the size wanted, or they may be traced onto wide sheets of paper. A lightweight pattern paper is sold in some fabric stores for this purpose.

Patterns designed for knits have arrows (⟵⟶) which are marked "stretch," indicating that they should be placed on the crosswise grain (the direction of greater stretch in tricot and most knits, power net being one exception; if patterns are transferred to tracing paper, these arrows should also be transferred).

It is always helpful to cut away pattern margins—even when using tissue-paper patterns—as they make it more difficult to get a clean, even sweep with the scissors.

USING OTHER PATTERNS   *cop.1*

Patterns that are designed for woven fabrics can also be used for tricot, but they will normally be too large. Because of the stretchy nature of tricot, it is wise to select a pattern that is a size or two smaller than you would normally wear. When a pattern has a diagonal arrow, indicating it is intended to be cut on the bias, it is not designed for tricot. It is not feasible to cut tricot garments on the bias—there is too much variation between the lengthwise and crosswise stretch of tricot. So ignore diagonal arrows and cut the garment with the stretch going around the body.

MAKING YOUR OWN PATTERNS

Because tricot is supple and because lingerie fitting is not as exacting as that of outer garments, it is quite easy to make your own patterns—using as your guide a purchased garment that fits well. There are two methods for doing this.

THE RUB-OFF METHOD WORKS WELL FOR SLIPS, PANTIES, SIMPLE GOWNS, AND PEIGNOIRS:

MATERIALS NEEDED:
- Plain paper.
- A large sheet of styrofoam (as large as largest section of garment to be copied) or other spongy surface, such as padded ironing board or foam-backed rug.
- Hat pin or large darning needle.
- Dressmaker pins.

DIRECTIONS:
- Over styrofoam (padding), place sheet of paper. Over that, place the garment.
- Smooth out garment to full width and pin around all edges of section to be copied—pinning through all three surfaces.
- Punch holes with hat pin or large needle along seam line, outlining entire section of garment.
- Remove pins, add new paper, and readjust garment to copy next section.
- Pivot garment for darts. Put a pin at the pivot point of the dart and swing garment around the estimated amount of the dart.

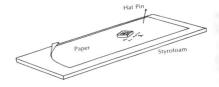

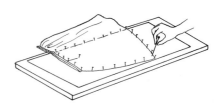

Fig. 18-1. The rub-off method.

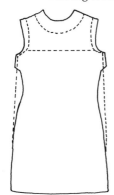

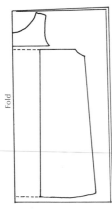

Fold

Fig. 18-2. Cutting pattern for layered gown.

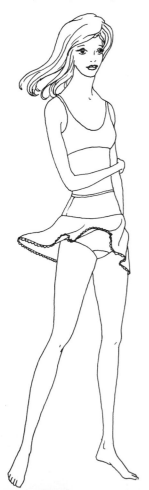

- When removed, paper will act as a pattern, the series of holes indicating the seam line. Add ¼ inch for seam allowance on edges.

RIP-APART METHOD:

- Use an old garment for a pattern. But before ripping garment apart at the seams, make one or two marks across each seam and dart to use as matching points (in lieu of pattern notches). Mark center front and center back of garment. Make a grainlike marking on each section that is not to be placed on the fold.
- *To mark grain,* lay each section out flat, ribbed side up. Hold material taut and run a sharp pencil along the fabric in the direction of the rib; the pencil point will rest between two ribs and automatically form a straight line. Mark fabric a few inches at a time.
- *Cut the garment apart* along the stitching line on the wrong side, removing the entire seam allowance. Do not remove the lace or other trim, but cut off elastic.
- *Press each section flat* and pin to pattern paper. Trace around edges of each section, adding necessary allowances for edge finishes at top and bottom of garment. Allow ¼ inch for all seams.

PATTERN VARIATION TIPS

It is quite possible to make attractive lingerie by using patterns designed for outerwear and modifying them. A layered nightgown may be made from a basic pattern as follows:

MAKING LAYERED GOWN FROM BASIC DRESS PATTERN

PATTERN ADJUSTMENTS: choose a basic pattern that fits through shoulder and bustline. Reshape arm and neckline to enable garment to slip over the head easily without addition of a zipper. The pattern may be made on plain brown wrapping paper.

If extra fullness is desired in bust, a yoke may be added by splitting pattern about halfway down the armscye and adding a seam allowance to both pieces of pattern. Add fullness to skirt.

CUTTING OUT LINING: lay the adjusted pattern on tricot or whatever fabric you have chosen for the lining—or underlay–portion of the finished gown. Eliminate any front or back seams by placing center front and center back on the lengthwise fold. (Since bias seams tend to pucker more than straight seams, it is sometimes desirable to straighten side seams as much as possible for the first attempt.) If more fullness is desired in skirt portion of the lining, place pattern away from the center fold.

CUTTING OUT SHEER OVERLAY: use the same pattern pieces to make overlay. More fullness is required in the sheer layer, however, so place

Fig. 18-3. Slip-panty.

the center front of pattern away from fold at least 4 inches to give the desirable fullness.

MAKING A SLIP-PANTY

A one-piece combination slip-and-panty garment may be made by using both the pattern pieces from a panty (or girdle) and a half-slip.

- Lay out and cut panty in usual manner, marking fabric to indicate a future stitching line for attaching slip 5 inches down from the waistline.
- Cut pattern for half-slip, making it 5 inches lower at the waist-line.
- Stitch side seams of slip and attach a 1-inch wide stretch lace to the top of the slip.
- After panty is completed, join other edge of stretch lace to the indicated seamline (5 inches down from waistline) on panty.

MAKING A PANTS LINER

A liner to wear under slacks to keep them from clinging to panty hose, may be cut by using the slack pattern and cutting the liner of lingerie fabric. It might be made of tricot or non-cling tricot. Lingerie elastic may be applied at the waist. Eliminate hem at bottom and add lace, if desired.

Fig. 18-4. Pants liner.

MAKING A BODY SUIT

Combine a favorite slip or camisole with a panty or girdle pattern.

Lower waistline on panty pattern approximately 2 inches when cutting, and cut off pattern for slip or camisole approximately 2 inches below waist (leaving seam allowance), and join the two with a seam. Or cut as one, overlapping the two patterns on the fabric so that the correct length of suit can be cut. This is possible if slip pattern is chemise style and requires side seams only. Add snaps to crotch seam.

Fig. 18-5. Body suit.

19

LINGERIE FABRICS

It is important when selecting lingerie fabric to remember a basic rule of sewing: choose fabric that is compatible with the design of the pattern.

In order to achieve pleasing results, it may be necessary to spend some time familiarizing yourself with the lingerie fabrics now available. The following are some knit fabrics adaptable to lingerie sewing:

TRICOTS

Tricot (pronounced tree'-ko from the French word *tricoter* meaning: *to knit*) is probably the most popular knit lingerie fabric. It is easy to care for, durable, drapable, has a comfortable stretch, and a silky appearance. Tricot's strength and resiliency come both from the fibers (nylon and Arnel triacetate are the most common) and the way in which it is knit. Each yarn forms a loop which is interlocked with the loop above, below, and alongside it. This causes tiny ribs in the fabric. The ribs running lengthwise on the right side are called "wales," and the ribs running crosswise on the wrong side are called "courses." The crosswise "courses" have greater stretch.

Lingerie tricots, taken as a group, are relatively light in weight, but they may range from sheer to opaque in appearance. They are available in widths from 44 inches to 108 inches. They may be found in solid colors and prints at department stores, through mail-order houses, mill-end and factory-outlet shops, and most fabric stores. They are often grouped according to weight. Personal taste and the design and function of the garment will direct their use.

HEAVYWEIGHT TRICOT of 50 to 60 denier has an opaque quality that makes it suitable for men's pajamas, robes, single-layer gowns, and slips to be worn under sheer dresses.

MEDIUM-WEIGHT TRICOT of 30 to 40 denier is a more popular choice for slips. It is suitable for the garments mentioned above and also for panties. (This weight may also be used for dresses.)

LIGHTWEIGHT TRICOT is more translucent fabric. It is good as a lining fabric, is used for some types of nightwear and panties. It is not particularly good for slips.

SHEER-WEIGHT TRICOT of 15 to 20 denier is often called nylon chiffon. It has a filmy transparency that makes it a favorite for overlays and peignoirs. It is used extensively for binding neck and armhole edges, backing laces, and fashioning delicate looking trim for intimate apparel.

SATIN TRICOT is a luxurious fabric with the shiny appearance of a woven satin. It is popular for pajamas, gowns, slips, panties, and robes.

CREPE TRICOT looks like a fine georgette. It usually falls between light-weight and sheer in weight. It has a frosted look and a slightly pebbled texture. It makes elegant looking gowns, peignoirs, overlays, panties, and slips. (Crepeset and Crepelon are two tradenames for crepe tricot.)

STRETCH TRICOT is a soft stretch fabric with a high content of nylon and a small amount of Spandex added. It is usually found in pastel colors and is used for bras and girdles where a soft, natural look is desired. Garments made from it will usually stretch to fit a number of sizes.

NON-CLING TRICOT is a tricot that has been treated with a non-cling substance so that it will be relatively static free when worn under other synthetics and wools. It retains some degree of stretch.

OTHER TRICOT VARIATIONS are seen in such fabrics as permanently ruffled or pleated tricot, tricot with allover clipped dots, or tricots made of yarns such as Banlon or Taslan that are crimped and thus give the fabric a textured effect.

OTHER LINGERIE FABRICS

STABILIZED NYLON is a knit nylon with the look and body of taffeta. It is especially constructed and treated to prevent clinging. It must be treated differently from the above-mentioned fabrics as it has almost *no stretch*. It is used primarily for slips to be worn under knits. It comes in pastels, prints, and white.

ALLOVER LACE is a lace-patterned fabric available by the yard for making peignoirs and the bodice portions of gowns and slips. When backed with sheer tricot or nylon marquisette it is often used for panels on the front of girdles, or to add decorative touches to bras, bra gowns, or panties.

PREBACKED LACE is a term for allover lace fabric that is fused to a backing of nylon chiffon or nylon marquisette. It is used to make decorative support panels for girdles. Lingerie fabric shops often cut this fabric into squares and sell them as "girdle panels." (Don't confuse it with squares of softer lace—bonded to fiberfill—which are for bra-making.)

POWER NET is a two-way stretch fabric made of nylon-covered Spandex and is most commonly used for girdles. It ranges in weight from 36 gauge for heavier yarns and fabrics, which give firm control, to 56 (or even 66) for finer fabrics offering less control. The control comes from the elasticity of Spandex yarns which have in recent years almost completely replaced the old-fashioned rubber.

Power net comes in black, white, colors, and prints. It is also available in jacquard patterns. These have a lace-like quality and are used for the same purposes as regular power net as well as for decorative purposes.

Newly developed power net made with a blend of Qiana and Lycra promises a more silk-like girdle fabric in the near future.

[Note: Power net containing Lycra Spandex is often referred to as simply "Lycra" in lingerie-making circles.]

SATIN ONE-WAY STRETCH FABRIC is used (with the stretch going up and down) to make girdle support panels. It has one satinized side, is available in colors to coordinate with those of power net. It offers maximum control.

BRUSHED KNIT is a knit fabric with a brushed, or napped, surface on one side. (Brushing abrades the yarns, making the fabric warmer by literally trapping the air and holding in body warmth.) The brushed surface is usually turned outward for the sake of appearance. It is most often found in 100 percent nylon or combinations of nylon and polyester or rayon/ acetate. The addition of polyester adds to the wearing quality. Rayon and acetate soften the fabric and increase its absorbency.

Brushed nylon comes in widths up to 108 inches in both colors and prints. It is popular for granny gowns, pajamas, robes, and infants' wear.

Astrella Cloth and *Cuddle Cloth* are names given to two of the heavier brushed fabrics—containing 75–80 percent Arnel (triacetate) and 20–25 percent nylon yarns. A bit warm for most sleepwear, they make luxurious winter-weight robes and lounging wear, come in lovely colors and prints.

QUILTED FABRICS are three-layer fabrics consisting of a plain or print shell (face fabric), a layer of fiberfill (or other batting), and a lining of compatible fabric. The layers are joined with quilting stitches by a machine during the fabrication process. The quilteds most popular for sewing at present are made of all-synthetic fibers. They are lightweight and have valuable insulating properties; make excellent winter-weight robes, hostess skirts, and other lounging wear. Frequently, there are coordinating fabrics available from which to make matching gowns, pajamas, and blouses. All-cotton quilteds, also available, are still preferred by some.

[Note: Recently some quilteds have been fabricated by a chemical process resulting in a simulated quilted look. Double-faced quilted fabrics—another recent development—make attractive wraparounds or overskirts with slits because they are equally pretty from either side.]

USING WOVEN FABRICS

Although we are detailing only knit procedures in this book, lingerie sewing is by no means limited to knit fabrics. Several woven fabrics have always been, and will continue to be, popular for lingerie making. Cotton batiste and blends are long-standing favorites because of their softness and absorbency.

Many of the washable synthetic lining fabrics also make appealing underfashions. Among them are lightweight polyester crepes, lightweight rayons and rayon blends, and relatively new silky fabrics of Qiana nylon. All are easy-care fabrics and come in widely varying colors and prints.

Of course, the techniques for handling seam finishes will be different since some of these fabrics may ravel. Pattern sizing will also be different—due to the fact that wovens do not stretch as knits do.

20

LINGERIE FINDINGS

The beautiful lingerie findings at her disposal make it possible for the home sewer to coordinate all the parts of her lingerie wardrobe. Learning to select them can be fully as important—and equally as satisfying—as selecting the basic fabric.

ELASTICS

LINGERIE ELASTICS considered most compatible with tricot are made of 100 percent nylon. They are softer and more resilient than the rayon blends commonly used a few years ago. They are often finished with one fluted (picot) edge. Widths vary, but most common are the ¼- and ½-inch widths. The wider of the two is used at the waist of a half-slip or panty. The ¼ inch is normally used for panty legs. Lush pastel shades, vibrant reds, black, white, and navy are among the colors to be found.

PLUSH ELASTIC is an elastic webbing that has a velvety nap on one side —the side intended to be worn next to the skin. It may have picot trim on one edge or both edges. It comes in colors to coordinate with power net and is used in bra and girdle making. It varies in width and stretchability. The firmer elastics are used for girdle waistbands. The softer and narrower plush elastics are more suitable for girdle legs, for edging body suits, for panty legs and waistbands.

ELASTIC LACE is a strip lace made of power net in a coarse lace pattern. It comes in widths from 1 to 5 inches, finished on both edges so that it may be appliquéd to fabric. It molds to curved edges, is soft and decorative. It is used for leg finishes on girdles. It may also be used for waist elastic on natural-look girdles. Other uses are for the waistband on hip-hugger or bikini pants, or to finish tops of slips and camisoles to make them hug the body. It comes in a variety of lacy patterns and colors, may be split and used for decorative purposes.

GARTERLESS ELASTIC can be an elastic lace or other fancy elastic which is backed with rows or swirls of gripper (such as familiarly seen on no-slip belting). It is used on girdle legs—in place of garters—to hold stocking or panty hose in place.

Fig. 20-1. Assorted lingerie elastic

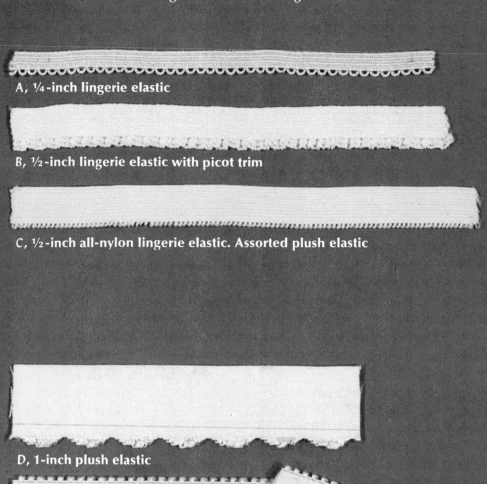

A, ¼-inch lingerie elastic

B, ½-inch lingerie elastic with picot trim

C, ½-inch all-nylon lingerie elastic. Assorted plush elastic

D, 1-inch plush elastic

E, ¾-inch plush elastic

F, ½-inch plush elastic

G, double-faced plush

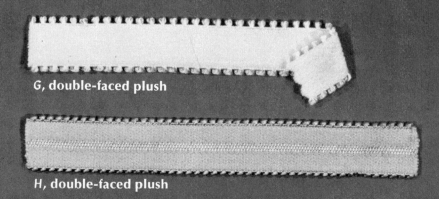

H, double-faced plush

Fig. 20-2. Elastics

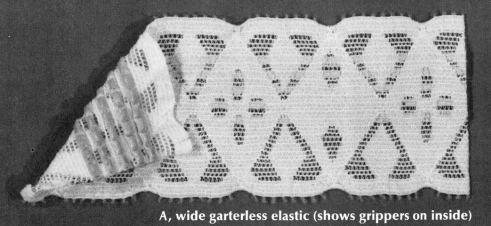

A, wide garterless elastic (shows grippers on inside)

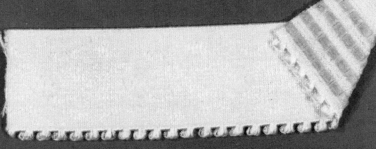

B, 1-inch garterless elastic (shows reverse side). Baby elastic

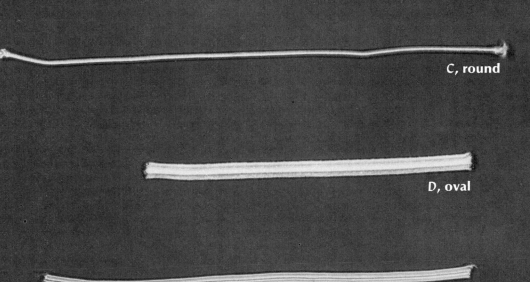

C, round

D, oval

E, flat

F, elastic webbing

GARTER ELASTIC is a very firm elastic used for making garter tabs and stretch shoulder straps. It does not possess the degree of stretch necessary for use on the waist or leg of girdles.

OVAL ELASTIC, ROUND ELASTIC CORD, OR FLAT "BABY ELASTIC" may all be used for gathers, ruffles, shirring and smocking effects in lingerie making. These small elastics are sold in packages of 6 or more yards and consist of rayon-covered rubber.

ELASTIC THREAD (nylon or rayon-covered) may also be used for the same effects mentioned above. It may be wound on the machine bobbin while regular thread is used on top of the machine.

ELASTIC WEBBING is a sturdy, heat-resistant, terry-textured elastic made of mercerized cotton and heavy rubber strands. It comes in 1¼ inch widths and is used mainly for men's pajamas and underwear.

FILLING AND BACKING MATERIALS

POLYESTER FIBERFILL is a lofty (resilient) and lightweight batting sold either by the yard or in squares for use as bra filler or for trapunto work.

FUSED-TO-FABRIC FIBERFILL is fiberfill already bonded to nylon fabric. It may be double-faced, have decorative fabric (such as allover lace) on one side and a plain tricot backing, or plain tricot on both sides. It is used for the face fabric on shaped bras or it may be inserted in bust cups made of other fabric to serve as padded lining. It is often sold in squares big enough to make one or two bras.

POLYESTER FLEECE is an all-bias sheet-like padding with a slight degree of loft, available by the yard in 45-inch widths for use in padding.

QUILTED FABRIC: (See Fabrics, p. 116) used in bra shaping.

FOAM, made of rubber latex or urethane, available in sheets from arts and crafts dealers if not obtainable in fabric stores, is used for padding.

NYLON MARQUISETTE is a sheer, woven nylon fabric that may be used for firming, backing, and taping of lingerie fabrics.

STRAPS

SHOULDER STRAPS of ready-made nylon satin straps with adjustable sliders can be used for slips and camisoles. Banlon straps with elastic inserts or plush elastic straps are good for bras.

ADJUSTABLE SLIDERS are small metal or plastic sliders which may be added to straps made of nylon ribbon or tricot fabric to make them adjust to different lengths. May be purchased or saved from old garments.

RIBBON

NYLON RIBBON is widely sold by the yard in all colors, used for shoulder straps and many lingerie trims. Rayon satin may also be used.

Fig. 20-3. Adjustable shoulder straps

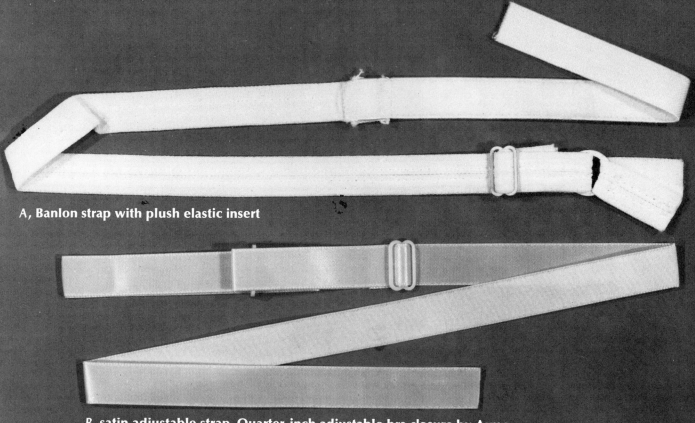

A, Banlon strap with plush elastic insert

B, satin adjustable strap. Quarter-inch adjustable bra closure by Armo

F, bra-back replacement kit

D, hook half

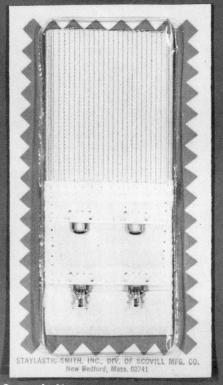

STAYLASTIC-SMITH, INC., DIV. OF SCOVILL MFG. CO.
New Bedford, Mass. 02741

C, eye half

E, garter; with elastic by Armo

Fig. 20-4. Assorted stretch laces

A, ½-inch decorative stretch lace

B, ⅞-inch elastic lace (Armo)

C, 1⅛-inch elastic lace (Armo)

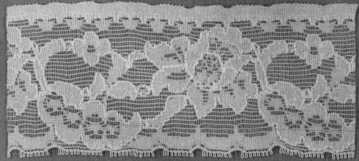

D, 2-inch color stretch lace

G, 5-inch stretch lace for girdles

E, 2½-inch stretch lace by Numa Spandex (350 denier)

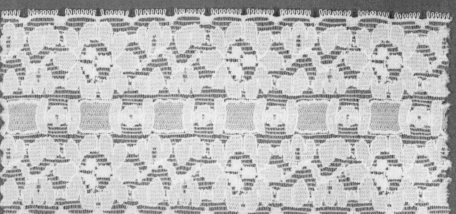

F, 2¾-inch decorative stretch lace by Numa Spandex (420 denier)

Fig. 20-5. Assorted trims used for lingerie

A, B, C, rosettes and bows

D, appliques

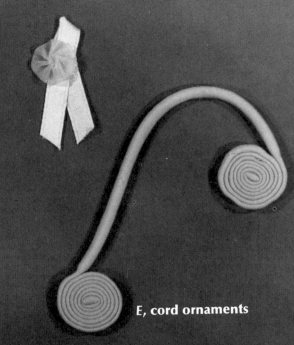

E, cord ornaments

F, G, H, I, assorted edgings

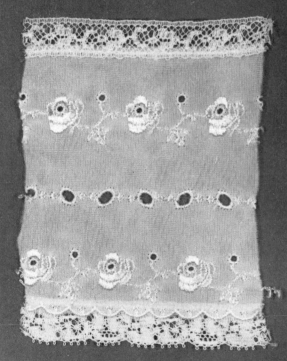

Fig. 20-6. Laces

A, beading

B, seam binding

C, galloon lace

D, galloon lace, 1-inch wide

E, insertion lace

Fig. 20-7. Assorted edgings

A, extra-wide border lace

B, 3-inch wide border lace

C, narrow border lace

D, flouncing

CLOSURES

HOOK HALVES AND EYE HALVES may be purchased separately in some fabric shops and wholesale supply houses. Made of woven nylon, they come on rolls in the same way that lace or ribbon does and are snipped off and sold by the number of eye halves or hook halves the customer requests. This type of closure has no elastic attached.

BRA REPLACEMENT KITS are widely available at notions counters and consist of sections of elastic webbing to which a firm cotton has been stitched. Two sections are contained in one package—an eye half and a hook half. Elastic is attached, but may be cut off when used with power net. Usually found in white only.

GARTERS may be purchased or transferred from another girdle. Four or six are needed for holding up regular hose.

PLASTIC BONING

Boning is an optional finding for bras. It may be purchased or saved from an old bra and taped into bra seams for extra firmness.

THREAD

For tricot sewing, *nylon-machine-twist thread* or *Dual Duty Plus Extra Fine* (a synthetic/cotton core-spun) are the most satisfactory. Economical large cones of 1185 to 7200 yards may be found in most standard colors. White-nylon machine-twist thread is fairly transparent and may be used for sewing many pastel color fabrics. The 100 percent polyester and polyester/cotton core-spun threads may be used on heavy tricots, brushed nylons, and quilteds. Power net may be stitched with either type—depending on the weight of the fabric.

LACE

Nearly all types of lace may be used to trim lingerie. Lace should be preshrunk with the fabric. The fiber content should be similar to or harmonious with the lingerie fabric to which it is stitched. Lace that is heavy or stiff may destroy the delicacy prized in most lingerie garments.

A soft nylon lace is the best choice for tricot sewing. Cotton and other laces may feel too stiff and scratchy—but are sometimes used successfully when backed with or encased in sheer tricot. The more supple nylon lingerie laces are sold by the yard in lingerie fabric stores. Many are also available, prepackaged, at notions departments. The color range is unlimited.

Here are some common types.

BEADED LACE: has eyelets through which ribbon may be threaded.
GALLOON: has scalloped finish on both edges.
BORDER LACE: has one straight and one scalloped edge.

INSERTION LACE: has two straight edges, is often inserted between two sections of fabric.

FLOUNCING: has one straight and one scalloped edge, a wide lace used for trimming bottom of slip.

MEDALLION: is a single detached motif or design.

STRETCH LACE SEAM BINDING: is prepackaged lace, most often used for hems in dressmaking, works well on curved edges.

OTHER TRIMS

Many other types of lingerie trim may be purchased, including a variety of nylon-embroidered edgings, appliqués, nylon roses, Chinese ball buttons, and dainty frogs.

21

LINGERIE EQUIPMENT AND SUPPLIES

Your usual sewing equipment may be used for lingerie sewing with a few simple additions.

SHEARS must be sharp to cut tricot, power net, and most lingerie fabrics accurately and without giving the fabric edges a chewed look. Those with bent handles work well because they lift the fabric less as it is being cut. Shears must be kept sharp. Tricot and stretch fabrics dull them rather rapidly. Wipe lint from the blades frequently.

Some authorities suggest cutting through #00 sandpaper once in a while to keep scissors sharp.

Some companies have designed special shears with *serrated blades* for cutting synthetic knits. *Barber scissors* are often recommended for cutting tricot. *Electric shears* also work well for many women.

SMALL TRIMMING SCISSORS with a sharp point for getting into corners are very helpful for cutting threads and trimming close to seams.

PINS used in lingerie sewing should be the fine-pointed dressmaker silk pins or ballpoint pins. Colored plastic heads are convenient because they are easy to see when inserted in colored or printed fabric. Glass-head pins are more apt to break when dropped.

BALLPOINT SEWING MACHINE NEEDLES are preferred. A number 70,

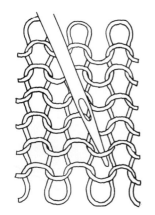

Fig. 21-1. Ball-point needle going through tricot.

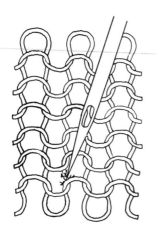

Fig. 21-2. Regular sharp-point needle going through tricot.

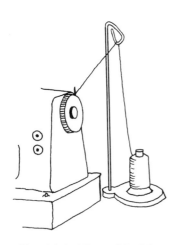

Fig. 21-3. Thread holder.

or its equivalent, is good for fine lingerie sewing. A number 90 may be required for some of the heavier girdle fabrics.

A fine-pointed needle in size 9 to 11 will also give satisfactory results in most machines.

The slightly rounded tip of the ballpoint needle, however, parts the individual threads and allows the needle to pass by rather than puncturing them.

HAND SEWING NEEDLES: For hand stitching on tricot, use a size 7, 8, or 9 sharp needle. (A milliner's needle comes in handy for some hand work.) As with the machine needle, a fine point will slip more easily between knit yarns.

Tailor's tip: Running the needle through hair will make it slide more easily through some fabrics.

MAGIC TRANSPARENT TAPE: may be used in place of pins to hold lace in position while stitching. It also serves as a guide for seamlines. It is useful for labeling various sections of a garment as it is cut out. A piece of tape which has been penciled with such notations as "right," "wrong," "front," and "back" may be easily removed as garment is completed. The frosted transparent tape comes off more easily, without leaving sticky residue, than clear tape.

MARKING PENCIL: Soft, chalk-like marking pencils of red or blue will be helpful in marking and labeling fabric, as they will wash out later. (Carbon paper and lead pencil may not.)

PATTERN PAPER is available in 45-inch-wide paper in some knit-fabric stores for the purpose of tracing the correct size off a multiple size pattern. It has lines at 1-inch intervals indicating lengthwise and crosswise stretch.

SPRAY STARCH or other aerosol fabric sizing can be helpful in dealing with sheer fabric or nylon laces which have a tendency to curl at inconvenient times. Spray on starch and press with a barely warm iron to give body to edges that are to be stitched. The sizing washes out and softness returns to finished garment.

A STEAM IRON is used less in lingerie sewing than most other types of sewing, but is helpful for pressing some seams and in making bias-fold tape.

A SEAM GAUGE is a six-inch ruler, notched at various intervals, with a sliding gauge.

A LOOP TURNER is a long metal device with a hook on one end and a latch point on the other, used for turning tubing.

A BODKIN is helpful for threading elastic.

AN EMERY BOARD should be kept handy as rough fingernails have a way of snagging tricot.

A THREAD HOLDER is an optional accessory for the sewing machine; holds large cones of thread and keeps thread from becoming tangled by guiding it as it is fed into tension mechanism.

[Note: one may make a substitute thread holder by placing thread cone in a can with a hole in the cover.]

22

THE PREPARATION, LAYOUT, AND CUTTING OF LINGERIE

As lingerie is expected to be washable, most reliable sources advise shrinking lingerie fabric before sewing—especially fabric that was purchased at a bargain price. Many fabrics sold by factory-outlet stores are from stock that was milled for ready-to-wear manufacturers and it may vary greatly in quality. Shrinking also helps tricot return to its normal state—it may have stretched on the bolt. Excess finishing solution may also be washed away by taking this step.

TO SHRINK: submerge fabric so that it soaks thoroughly in lukewarm water (or gently wash by machine) along with the findings that may be susceptible to shrinkage (lace, zippers, etc.). Add fabric softener to reduce static electricity.

TO DRY: gently squeeze out excess moisture with a towel. Then dry naturally—preferably on a flat surface—or place in clothes dryer on a low (or "no heat") setting with a damp towel. May spray dryer drum with anti-static fabric softener before loading, to prevent static build up.

　　[Note: Never expose nylon to sunlight in drying. It causes yellowing.]

TO IRON: press with "warm" setting, once over lightly. Avoid high heat in washing, drying, and ironing. It will melt (or fuse) nylon fabric.

TO LAY OUT: place lingerie fabric on a non-slip surface—a ping-pong table, carpet, or fabric-covered cutting board. Roll up any extra fabric at end of table. Don't allow it to hang off the edge.

TIPS FOR TRICOTS

Establish right and wrong sides of tricot fabric before cutting. Stretch an edge of the fabric cut *on the crosswise rib* by grasping it between both hands and pulling. The fabric will always roll toward the *right side.*

　　[Exception: some knit designs are purposely printed on the wrong side of the knit.]

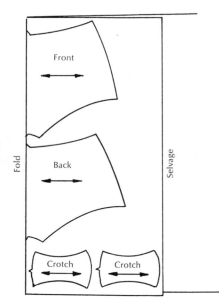

Fig. 22-1. Laying out tricot.

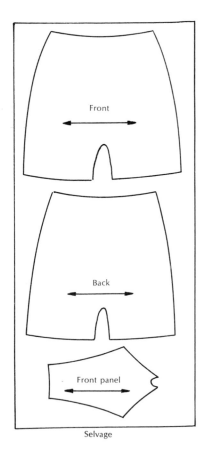

Fig. 22-2. Laying out power net.

- Lay pattern on fabric so that arrows (indicating "stretch") are placed on crosswise grain, or direction of greater stretch.
- If fabric is to be cut double, fold it on the lengthwise grain. Follow one of the ribs carefully with the eye and place right sides of tricot together on this line, or "wale."
- Pin pattern to fabric with sharp dressmaker pins or ballpoint pins. Whenever possible, pin within the seam-allowance margins to prevent pin pricks from showing.
- Cut out pattern with sharp scissors. Notches should be cut outward, not into seam allowances which are usually quite narrow.
- Make a habit of cutting notches (outward) at center front and center back of each pattern piece, even though they may not be indicated by pattern. These notches are extremely helpful later in matching pattern pieces and distributing fullness.
- Label pieces of pattern with magic mending tape before removing pattern paper.
- Save fabric scraps as you cut out lingerie garments. Leftovers from one garment may often be used to trim another garment.

TIPS FOR POWER NET

Determine the right and wrong side of power net before cutting. The right side has a slightly raised texture. The wrong side is smooth. Test by running a finger over the fabric.

- Lay the girdle pattern on the fabric so that the greater amount of stretch will go around the body. As power net stretches *with the selvage*, the top of the pattern and the arrows will run parallel to the selvage.
- If in doubt as to which direction on a piece of power net has the greater amount of stretch, test by stretching fabric between your hands. When fabric is being pulled in the direction of greatest stretch, the tiny holes in the knit will close. If pulled in the direction of lesser stretch, the holes will open.
- Power net and other girdle fabrics such as stretch tricot should be spread out on the cutting surface and left to relax for some time before they are cut. They will then resume their normal degree of recovery.

TIPS FOR QUILTED FABRICS

Whenever possible, lay out patterns on quilted fabric so that unnecessary seams may be eliminated. It cuts down on the bulkiness of the garment and saves sewing time. It should not be done, however, if it will spoil the design line of the garment.

- It may be possible on a bathrobe to extend the front of the pattern at center front so that it may be turned back as a facing, thus eliminating a separate facing and a bulky front seam. Do this at the cutting table by overlapping the pattern pieces for the robe front and front facing.

- Center-back seams may also be eliminated if the back seam is cut on the straight of the grain. However, if garment is meant to be flared, this step will destroy the fit and style. (Center-back seams serve a useful purpose in that they prevent a garment from sagging out of shape when one sits in it.)
- To transfer pattern marking onto a quilted fabric, it may be necessary to use tailor's tacks in order to mark through the thickness of the layers. Otherwise markings may be traced to the back of the quilted fabric—one layer at a time—with tracing paper.

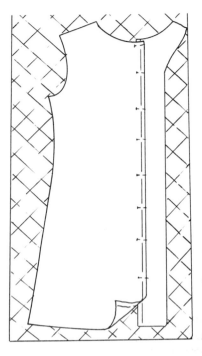

Fig. 22-3. Laying out and cutting quilted fabric.

23

SEWING LINGERIE SEAMS AND DARTS

THINGS TO CHECK BEFORE BEGINNING TO SEW LINGERIE SEAMS

Be sure the sewing machine is *clean* and oiled. Frequent cleaning is necessary when sewing tricot, brushed knits, or quilted fabrics as all of them create clouds of lint.

- Insert sharp new *needle* or ballpoint needle in machine. Be sure that it is inserted *correctly*.
- *Check* the machine cabinet, other sewing areas, and fingernails *for rough spots* that cause fabric to snag.
- *Check pressure* on presser foot. It may need to be increased slightly.
- *When winding synthetic thread on bobbin,* stop winding before bobbin is entirely full, because nylon and polyester threads stretch and have a tendency to cause the bobbin to spin backward in the bobbin case if wound completely full.
- *Test stitch* on a piece of the fabric that is to be used. (Using a different color thread in bobbin will help detect unbalanced

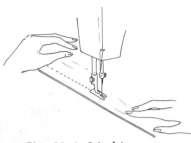

Fig. 23-1. Stitching tricot.

Fig. 23-2. Beginning row of stitching.

Fig. 23-3. Double straight stitch.

stitches.) Most repairmen say to leave bottom tension alone, if possible, but it may be necessary on some machines to lower the upper tension.

HOW TO SEW TRICOT

SETTING STITCH LENGTH: before you begin a tricot seam, establish a stitch gauge of 10 to 12 stitches per inch. If stitches shorten as you sew tricot, lengthen them to 8 to 10 per inch. Test stitch for length on a scrap of tricot before sewing garment.

TO BEGIN ROW OF STITCHING: hold the top and bobbin threads between finger and thumb. Lower the presser foot and needle into the fabric, start the machine, and pull slightly on the two threads—toward the back of the machine. This prevents static electricity—generated by sewing on synthetic fabric—from drawing the thread down to the bobbin and causing bunching.

STITCHING THE SEAM: to stitch a lengthwise seam on tricot, place the left hand behind the presser foot and grasp the fabric with thumb and forefinger. Keep the right hand in front of presser foot, holding fabric at seam allowance. Pull fabric slightly in front and in back of presser foot with a gentle, even pressure. By doing so you build extra thread (stitches) into the seam and produce "give" to correspond with the "give" of the knit fabric. Keeping the fabric taut also prevents it from "bouncing" up with the needle and causing skipped stitches. Stitch at a slow, even pace. Fast stitching can cause fabric to rise and fall, resulting in uneven and skipped stitches.

DON'T STITCH OVER PINS: while it is a good practice to pin-baste lingerie fabric at regular intervals along the seam line, don't stitch over pins with machine. There is danger of damage to both needle and fabric in so doing. Instead, stop sewing as you approach the pin. Keeping needle down in fabric, remove the pin and continue to stitch.

"STITCH-AND-PULL": always leave several inches of thread at the beginning and end of each tricot seam. If the seam appears puckered when stitching is finished, the puckers may be eased out to the ends of the stitching line. Starting at the center of a seam, slide the fabric gently with the fingertips toward the end of the stitching line. Nylon thread is slippery enough to allow this trick to work.

[Note: Seams tend to pucker more when sewn on the diagonal than on the straight of the goods.]

CHANGE NEEDLES FREQUENTLY: machine needles sometimes get hot from stitching lingerie fabric. They may also become nicked or bent for various reasons and cause snagging of fabric or skipped stitches. Check to make sure you have the correct size of needle for the weight of fabric you are using.

FASTENING THREAD ENDS: as a general rule, backstitching is not recommended as a means of securing thread ends when sewing tricot. It has a tendency to poke fabric down into the needle plate on some machines.

A more common means of securing thread ends in tricot is to pivot the fabric on the needle at the conclusion of a seam and retrace a few stitches—sewing in a forward position.

Tying of thread ends is unsatisfactory as synthetic threads are slippery and do not hold a knot well. On some machines it is possible to drop the feed dog or to set the stitch length at 0 (zero) and make a bar tack at the beginning or end of a seam.

TYPES OF LINGERIE SEAMS

Since lingerie knits do not ravel, seams may be narrow and do not need to be finished in any way. Following are the most often used lingerie seams:

THE DOUBLE STRAIGHT STITCH:
- Make a straight stitch on the seam line.
- Make a second row of straight stitching ⅛ inch from the first (nearer the cut edge).
- Trim seam allowance to within ¼ inch of second row of stitching.

THE ZIGZAG OVERCAST:
- Stitch with a straight stitch or slight zigzag on seam line.
- Trim seam allowance to ¼ inch.
- Overcast edge, through both thicknesses, using some form ·of zigzag stitch. (On machines with automatic blindstitch, fabric may be reversed for second row of stitching so that the seam edge is to the *left* of the presser foot and edges may be overcast with a medium-width blindstitch.)

THE OVEREDGE STITCH (Imitation Overlock):
  A special feature of some machines, sews fabric pieces together and overcasts edges at the same time.

THE FRENCH SEAM (particularly good for seaming sheers):
- For the first row, place *wrong* sides of fabric together and straight stitch in a narrow seam (or trim seam to ⅛ inch after stitching).
- Turn fabric inside out and fold along stitching.
- Stitch a second row of straight stitching just far enough from the fold to enclose the raw edges. Keep seams narrow to avoid a "homemade look."

THE WELT SEAM (flattens and gives a smooth finish to such stiff fabrics as stabilized nylon):
- With right sides of fabric together, straight stitch along the seam-allowance line.
- Trim seam allowance to ¼ inch.
- Turn both seam allowances toward back of garment.
- From right side of garment, stitch through all three thicknesses.

MOCK FLAT FELL (may be used to join lace ends):
- Place two right sides of material together.
- Fold ends under, twice, making two ¼-inch folds and turn toward back of garment.
- Topstitch with a double row of straight stitching or a zigzag stitch.

Fig. 23-4. Zigzag overcast.

Fig. 23-5. Overedge seam.

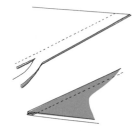

Fig. 23-6. French seam.

Fig. 23-7. Welt seam.

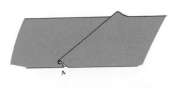

Fig. 23-8. Mock flat fell.

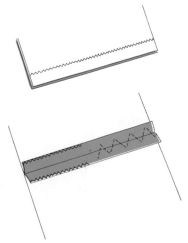

Fig. 23-9. Reinforced girdle seam.

Fig. 23-10. Overlapped girdle seam.

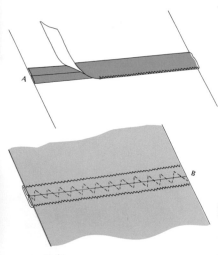

Fig. 23-11. Taped girdle seam.

SEAMS FOR POWER NET

The best stitch to use on power net or any of the stretch fabrics used in lingerie sewing is the "stretch" stitch which differs with the make of the sewing machine—most now have a recommended stretch stitch.

If a machine does not have a stretch stitch, stretch may be imparted to an ordinary zigzag stitch in these two ways:
- Widening the stitch width
- Shortening the stitch length

Usually a combination of the two is used. Synthetic thread is a must. Use a number 80 or 90 ballpoint needle (depending on the weight of the power net) or the equivalent thereof.

A straight stitch is not recommended because the thread is apt to break during wear of the garment. But it is sometimes used if a great deal of stretch can be built in by the seamstress and if each seam is *triple stitched.*

THE PREFERRED GIRDLE SEAMS

THE REINFORCED GIRDLE SEAM:
- Stitch a plain seam with stretch stitch or narrow zigzag (2 to 2½ stitch width, 15 to 20 stitch length). Press seam open with fingers or warm iron.
- Topstitch from the right side with a plain zigzag—set at a wide setting and short-stitch length—or other decorative open-stitch pattern.

THE OVERLAPPED GIRDLE SEAM (flat joining seam):
- Lay seam allowances of two sections of fabric so that they overlap each other approximately ¼ inch.
- Overstitch both raw edges as shown.

TAPED GIRDLE SEAM (good for center back and side seams of girdle):
- Sew plain girdle seam and press open.
- Cut lengthwise strip of self-fabric or plush elastic the length of seam to be taped.
- Place strip of tape (fabric or elastic) over the girdle seam on inside of garment, centering it so that it is the same width as the opened seam (trimming seam allowance to fit if necessary).
- Zigzag the tape and seam edges together along edges, stitching through all three thicknesses.
- On right side of girdle, stitch with a large zigzag or multiple stitch through center of seam and tape.

SEAMING QUILTED FABRICS

Because of their thickness, quilted fabrics must be handled differently from other fabrics on some machines. To stitch quilteds made of nylon and Dacron it is recommended that a small needle be used in the machine and that nylon or polyester thread be used. It may be necessary to lower the tension and pressure on the presser foot.

The seam edges of quilted fabrics must be enclosed in some way to keep the fiberfill from oozing out during the washing and wearing of the garment.

SUGGESTED SEAM FINISHES FOR QUILTEDS:

- Make a plain ⅝-inch seam and then zigzag or straight stitch the outer edges of the seam or use *imitation overlock* seam.
- Bind the seam edges with a crosscut binding, bias tape, rayon or nylon seam tape, or use Hong Kong Finish.
- *Mock French seam:* Stitch a plain seam, then pick away all fiberfill outside the stitching line. Turn the two seam edges inward. Press, and hand stitch together.

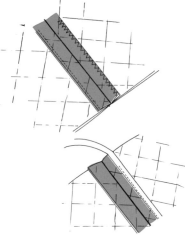

Fig. 23-12. Quilted seam finishes.

MAKING ENCLOSED SEAMS

There are times in lingerie sewing—when a double layer of fabric is involved—that sections of a garment may be stitched in place by machine without the stitching showing.

CONCEALED YOKE SEAM (used on gown or peignoir):

- Cut two layers of fabric for each yoke section—may be two layers of tricot or one layer of fancy fabric, such as allover lace for outer layer, and one of tricot for inner (lining) layer.
- Join side seams of yoke and yoke lining separately.
- Complete construction of skirt section and then pin the yoke lining to the inside with the right side of the yoke lining to the wrong side of skirt.
- Pin the right side of the yoke to the right side of the skirt.
- Stitch both sections of yoke to the skirt on the designated seam line. At the side seams, turn the least noticeable seam forward and the other toward the back. Trim seam allowance to ¼ inch.
- Pull yoke into position, matching shoulder seams, again turning least noticeable seam toward front and other back.
- Pin yoke and yoke lining together at neckline and armholes. Finish raw edges with binding or lace.

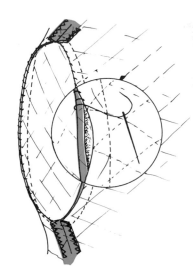

Fig. 23-13. Mock French seam.

ENCLOSED CROTCH SEAM (for tricot panty or tricot girdle crotch):

- Cut double layer of tricot for crotch.
- Place right sides of two crotch pieces together.
- Insert back of panty between crotch pieces, matching the seam lines. (The panty will have an "inside curve" and the crotch an "outside curve," but don't panic—just match the center notches and key the seam ends, then pin-baste at right angles to the seam edge.)
- Sew back crotch seam with a straight stitch (or desired stretch stitch). Make a second row of stitching if you wish to insure long wear. Back-tack or leave long thread ends. Trim seam allowance to ¼ inch.

Fig. 23-14. Concealed seam in yoke.

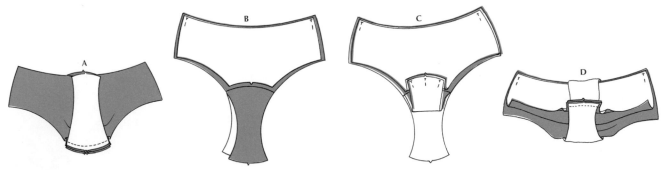

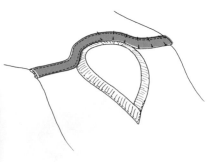

Fig. 23-15. Enclosed
crotch seam.

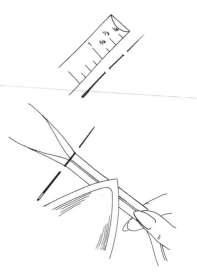

Fig. 23-16. Making
fabric tape.

- Pin right side of inner crotch to wrong side of panty.
- Fold top of panty down and flip outer crotch back and around entire panty. Pin with right sides together—through all three seam allowances.
- Sew the front crotch seam the same as the back and trim the seam.
- Turn panty right side out, pulling it out from between the crotch pieces. Seam will be hidden.
- If desired, the two raw edges of crotch may be edgestitched together on both leg edges before elastic is applied.
  [Note: Some seamstresses prefer to apply the crotch while side seams are still open so that elastic may be applied before side seams are stitched.]

TAPING SEAMS

The practice of taping seams serves to reinforce a garment at stress points. Taping is frequently used to reinforce seams in men's and children's knit nightwear, particularly across the shoulders and back neckline.

TO MAKE SELF-FABRIC TAPE:

- Predetermine width of tape wanted. Then cut strips of self-fabric on the lengthwise grain. Press under edges.
- To speed pressing, insert two darning needles on padded ironing board—or other padded surface. Have exposed center section of needle the exact width you want your finished tape to be. Draw fabric strips through space under center section of darning needle and press with warm steam iron.

THE TAPED SHOULDER SEAM (using ½-inch tape):

- Cut strip of self-fabric on lengthwise grain that is 1 inch wide and at least 2 inches longer than the measurement across the shoulders and around the back neckline.
- Press under ¼ inch on each side of tape.
- With wrong side of garment up, place the "tape" directly over the shoulder and back neckline seams with wrong sides together and pin in place.
- Stitch along one folded edge. Keep tape and fabric relaxed.
- Repeat for other edge of tape.

Fig. 23-17. Taping
shoulder seam.

THE TAPED BRA SEAM:

Taping bra seams adds both firmness and support. It also helps in the shaping, as the bra may be molded to the correct body contour while the seam tape is being applied. Bra tape may be the commercial type or may be made of strips of fabric cut ⅞ inch to 1 inch wide. *Lengthwise* strips of tricot, sheer, satin tricot, or *bias* strips of marquisette and stabilized nylon may be used. Two methods follow:

METHOD A:

- Apply the wrong side of folded tape over all cup seams that have been stitched. Topstitch along both edges of tape maintaining the bra's cupped position. Never stitch flat.
- After bust-cup seams are taped, join front and back of bra at side seam, turn seams toward back and tape them also.

METHOD B (applicable to double-fold sheer or marquisette):

- Cut strips of fabric on lengthwise grain, 1 inch wide.
- Fold in half lengthwise, wrong sides together.
- Pin tape along seamline with raw edges even—working from lower-cup side. Stitch tape along seam-allowance line, over top of previous stitching.
- Turn folded edge of tape over to upper-cup side of seam. Topstitch near folded edge and again near seam edge.

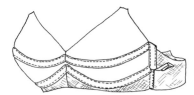

Fig. 23-18. Taping bra seam—Method A

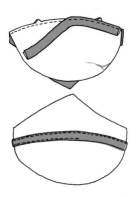

Fig. 23-19. Taping bra cup—Method B

SEWING DARTS IN TRICOT

It is recommended that darts in tricot slips and gowns be double stitched. Here are two methods; the first for the beginner, the second for the more advanced lingerie seamstress.

METHOD A:

- Sew from wide part of dart to point.
- Pivot material at the tip of the dart, keeping needle down in fabric, and stitch back to seamline. Keep this second stitching line inside the first seam, tapering from ⅛ inch to ¼ inch as the base of the dart is approached.
- Trim away excess tricot from dart.
  [Note: Zigzag stitch may be used for second row of stitching.]

METHOD B (pre-trimmed dart):

- Trim dart to remove all but a narrow seam allowance.
- Sew from wide part of dart to point.
- Pivot at point and reset machine so that it will overcast the raw edges of dart-seam allowance as you make the return row of stitching.

SUBSTITUTING GATHERS FOR DARTS:

Sometimes substituting gathers for darts results in a softer look to a lingerie garment (for example, a slip bodice). It may also be a time-saver for those who find tricot darts difficult to execute.

- Along seamline where dart would normally be located, run 2 rows of machine-gathering stitches (elongated straight stitch)—

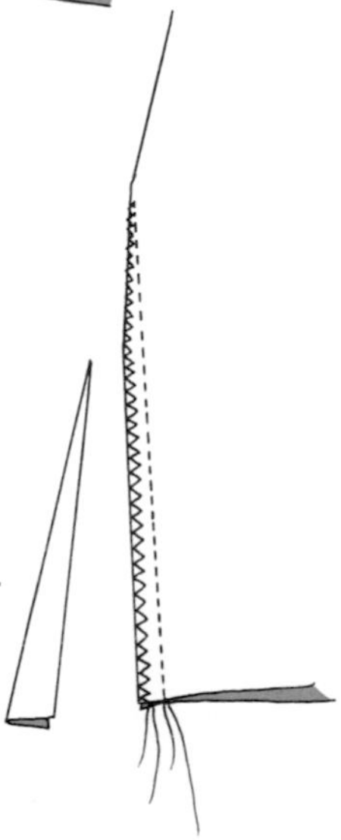

Fig. 23-20. Dart—Method A.

Fig. 23-21. Dart—Method B.

Fig. 23-22. Substituting gathers for darts.

one on the designated seam-allowance line and another between the seam and the edge.

- Pull up the bobbin thread to ease in the amount of fullness that would otherwise be taken up by a dart, so that notches and edges are keyed to those of the seam to which the gathered section will be joined.
- To anchor gathering threads firmly in tricot, place round-head pins at both ends of row of gathers. Wind gathering thread ends in a figure 8 around the head and point of pins several times, as shown in Figure 23-22.

24

LINGERIE ELASTIC

Lingerie elastic that is ½ inch wide is usually considered "waist elastic." Elastic that is ¼ inch, or narrower, in width is referred to as "leg elastic," but the two may be used interchangeably. Waist elastic usually has four ridges which act as helpful guides when it comes to topstitching. Leg elastic has only three ridges.

The fluted—or picot—edge, seen on most lingerie elastic, may be placed either off the edge of the garment or down toward the body of the garment. The former is, perhaps, a bit more decorative, but the latter is less apt to curl after washing.

TAKING MEASUREMENTS

MEASURING FOR WAIST:

To determine the length of elastic to be applied to the waist of a half-slip or panty, subtract from 4 to 6 inches from the body measurement—depending on the amount of "give" in the elastic you've chosen. Or—still more reliable—actually fit the elastic around the waist, tightening it until it is comfortably sung.
[Note: If elastic is to be topstitched, it should be cut shorter than elastic that is to be threaded through a casing, as topstitching robs elastic of some of its resiliency.]
A heavy fabric will also take up more of the elasticity than a sheer fabric, making it necessary to cut elastic shorter for heavy fabrics, such as satins, and longer for sheer tricot.

MEASURING FOR LEG:

>To measure elastic for a brief panty leg, measure around top of leg and cut to this length, or slightly shorter. Subtract some length for topstitching. Casing elastic may be cut to same length as leg measurement. For bikini legs, which may be cut at varying angles, it is best to try on panty after the waist elastic has been attached and measure around the leg for the actual size of the opening.

MEASURING FOR HIPS:

>To determine length of elastic sewn at top of a bikini or hip-hugger, try on panty to see where top edge comes and then measure around hip at this point. Deduct 6 to 8 inches—depending on method of application and stretchiness of elastic. (Elastic lace is a popular choice for the bikini or hip-hugger.)

JOINING ELASTIC ENDS

Elastic may be attached to a garment before side seams or the center-back seam is stitched—while the garment is still open, so that the work will be flat. This is a trade technique and is often used in attaching elastic webbing to men's pajamas and applying elastic lace to girdle legs. For most lingerie garments, however, it is a more acceptable practice to *join the elastic ends before applying elastic* to the waist or leg, using one of the following methods:

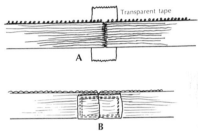

METHOD A:

>Butt ends of elastic together—*putting both edges on a piece of magic tape*—and zigzag or handstitch back and forth.

METHOD B:

>Stitch elastic ends together in a ¼ inch seam. Open seam and topstitch in a rectangle.

METHOD C:

>Overlap the ends a good ¼ inch and sew them together securely on the three open sides. The picot edge does not have to be overstitched, but it is a good idea to overstitch the other edges.

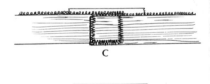

METHOD D:

>Make a false flat-fell seam at joint by turning the two edges in ¼ inch—one up and one under—so that they may be locked together and enclose the raw edges. A hair clip may be used to hold the joint together while it is being sewed.

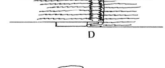

RIBBON TABS OR LABELS

To hide the elastic joint from view, a tab of satin ribbon or folded tricot may be placed in the garment It also serves to identify front and back of a garment, if placed at center-back seam. Personalized dressmaker's labels may also be used. They may be applied by hand or machine after the garment ·is completed, or inserted as elastic is applied.

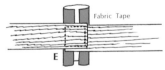

Fig. 24-1. Joining lingerie elastic.

If a ribbon or self-fabric tab is used, it may be stitched directly to the elastic by placing it at right angles to the elastic, just under the joint. Stitch down both sides of the joint, securing elastic to ribbon. Leave enough ribbon at top and bottom of elastic to fold over and join into seam as elastic is applied.

METHODS OF APPLYING LINGERIE ELASTIC

TOPSTITCHED METHOD

This is the quickest method—the one most often seen on ready-to-wear garments. Elastic is stitched directly to outside of garment and, as it remains clearly in evidence, is usually of a well matched or coordinating color.

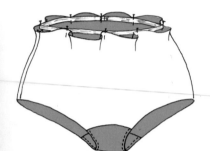

Fig. 24-2. Dividing elastic for waistline.

FOR WAIST OF SLIP OR PANTY:

- Divide circle of elastic into quarters. (For the beginning sewer, *eighths* is even easier.) Mark each of these equal divisions with a pin.
- Divide the waistline into quarters—or eighths—marking it with pins also (or use side seams and center front and back notches as guides).
- Placing joint of elastic at center back (or side seam), pin elastic along top of garment—wrong side of elastic to right side of garment—having edges even. Match each quarter marking.
- Place garment on sewing machine with tricot down toward feed dog. Using a straight stitch or small zigzag, start stitching at one set of pins, between the first 2 ridges of elastic. Stretch both elastic and tricot to make them meet at each of the quarter markings. Stitch slowly, a small section at a time, keeping needle down in elastic when stopping to remove pins so that elastic will not pull out from under presser foot. (Turn side seams toward back of garment.)
- Stitch an inch or two past the starting point to reinforce ends of stitching.
- Make a second row of straight or small zigzag stitches along upper edge of elastic (or one wide zigzag stitch down middle of elastic), making sure elastic is stretched the same amount as it was on the first stitching.
- Trim away any excess tricot at the top of the garment.

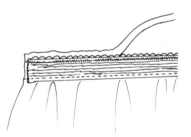

Fig. 24-3. Topstitched method of applying elastic.

FOR PANTY LEG:

The same method as above may be used, but as leg elastic is narrower, the two rows of stitching will be closer together. If a single row of zigzag stitching is used, stitch down the middle of the elastic keeping stitch width half the width of the elastic.

STITCHED AND TURNED METHOD

This method gives a more finished look to lingerie as there are no raw edges exposed when it is completed. It may be executed so that the finished elastic will appear on the outside of the garment, or so that the elastic is inside and only the picot edge appears outside. The latter is effective for use of contrasting color elastics. Decide in advance the desired look and then apply elastic to the opposite side.

FOR WAIST OR LEG:
- Measure elastic, join ends, and quarter, as above.
- Pin elastic to inside of garment (or opposite side from which you wish finished elastic to appear). Have edge of elastic even with the edge of garment—wrong side of elastic toward tricot.
- Straight stitch between two ridges along the inner edge. Stretch the elastic to meet each marking. Stitch beyond starting point.
- Remove work from machine. Trim away tricot close to stitching. Fold elastic to opposite side of garment.
- Stitch along other edge of elastic with a zigzag or straight stitch, stretching to same degree as before. Be careful that fabric on underside lies smooth so that no extra tricot gets bunched under elastic as it is sewn.

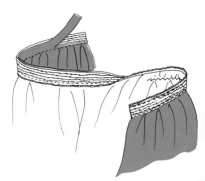

Fig. 24-4. Stitched-and-turned elastic.

CASING METHOD

The quick application of the above two methods and their lack of bulk have made them more popular recently than the casing, but a casing may still be used where lingerie elastic may not be available. It has the advantage of long wear and easy replacement of elastic.
- Fold edge of garment to wrong side in a hem that is the width of elastic plus ¼ inch.
- Pin folded-over tricot in place and stitch close to the raw edge, using either a straight or a narrow zigzag stitch. Leave a small opening for inserting elastic.
- Insert elastic with a safety pin or bodkin. Secure ends of elastic. Close opening with hand stitches.

LACE CASING:
> This method may be used when lingerie elastic is not available and there is an insufficient amount of fabric left to make the usual fabric casing—or just to add a dressy touch to lingerie. You may use a stretch-lace seam binding. For ½-inch elastic, use lace that is ½ to ¾ inch wide.
- Lap wrong side of lace ¼ inch over wrong side of garment edge. Straight stitch close to edge of lace.
- Fold lace to right side and stitch along bottom of lace with either straight stitch or narrow zigzag. Leave an opening for elastic.

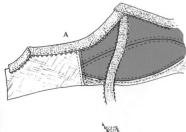

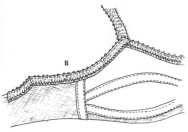

Fig. 24-5. Applying plush elastic to power net.

Fig. 24-6. Applying stretch lace to girdle leg.

- Insert elastic, overlap ends of elastic. Stitch them securely. Close the opening.

APPLYING PLUSH ELASTIC TO POWER NET

Plush elastic is used to finish the edges of power net in bra making. It is applied as follows:

FOR UPPER EDGE OF BRA:
- Pin elastic, nap side up, to right side of top edge of bra and front V. The picot edge will be down. Overlap the edge ¼ inch. Stitch close to the picot trim.
- Trim elastic to the wrong side and stitch along the other edge of the elastic with a straight, elastic, or zigzag stitch.

FOR BOTTOM EDGE OF BRA:
- Use same procedure as for top edge, stitching first to outside of bra and then turning so that napped side of elastic is toward body when second row of stitching is complete.

APPLYING PLUSH ELASTIC TO GIRDLE

In girdle-making, plush elastic is applied in the same manner as for bra-making. To apply to *waist,* observe the following steps:
- Measure and cut picot girdle elastic (most will have picot trim on one edge) so that it fits waist opening comfortably without stretching. (Some fitters suggest that it may be snugged in as much as 4 inches, but this is a highly individual matter.) Allow an extra ½ inch for joining.
- Stitch ends of elastic to form circle.
- Divide elastic and girdle top into fourths. Mark with pins.
- Placing elastic seams at center back, overlap elastic ¼ inch over right side of girdle—nap side up and picot edge down. Stitch as close as possible to the picot edge of elastic, stretching both elastic and fabric as you zigzag.
- Turn elastic to wrong side and zigzag stitch bottom edge of elastic, again stretching both elastic and fabric.
  [Note: May also be applied to *leg* in same manner.]

APPLYING ELASTIC LACE

Stretch lace may be sewn to a *girdle leg* before the side seams are stitched. Or it may be joined and applied after the leg is closed. Measure stretch lace for leg openings, using the same measurement as the girdle leg.
- Place stretch lace on right side of girdle fabric, overlapping the leg edge about ½ inch. Stitch along the upper edge of elastic with wide stretch or zigzag stitch.
- Trim away excess girdle fabric ¼ inch from stitching. Repeat for other leg.

GATHERING WITH NARROW ELASTIC

Narrow elastic, ⅛ inch wide or less, may be applied to intimate apparel to give a softly gathered or shirred effect. The yoke or sleeves of a granny gown, the empire waist of a bodice gown, the bloomer leg of a shortie nightie are some places this might be used.

Apply *"baby elastic"* by placing the elastic under the machine presser foot and catching it with two or three stitches. Then stretch elastic and zigzag over it. This may be done in a sleeve or panty leg before the seam is closed. Finish the edge of the garment before applying elastic.

Round elastic usually has more give than the flat kind. If *flat elastic* is used, more than one row will be required.

Elastic thread may also be used. On some machines it is possible to thread it through a small hole in the machine embroidery foot and pull it while it is being stitched. The more it is pulled, the tighter the gathers. (To make a second row—stitch one presser-foot width away, pulling material straight while sewing.)

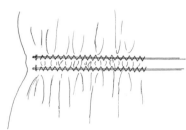

Fig. 24-7. Gathering with baby elastic.

25

EDGE FINISHES FOR LINGERIE

The open-ended possibilities for finishing the edges of garments is one of the things that keeps lingerie sewing from ever becoming a bore. The imaginative seamstress will soon devise her own version of many of the methods listed in this section. Individual pattern instructions, the shape and location of the garment edge to be finished, and one's own personal preferences will dictate at what point in the construction of the garment the edge finish should be applied. Whenever feasible, it is considered time-saving to finish edges while the garment piece is still flat.

COLLARS

Collars may be stitched and turned in the usual dressmaker method—the enclosed seam, turned, clipped, and graded. A lightweight or feather-weight nonwoven interfacing will keep tricot collars from curling.

The trade technique used very often is to place the collar and facing wrong side together and stitch around the outer edges with a fancy

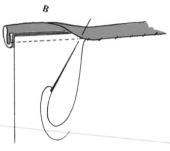

Fig. 25-1. Crosscut
binding.

stitch. Cut away excess fabric close to fancy stitching. Collars constructed this way may be finished around the edges with various types of trims and bindings.

For another method of applying a convertible or non-convertible shaped collar to tricot robes, pajamas, and other tricot garments, see Chapter 12, page 85.

On heavier, quilted or bulky *fabrics,* collars may be made of only one layer of fabric. The facing is eliminated to reduce the bulk. A single-layer collar may be finished with an overedge stitch so that it will not ravel and then trimmed with binding or some form of edging.

CROSSCUT BINDING

For finishing curved edges—such as the neck or armhole—on tricot fabric, a self-fabric binding, cut on the crosswise grain, is flexible and easy to apply. Sometimes called *French binding,* it may be applied entirely by machine or finished by hand.

HAND FINISHED METHOD:

- Cut strips of chiffon or regular tricot across the width of fabric, making it 1½ inches to 2 inches wide and as long as needed. (This will usually be an inch or two longer than the opening.)
- Fold strip in half lengthwise, wrong sides together.
- Pin folded strip to *right* side of garment, matching raw edges.
- Stitch ¼ inch from the raw edge with a straight stitch.
- Fold binding over the raw edge and sew folded edge to seam line on inside by hand.

MACHINE FINISHED METHOD:

- Reverse above procedure, applying the crosscut strip to *inside* of armhole or neck edge. Then, as you turn folded binding to the *outside* of the garment, topstitch in place.
- Narrow lace may be inserted between binding and garment before it is stitched the second time.

SHELL EDGING

This is a popular method of finishing both straight or curved edges. Following are three methods:

HAND METHOD:

- Trim seam edge to ¼ inch, fold to wrong side.
- Working on wrong side, take 2 or 3 small running stitches along raw edge within the seam allowance only.
- Take two stitches over edge of hem, pulling thread taut as you do so.
- Repeat to end of hem.

MACHINE METHOD:

- Trim hem to ¼ inch, fold to wrong side.
- Set machine for automatic blindstitch; stitch length at approximately 15 stitches per inch, needle at center position.

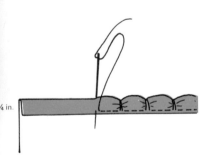

¼ in.

Fig. 25-2. Hand-sewn
shell edge.

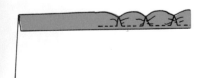

Fig. 25-3. Machine-sewn
shell edge.

- Insert fabric in machine so that the fold of the hem is to the left of presser foot, wrong side up, and stitch around entire hem.

MOCK SHELL:

- Insert fabric with fold edges to left of presser foot, as described above.
- Stitch from wrong side with wide zigzag or universal stitch.
- Stitch second row of straight stitches or tiny zigzag along inside edge of the wide zigzag.

EDGING WITH NARROW LACE:

This method works well for smooth edges rather than gathered ones. It may be used to finish armhole, neck edge, collar, pockets, etc., on tricot or any non-raveling fabrics. Use a soft ½-inch lace.

- Stay-stitch the edge of the garment by straight stitching ¼ inch from cut edge.
- Gather lace slightly by pulling a thread along straight edge of lace, or by running a machine-gathering thread through lace to ease in slightly.
- Pin the straight edge of the lace to the right side of the garment so that it overlaps the edge ¼ inch.
- Topstitch lace to garment using either zigzag or straight stitch.
- Finish raw edge of lace at ends, by folding under ¼ inch twice and stitching. See Mock Flat Fell, page 133.

EUROPEAN TECHNIQUE (for a firmer edge):

- Place narrow lace along the edge of garment—wrong side of lace to right side of garment. Have outer edges even.
- Stitch along inner edge of lace.
- Fold back the tricot on stitching line. Stitch with a small zigzag on top of the straight stitch.
- Trim away tricot close to stitching line, on wrong side.

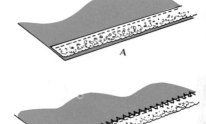

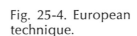

Fig. 25-4. European technique.

BAND TRIM

The following is a good finish for straight edges, using self- or contrasting fabric. It may be used for finishing a panty leg, sleeve edge, hem, or garment front opening. The following directions are for a 1-inch band for finishing a *panty leg*.

DRESSMAKER METHOD:

- Cut strip of crosscut fabric 2½ inches wide and the measurement of the opening, plus a seam allowance.
- Join in circle with a narrow seam.
- Quarter panty leg and band.
- Place circular band so that one edge of the right side is to the wrong side of the panty leg. Stitch in ¼-inch seam, stretching both panty and band.
- Trim seam and turn to right side. Fold under raw edge at seamline. Pin in place and sew, using either a zigzag, decorative, or straight stitch. Stretch as you sew.

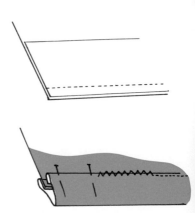

Fig. 25-5. Band trim.

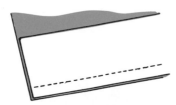

TRADE METHOD ("quickie" technique):
- Cut band and join ends as above.
- Fold band in half, wrong sides together, and stitch the double band to the right side of the panty, stretching both panty and band as you sew.

HONG KONG FINISH

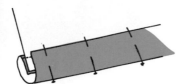

This is a quick trade technique for finishing hems, facing edges, trimming collars, cuffs, pockets, and quilted seams.
- Cut a strip of fabric (any non-raveling material) at least 1 inch wide to use as binding.
- Place strip of binding so that the right side faces the right side of garment, raw edges matching. Stitch in ¼-inch seam.
- Turn binding to inside of garment, folding it over the top of the seam so the ¼ inch will remain exposed to view.
- Stitch a second time from the right side, in the groove or "well" made by previous stitching. (The raw edges of this binding do not need to be turned under or finished in any way.)

Fig. 25-6. Hong Kong trim.

HEM FINISHES

ROLLED HEM (a hand finish for circular skirts or sheer fabrics):
- Trim seam allowance to ¼ inch.
- Fold under raw edge ⅛ inch to inside.
- Take a ⅛-inch stitch along the fold and anchor the thread.
- Take a tiny stitch in the garment directly below the raw edge (catching a single thread of garment).
- Slip needle through fold for about ¼ inch.
- Repeat around hem, pulling up thread to form roll about every 8 stitches.

TAILORED HEM (works best on garments with very little stretch):
- Turn bottom edge of garment up 1 inch toward wrong side and pin in place from wrong side.
- Zigzag or straight stitch close to raw edge on wrong side, keeping fabric relaxed while stitching.
- Fasten thread by overlapping 1 inch at the end.

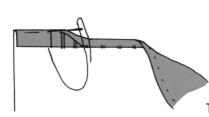

Fig. 25-7. Rolled hem.

MACHINE-EMBROIDERED HEM:
- Choose an open-stitch design. Close stitching is too stiff and the sewing action may jam fabric in needle plate.
- Turn under lower edge 1¼ inches to wrong side of garment. Pin in position from right side.
- Place a narrow strip of typing paper under hem.
- Select a machine-embroidery stitch, setting machine at a short stitch length and a wide bight. (Test stitch on a double layer of fabric.)
- Working from the right side of garment, embroidery-stitch hem in place 1 inch from the fold.

- Tear away paper from wrong side of hem.
- Trim away excess fabric above stitching line (on wrong side).

HEMS ON QUILTED GARMENTS:

Stitch by hand after the edge has been finished by one of the following means:

- Bias binding or crosscut binding.
- Zigzag or overedge stitch.
- Hong Kong Finish.

LACE HEMS

OPAQUE LACE HEM:

This method of applying wide lace may be used at the hem of a slip after one side seam has already been stitched. The garment may be laid flat while lace is stitched to hem. The second side seam—when stitched—will then incorporate the raw edges of the lace.

- Measure enough lace to go around hemline, keeping in mind that tricot has more "give" than lace. Allow an extra ½ inch of lace for joining seam allowance.
- Place lower (or scalloped) edge of lace even with lower edge of garment. Pin or tape in position. (If desired, scallops may extend below edge of tricot.)
- Stitch along top edge of lace, following the lace design with a straight or zigzag stitch.

Stitch again at lower edge of lace, using one of the following methods:

a. Stitch ¼ inch from scalloped edge and trim away fabric with small trimming scissors.

b. Stitch ⅛ inch from scalloped edge and allow fabric to remain, as a peek-a-boo trim.

FREE-HANGING LACE HEM ("quickie" method):

- Measure enough lace to go around hemline, allowing ½-inch extensions for joining at side seam.
- Place scalloped edge of lace even with lower edge of garment. Pin or tape in position.
- Stitch along inner edge of lace, following the design with a zigzag or straight stitch.
- Trim fabric behind lace, close to stitching.
- Join lace ends separately from tricot side seam, using mock-flatfell seam or hand stitching.

FREE-HANGING LACE HEM (couture method):

- Trim hem to desired length *before* applying wide lace.
- Placing scalloped edge of lace up toward body of garment, pin wrong side of lace to wrong side of hemline so that the straight edge of the lace extends ¼ inch beyond the raw edge of tricot.
- From wrong side of garment, stitch ½ inch from straight edge of lace.

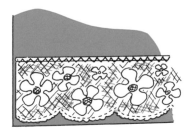

Fig. 25-8. Opaque lace hem.

Fig. 25-9. Free-hanging lace trim.

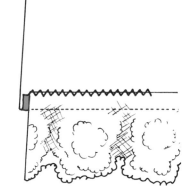

Fig. 25-10. Free-hanging lace, couture method.

- Turn the lace to right side of garment and topstitch straight edge of lace to garment. (The raw edge will then be enclosed in the stitching.)
- Join lace ends in mock flat fell or by hand stitching.

FREE-HANGING OVERLAY:

This is particularly good for emphasizing contrasting colors—lace of one color against a garment of another.
- Pin the lace to the slip, matching the lower edge of lace to the lower edge of garment.
- Stitch only the upper edge of the lace.
- Join lace at side seams.
- Finish bottom edge of tricot with a rolled hem.

DOUBLE-LACE HEM:

- Stitch a narrow lace to the lower edge of the finished slip using the European technique or simply overlapping the edge.
- Choose a wide lace. Pin it to the garment so that the lower edge of the wide lace and the lower edge of narrow lace match exactly.
- Stitch the wider lace to the slip at the upper edge only—following the contour of the lace.
- Join the wide lace in a mock flat fell at side seam.

FINISHING SLITS AND VENTS

A slit or vent in a slip allows for greater ease in walking or bending in below-the-knee fashions. They may be as short as 3 inches or as long as you like. A slit may be added to a garment by leaving the side seam open a few inches at one or both sides. Or it may be added to a pattern above one knee, at the center front, or center back.

Decide on the position and length of the slit desired and mark the position on the slip with a ruler or soft lead pencil.

A ribbon bow or lace appliqué at the top of a slit will add a touch of glamor and also help to reinforce the slit at its most critical point of stress.

Following are methods of finishing slits and vents:

BOUND LACE SLIT:

This is a quickie method for a wide-lace hem. Join side seams of garment but leave lace unseamed—at one or both sides.
- Cut enough wide lace to go around bottom of garment.
- Apply to bottom edge of garment in one of the methods previously shown. Do not join lace at side seam where slit is desired.
- For each slit, cut 2 strips of lace to use as binding. (A 1-inch-wide lace, lace seam binding, or an allover lace-fabric strip may be used. If using lace fabric, cut strip wider to allow for turning under edges.) Cut lace strip about ½ inch longer than lace hem is wide and turn ends under ¼ inch.
- Fold the binding lace in half, lengthwise (turning under any raw edges), and press with lukewarm iron.
- Using the narrow lace strip as binding, encase the raw edges of

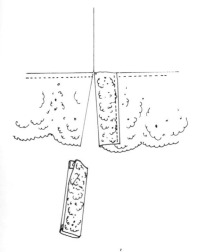

Fig. 25-11. Long slit (in slip).

Fig. 25-12. Bound lace slit.

the wide lace. Topstitch along the loose edge of binding, making sure that stitching goes through all layers.

MITERED LACE SLIT:

When wide lace trimming used at the hemline is extended up the garment to trim the slit, the lace needs to be mitered at the corner.

METHOD A:

- Mark position and length of slit—if at other than seamline.
- Measure and cut enough lace to go around the hemline and up both sides of slit, allowing extra for mitering corners and turning under at top of slit.
- Line up lace at the top of slit. Fold cut end under ¼ inch (either straight across or on an angle) and pin lace along edge of vent, having outer edges of lace even with edge of vent.
- Form a miter at the bottom corner of the slit by folding the free end of the lace back, temporarily, right sides together. Hold in place with thumb and pin the miter—pinning only through the lace.
- Continue pinning lace in place around hemline. Then stitch lace to garment along inner edge of lace.
- As you approach corner on opposite side, miter lace without removing material from machine.
- Topstitch miter separate from tricot, trimming excess lace close to stitching on wrong side.
- Reinforce top of slit with two lines of straight or zigzag stitching.
- For free-hanging look, trim away tricot from behind lace. For opaque look, stitch again, along outer edge of lace.

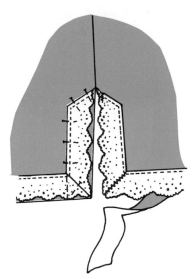

Fig. 25-13. Mitered lace slit—Method A.

METHOD B:

- If slit is in side seam, stitch seam down to point where you want slit to end, fastening thread ends securely.
- Starting at slit, pin lace to hem of garment, keeping scalloped edge of lace even with raw edge of fabric.
- Miter corner of slit as you reach it and continue pinning lace up the edge of slit.
- At top of slit, fold lace to form a triangle, as shown.
- Pin lace along other edge of slit and join ends of lace at corner on an angle to form a miter.
- Unpin lace from tricot at corners while you topstitch and trim miters.
- Replace pins and stitch around entire inner edge of lace.
- For free-hanging look, trim away tricot from behind lace; or appliqué by stitching again, along outer edge of lace.

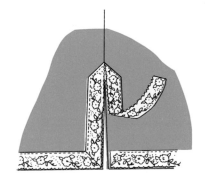

Fig. 25-14. Mitered lace slit—Method B.

OVERLAPPED VENT:

Overlapping the two vertical edges of a slit gives a more finished look. Whether a vent laps to left or right of garment depends on its placement. If vents are placed at both side seams, both should lap toward back.

- Mark position and length of vent.

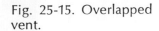

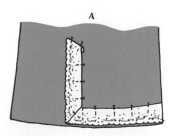
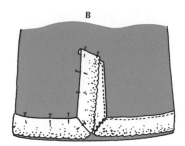
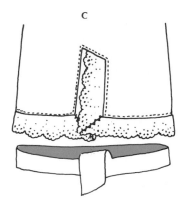

Fig. 25-15. Overlapped vent.

- Line up lace at top of slit, estimating generously to allow for hem, miters, and both sides of slit. Pin in place down edge of vent.
- Stitch around entire hemline, keeping outer edge of lace even with lower edge of slip.
- As you approach other side of vent, miter other corner so that it falls somewhat short of the stitched edge of the first side of vent —offsetting two sides so vent will open easily.
- Continue stitching up second side of vent, finishing top by turning under lace and stitching on diagonal, catching both layers of lace. Trim away tricot close to stitching.
- Topstitch miters and trim out excess lace from underside.

VENT WITH CHIFFON UNDERLAY:

A true *couture touch* for slips. The following directions are for a 6-inch slit in left-side seam:

- Cut a strip of chiffon (sheer tricot) that is 6¼ inches long and twice the width of lace used to trim hemline.
- Fold chiffon strip in half lengthwise, wrong sides together. Pin folded strip to right side of back-seam allowance. Stitch ¼-inch seam from Point A to Point B (¼ inch from top of chiffon).
- Leaving needle down in fabric and raising presser foot, fold back the extra ¼ inch of sheer. Pin the front of the slip into position, keying the front- and back-seam allowances. It is necessary to clip the front-seam allowance 6 inches from bottom. Slide the fabric above the clip under the chiffon. Then lay chiffon back

Fig. 25-16. Vent with chiffon underlay.

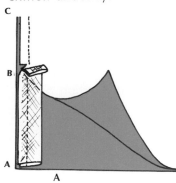
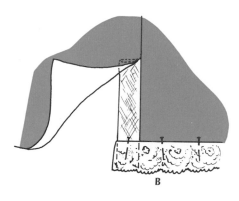

over the tricot and lower the presser foot. Stitch up entire seam to Point C (top of slip).

- Measure enough lace to go around bottom of slip and up front of vent, allowing extra for mitering. Starting at the back, pin lace to bottom edge. Leave ¼-inch extension beyond folded edge of chiffon for finishing later. Stitch lace around entire bottom edge.
- Miter front corner so that outer edge of vertical section of lace will overlap the underlay seam by ¼ inch. Pin and stitch lace vertically to top of vent.
- Turn under lace at top of vent ¼ inch—either diagonally or straight across—and stitch through lace, tricot, and chiffon.
- Trim away tricot close to stitching, stitch and trim mitered lace, turn under ¼-inch extension at back edge of lace and stitch.

APPLYING MITERED LACE TO A SLIP BODICE

Pin wide lace to the upper edge of the bodice. Have the outer edges of lace and bodice even. Form a dart in the lace on the wrong side at the high point of the bodice.

- Topstitch the lower edge of the lace to the tricot.
- Pull the tricot away from under the lace and topstitch the miter with either a zigzag or a straight stitch. Trim excess lace close to stitching at back.
- For free-standing lace, cut away tricot close to the stitching line at lower edge of lace. For appliquéd lace, repin lace and stitch to tricot along upper edge.

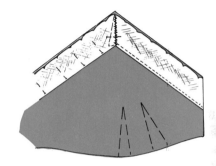

Fig. 25-17. Applying mitered lace to slip bodice.

26

LINGERIE TRIMS

FABRIC TRIMS

RUFFLES

One of the prettiest and softest trims for intimate apparel is the self-ruffle—particularly on garments of chiffon or those with chiffon overlay. Nylon chiffon (sheer tricot) ruffles do not have to be finished on the

edges. They will "feather" with wear, but only become prettier.
Ruffles should be cut on the crosswise grain.

- Cut strips of chiffon 1¼ inches wide across width of tricot. For extensive ruffling, fold fabric over and over, cutting several layers at once.
- Stitch down center of strip, using machine gathering foot or ruffler. The shorter the stitch length, the fuller the gathers. *Or*, make two rows of machine gathering stitches, ¼ inch apart on each side of center, and pull up thread to ruffle.
- Apply ruffles to garment by stitching down center of ruffle. Remove gathering threads.
- For variation, apply several layers of ruffles at one time or cut wider and fold for enclosed ruffles.

ROLLED TRICOT

Tricot that is cut lengthwise will roll of its own accord to form a tubing that has many uses. A strip cut approximately ¾ inch wide and pulled taut until it rolls will substitute for ribbon. It may be threaded through lace or used to make pom-pom trim for slippers, robes, or novelty items. It is also effective threaded through a lightweight metal chain for a belt on a robe or hostess gown.

POM-POM TRIM

Cut a strip of cardboard that is 2 x 4 inches. Cut a small window in it to one side of center.

- Cut strip of lengthwise tricot ½ inch or wider and stretch taut until firmly rolled.
- Wrap tricot strip around cardboard.
- Pull a 5-inch strip of rolled tricot through small window and tie it securely around wound strips.
- Cut the loops along both edges of the cardboard.
- Shake out tricot ends to make fluffy pom-pom.

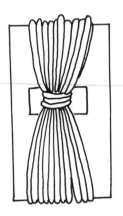

Fig. 26-1. Pom-pom trim.

SPAGHETTI TRIM

A tubing of either tricot or chiffon may be made by this simple cordless method and used for shoulder straps and a variety of trims.

- Cut strip of fabric on *crosswise* grain that is 2 inches wide (may be wider for chiffon) and whatever length is needed.
- Fold strip in half, lengthwise, right sides together. Begin stitching at the raw edge, angling to ¼ inch from folded edge. Continue stitching—¼ inch from edge—down entire length of strip, stretching as you sew. *Do not trim seam.*
- Cut a notch in the fold about ½ inch from upper edge of seam (at the point where angle sewing ended). Slip a bobby pin over the top of the seam and through the notch.

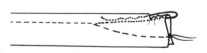

Fig. 26-2. Making spaghetti tubing.

- Turn fabric inside out by pushing bobby pin through tube. The fabric, following the bobby pin, will fill the tube out roundly, taking the place of cording.
- May be used for following trims: button loops, daisy trim, frogs, ball buttons, and straps. See *spaghetti straps,* page 159.

MILLINER'S ROSE

An ultra-feminine compliment to lingerie, easy to fashion out of bits and scraps. Sheers are particularly effective. Lighter weight tricots and Crepe-set may also be used. Lovely trim for nighties, peignoirs, slippers, granny caps.

TO MAKE THE FLOWER:
- Cut strips of chiffon on crosswise grain, 3 to 4 inches wide and 16 inches long.
- Fold strip in half lengthwise, wrong sides together.
- Beginning at one end, run a basting thread diagonally from folded edge to cut edge for about 6 inches, rounding off end of strip. Trim away sheer below basting thread.
- Pull basting thread, rolling the gathered fabric on an angle, to form center of rose. Secure by stab stitching at base of rose. (Mercerized thread will hold better than synthetic, here.)
- Baste another 6-inch section, stitching lengthwise along cut edge, rolling as you gather, and stab stitching to hold gathers in place. Continue across entire strip in 6 inch laps, being certain to keep raw edges even as you roll and stitch fabric.
- About 6 inches from end, taper stitching once again to fold. Trim away fabric below basting and finish rolling. Fasten securely with stitches.
- Attach a leaf or two at base of rose, if desired.

TO MAKE THE LEAF:
- For each leaf, cut a circle of chiffon 3 to 5 inches in diameter.
- Fold each circle in quarters.
- Run gathering thread along curved edge.
- Pull up gathering thread to form leaf. Secure with hand stitching.

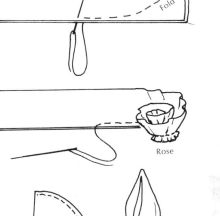

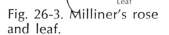

Fig. 26-3. Milliner's rose and leaf.

TRIMMING WITH LACE

Lace is the most popular lingerie trim. Yet it provides infinite opportunity for adding an individual touch to intimate apparel, as it comes in many colors, widths, and designs. Choose a matching color lace or—for added interest—one that contrasts with your fabric.

APPLYING LACE TO OUTER EDGES OF GARMENT

Wide lace is easier to apply to a flat section of the garment. At the top of a fitted garment it is wise to apply the lace before the side seams are stitched. At the bottom of an A-line garment, lace should also be applied

Fig. 26-4. Bra-gown trimmed with milliner's rose.

before the side seams are stitched because of the required tapering of the seams.

Take care to arrange scallops and pattern of lace so that they match where ends meet. Preplanning will also result in more attractive mitered corners.

Remember that tricot stretches more than lace as it is applied. Lace has a habit of becoming "used up" faster than anticipated. One way to prevent running short of lace is to wait until reaching the end of the seam to cut the lace.

There are two basic methods of applying lace to the outer edges of a garment.

- *Appliqué method* (for opaque look): stitch along both edges of lace and trim tricot close to outer stitching line.
- *Free-hanging* (for see-through look): stitch along inner edge of lace only. Trim tricot from behind lace.

SINGLE LACE MEDALLION

Fig. 26-5. Single lace medallion.

Close observation of a segment of wide lace will tell you it is made up of various small patterns or motifs—each outlined with a heavy thread, called *cordonnet*. (The cordonnet is more evident on the right than the wrong side of lace.)

To cut a single lace medallion to appliqué to a garment:

- Cut carefully around one of the individual designs in the lace—staying just outside the cordonnet with the trimming scissors.
- Pin the "appliqué" to right side of the garment in the position desired (transparent tape may be used).
- Topstitch the motif to the tricot, using either a straight stitch—just inside the cordonnet—or a medium-width zigzag—back and forth over the cordonnet.

The work will lie more smoothly when finished if stitching is done in a series of straight lines. Pivot the fabric on the needle rather than stitching rounded curves.

PEEK-A-BOO LACE

Fig. 26-6. Peek-a-boo lace.

Wide lace strips (or single lace medallions) may be given a peek-a-boo effect by cutting away the tricot from behind the lace after it is appliquéd to the body of a garment. But lace should first be mounted on sheer tricot to give it strength and to prevent discomfort:

MOUNTING LACE ON SHEER:

- Cut a strip of sheer that is the same width as the lace trimming. (Be sure that the direction of stretch on the sheer is the same as that of the garment. Choose matching or contrasting color.)
- Pin the wrong side of the lace to the wrong side of the sheer.
- Topstitch lace (straight or zigzag) to the sheer along both edges, following contours of lace. Keep both lace and fabric relaxed while stitching.
- Carefully trim away any excess fabric between scallops of lace.

APPLYING TO GARMENT:
- Pin the prepared lace to the garment in the desired position.
- Topstitch the lace to the garment along the edges. Keep both lace and fabric relaxed.
- From wrong side of garment, cut away the tricot behind the lace. If you have straight stitched, trim tricot to ¼ inch. If you have zigzagged, trim even closer to stitching.

CONTOUR LACE

When wide lace is applied to a curved edge—such as a rounded yoke, slip bodice, neck or armhole—it is sometimes necessary to cut slits in one edge of the lace.

Fig. 26-7. Contour lace.

- Cut slits in one edge of lace following design and cutting just outside cordonnet.
- Fit lace around curved edge of garment, overlapping the slits. Pin in place.
- Stitch the lace together along lap lines before stitching to the garment.
- Apply fitted lace to garment by appliqué method.

SHADOW LACE

The appearance of lace may be softened by sewing it between two layers of sheer. Some techniques are:
- Apply the lace to the under layer of a two-layered garment.
- Encase lace in a band of sheer and add it to edge of garment.
- When cutting out garment, extend outer edges so that fabric may be folded over and lace inserted in fold.

SHIRRED LACE

To achieve the full gathered look of lace ruffles often seen on the back of little girls' panties, stretch the tricot taut as the lace is applied. When tricot is relaxed, the lace will be ruffled. The amount of gathers is controlled by the amount the tricot is stretched. If lace is narrow, it may be stitched down the center for an interesting effect.

TIER LACE

Using narrow strips of lace, apply bottom layer of lace first. Add additional strips of lace by applying top edge of each strip so lace will overlap previous layers.

OTHER TRICKS FOR TRIMMING WITH LACE

- *Divide a wide lace* by cutting it lengthwise, being careful to follow the design. Apply one half as free-hanging lace at the bottom of a slip and the other as an appliqué above.

- *Divide an extra-wide lace* into three or four lengthwise strips and apply to a garment in rows—or part may be saved for another garment.
- *Fold wide lace lengthwise* so that under fold is wider. Stitch folded edge to tricot for a layered effect (especially pretty for galloon lace).
- *When a narrow lace edging is needed,* cut one from one edge of a wide lace. Save the remainder of wide lace to trim another garment.
- *To make a scalloped edge from a straight-edged lace,* trim lace into scalloped design, cutting carefully around each section of the lace pattern. Attach scalloped edge using appliqué stitches to cover all cut edges of lace so they will not fray.

USING ALLOVER LACE FABRIC

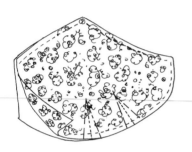

Fig. 26-8. Allover lace on slip bodice.

When allover lace fabric is used for an entire section of a garment, the usual procedure is to back the lace with another lightweight fabric to give it comfort and stability. Nylon sheer is the most commonly used backing fabric.

This treatment is often used for yokes on gowns and peignoirs, for slip bodices, and bra cups.

- Cut fabric for overlay and for backing from the same pattern piece, making sure that stretch direction is the same for both layers.
- Place wrong side of overlay to wrong side of sheer backing. Stay-stitch them together all around outer edge, keeping stay-stitching within the seam allowance. (Use a straight stitch, set between 8 and 12 stitches per inch.)
- Stay-stitch down *center* of any darts.
- Proceed with construction of garment, treating the double layer of fabric as one layer.
  [Note: Other fabrics that might be used for overlays are embroidered or pleated chiffon, or simply a second layer of nylon sheer.]

For a more sheer effect you may wish to use allover lace fabric without an underlining for a sleeve, overskirt, yoke, or entire garment. To prevent unsightly seams from showing through sheer lace, use either a French seam—suitable only for straight seams—(see Chapter 23, p. 133, 134–135) or Appliquéd Seam Method, below.

APPLIQUÉD SEAM METHOD:

- During layout, plan so that lace design will be unbroken where seams overlap.
- Lap edges of lace fabric, matching lace pattern, and trim around the motif of the top layer.
- Whip-stitch or zigzag stitch along edges of motif, forming a seam.
- Trim away underlayer close to stitching.

[Note: darts may be made the same way if their position and depth are planned carefully during layout.]

OTHER TRIMS

MACHINE TRAPUNTO

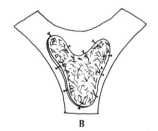

The inspiration for this padded embroidery came to us from Italy. Trapunto embroidery is often seen on the yokes of gowns, the collars and pockets of robes, and on the knees of children's garments. It may be done on a sewing machine.

The artistic individual may want to design her own trapunto. For the less gifted, a suitable design can be traced onto tissue paper from a greeting card or gift wrapping paper. For a child's garment, a coloring book is a likely source.

MATERIALS NEEDED are a piece of preshrunk organdy or marquisette, some polyester fiberfill or fleece, an embroidery presser foot or clear-plastic presser foot.

DIRECTIONS:

- Transfer the embroidery design onto a piece of organdy. If desired, the entire section of garment (collar, yoke, pocket) may be cut of organdy—the organdy then acts as an interfacing, adding body to that section of the completed garment. However, the organdy need only be slightly larger than the design.
- Place section of garment that is to be embroidered, wrong side up, on table.
- Place on top of it a layer of fiberfill for padding.
- Position organdy—onto which pattern has been traced—over the fiberfill with design side up.
- Baste the three layers together around the outer edges.
- From wrong side of garment (organdy side), stitch with very short machine stitches along all the lines designated on the organdy. The shorter the stitches, the puffier the finished trim will be. Avoid retracing stitches. Instead, raise needle, cut the thread—pulling the ends through to the wrong side—and begin afresh on another line of the design.
- After all stitching is completed, cut away excess padding from around outer edges.
- Complete garment in usual way, lining yoke with another layer of tricot to cover the organdy.

Fig. 26-9. Machine trapunto.

SMOCKING

Smocking is a decorative means for working fullness into lingerie garments. It may be used on sheer overlays. Cut the section of pattern you wish to smock about twice as wide as the finished piece will need to be. (Any extra fullness may be eased in with gathers.)

Fig. 26-10. Machine trapunto embroidery used on nightgown.

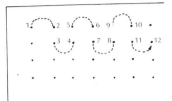

Fig. 26-11. Smocking markings.

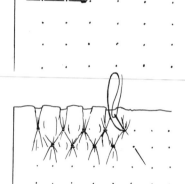

Fig. 26-12. Smocking markings.

HONEYCOMB STITCH (one of the most popular smocking techniques):

- Mark dots with a pencil on right side of fabric at ¾-inch intervals both vertically and horizontally, forming squares. Be sure dots are straight with fabric grain.
- Thread embroidery needle with 3 strands of embroidery thread.
- Work from right to left. Knot the thread and bring the needle up to the right side of fabric through the first dot in the top row.
- Take a small stitch at dot 1 and another at dot 2, keeping thread above needle.
- Draw together tightly.
- Insert needle in dot 2, carry thread under fabric and bring it up at dot 3 of the row below.
- Pick up dot 4 and dot 3 in the same way as you did dot 2 and dot 1, keeping thread below needle this time.
- Insert needle at dot 4 and carry under fabric to dot 5 in top row. Continue working in this manner, alternating the stitches from one row to the other until the end of row is reached.
- Bring thread out in dot 1 of third row and continue until pattern is completed, always keeping thread above or below stitching as indicated in Figure 26-11, B.

27

SHOULDER STRAPS AND CLOSURES FOR LINGERIE

Adjustable shoulder straps made of ribbon or plush elastic may be purchased for use in making slips, bras, and nightgowns. It is not always necessary, however, that straps be adjustable if the lingerie garment is fitted to the individual. There are many ways to make straps from lingerie findings—some simple, some fancy. Following are some suggestions:

TYPES OF STRAPS

RIBBON STRAPS:

- Use a single nylon satin ribbon of desired width and color. Add purchased adjuster or one removed from another garment.

- To form wider strap, overlap the edges of two lengths of ribbon slightly and stitch together.
- Overlay ribbon with strip of sheer. Cut sheer on lengthwise grain twice the width of ribbon. Turn under edge of sheer, but let it extend slightly beyond edge of ribbon. *Blindstitch sheer to ribbon on machine—with fold of fabric to left of presser foot—catching sheer to edge of ribbon. Repeat for other side.*

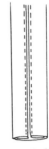

Fig. 27-1. Self-fabric strap.

SELF-FABRIC STRAPS:

Self-fabric straps are especially nice for garments of print fabric or colors for which ready-made straps are not available. Cut them lengthwise to prevent stretching. Make them any width.

Cut strip of lengthwise fabric about a yard long and three times the width the finished strap is to be. Fold under the long edges, twice, pressing with warm iron, and stitch down each folded edge. Add decorative stitch to edge if desired. Cut into lengths for straps.

Make straps of sheer—by above method—placing strips of lace down center before folding edges in and stitching.

Make self-fabric stretch straps. See page 201.

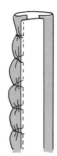

Fig. 27-2. Shoulder strap with sheer overlay and shell edge.

PLUSH ELASTIC STRAPS:

Cut into strap lengths and attach, with or without adjusters.

Cut plush elastic four inches longer than needed for bra straps. When finishing top of bra back, eliminate the usual edge finish between back closure and back straps. Instead, continue strap elastic across back, attaching it to the power net and topstitching.

LACE STRAPS:

- Select a lace from 1 to 3 inches wide and back it with tricot (cut on lengthwise grain) or ribbon that is slightly narrower than lace. Center ribbon or tricot with right side to wrong side of lace and stitch near each edge.
- Thread beaded lace with ribbon or rolled tricot.
- Make lace stretch straps by stitching lace to lingerie elastic. Stretch elastic as it is zigzag stitched to give shirred effect.

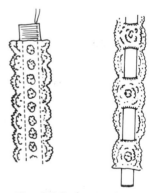

Fig. 27-3. Lace straps.

SPAGHETTI STRAPS:

See Trims, page 152. Use spaghetti tubing to make straps—single, double, looped one through another, or braided in strands of three.

    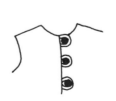 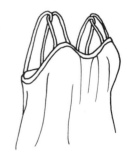

Fig. 27-4. Spaghetti tubing and some of its uses.

ATTACHING SHOULDER STRAPS

When attaching shoulder straps to a slip or gown, take care to anchor straps to fabric and not to lace alone. To provide a "stay" for security purposes, is especially important in garments worn by children or elderly persons who put a good deal of strain on the garment while dressing and undressing.

Pin strap in place. Then put a square of satin ribbon behind it, or use a circle, square, or triangle of nonwoven interfacing. Or a single lace medallion may be sewn to the right side of the garment at stress points.

BRA STRAPS:

Shoulder straps are positioned with right sides of strap and bra together. Tack strap in place before top edge of bra is finished. Purchased nylon adjustable straps may be made more flexible by removing the last 2 inches of strap and adding elastic.

Where it is not possible to insert strap between elastic and edge finish, turn under peak of bra and stitch securely to strap.

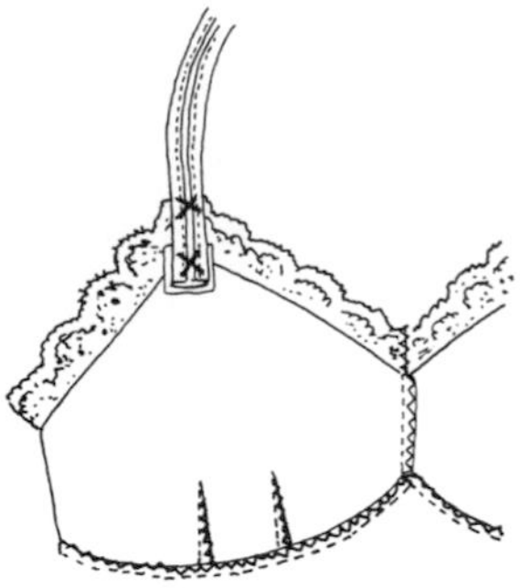

Fig. 27-5. Attaching shoulder straps.

USING A PAPER NECKLINE GUIDE

Some garments—such as nightgowns—which have no sleeves, may have a neck binding that continues on over the shoulder and serves as shoulder straps. It is helpful, in such cases, to cut a guide from paper to simulate a yoke. It holds the garment to the correct shape while the binding is applied to the neckline.

- Shape the paper neckline guide to the shoulder in the length and position desired. Place all markings—CF, CB, underarm—on the paper.
- Stitch the side seams and gather the fullness of the gown to match markings on paper. Pin paper to wrong side of gown.
- Using crosscut binding, stitch with the straight stitch to the right side of the gown through both fabric and paper. Continue around the garment and over both shoulders, starting and ending at center back.
- Tear paper away carefully so that no stitches are broken.
- *Place a seam tape or ribbon over the shoulders* on the inside of the binding, attaching it to the gown at end.
- Turn the binding to the wrong side. Fasten binding to the stitching line with a hand stitch (or topstitch). Lace may be inserted.

Fig. 27-6. Using paper neckline guide.

CLOSURES

BUTTONHOLES: Sheer practicality discourages our spending time making hand buttonholes on most of our intimate apparel. Machine buttonholes do nicely—with one improvement over ready-to-wear—the addition of interfacing on both the buttonhole and button side of your garment.

Use lightweight or featherweight bias nonwoven interfacing or a permanent-finish organdy.

In most cases, the interfacing may be applied directly to the facing portion of the garment and attached at the raw edge. This anchors the interfacing to the facing and keeps it smooth during laundering. The small additional time spent on this step adds to the life of the buttonholes, keeps the buttons from popping off, and saves touch-up ironing time.

[Note: Buttonholes seem to serve better stitched vertically rather than horizontally in lingerie knits. On some machines, typewriter paper placed between fabric and feed dog aids in making professional looking buttonholes.]

OTHER CLOSURES:

Grippers may be applied to front closings and concealed under strips of embroidered trim or pretty lace appliqués.

Loop buttonholes may be made of spaghetti or crosscut fabric. Neckline closing on a peignoir may be merely an extension of the binding at the neck edge into two tie ends long enough to form a bow.

28

TIPS ON BRA-MAKING

TYPES OF BRA

The home sewer can obtain the fit and look she wants in a bra by varying the methods of construction and the fabrics she chooses. What constitutes a satisfactory bra is a matter of individual taste. Generally speaking, bras fall into one of three categories:

UPLIFT: this type of bra is aimed at figure control. It offers a decided degree of support as well as uplift, comfort, and separation of the breasts. It is achieved by utilizing power net in the bra construction and by taping seams. In some bras, wire or featherbone may be added to seams.

SHAPED: this look is acquired by the addition of soft fiberfill or foam, which adds to the contour of the bra for the purpose of (a) building up a slight figure, (b) giving extra support to a full bust, or (c) compensating when one breast is smaller than the other.

NATURAL LOOK: simply constructed bras of stretch tricot with the emphasis on a rounded, natural look rather than firmness. Cups are usually one-piece or may have a vertical seam. One size will fit all average sizes.

PATTERNS

Patterns are now available for these three types of bras. In addition, many pattern companies also offer patterns for bra-gowns and bra-slips. Once learned, bra-making principles may also be applied to the making of bra-top dresses and jumpsuits.

It may be necessary to experiment—combining more than one bra pattern—to get the exact fit and style that suits an individual. Ripping apart a favorite old bra can be a useful step. Remember to rip apart only half the bra, though, leaving the other half intact so that construction methods may be studied. A pattern may be made from the old bra, or the information gained from studying the techniques used may be combined with the instructions given with a purchased pattern. This enables the sewer to create her own highly individualized bra pattern, thus achieving a perfect fit each time she chooses to make a bra.

DETERMINING CORRECT PATTERN SIZE

As with ready-to-wear bras, two factors determine the proper fit in a bra pattern: *bra size* and *cup size*. The following is one method of obtaining these two important factors. (A well-fitting bra should be worn while measurements are taken.)

To determine correct *bra size*—measure around chest, placing tape measure under the arm, just above the bust. If the figure you get is an uneven number—such as 35 inches—use either a 34 or 36 *bra size* pattern.

To determine correct *cup size*—measure around the bust at the fullest point. If measurement is:

½ inch more than *bra size* . . . . . . .buy AA *cup-size* pattern
1 inch more than *bra size* . . . . .buy A *cup-size pattern*
2 inches more than *bra size* . . . . . . .buy B *cup-size* pattern
3 inches more than *bra size* . . . . .buy C *cup-size* pattern
4 inches more than *bra size* . . . . .buy D *cup-size* pattern

MAKING THE BRA

BRA-MAKING MATERIALS

Fabrics used in the bust-cup section of bras are determined partly by the pattern style and partly by personal preference. Uplift or shaped bras may be made of a combination of fabrics. Most of them have more than one layer of fabric—one fabric acting as a lining for the other.

SUGGESTED FABRICS FOR OUTER CUPS:

- *Tricots:* stretch tricot, non-cling, sheer, crepe, satin, Qiana, or regular
- *Allover lace fabric*
- *Lace bonded to sheer or marquisette.* (It is not necessary to add lining to these unless a softer inside finish is desired.)

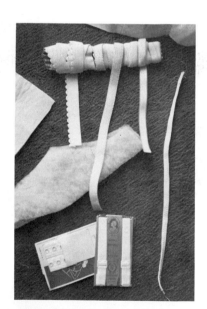

Fig. 28-1. Lingerie findings used in bra-making are easy to buy nowadays. Shown are napped back elastic, polyester fiberfill, adjustable shoulder straps, and bra-closure kit. Also shown is self-fabric stretch strap that you can make.

SUGGESTED FABRICS FOR LINING CUPS:
- *Tricots:* sheer, non-cling, crepe, Qiana, or satin
- *Stabilized nylon*
- *Marquisette*
  [Note: The last two provide most support as they have no stretch.]

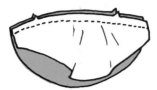

SEWING CUP SEAMS

The method of cup construction will vary with the pattern used, but some general tips are:
- If cups are constructed of 2 layers of fabric (such as lace over tricot) stitch the two together around the outer edge before joining upper- and lower-cup sections.
- When joining upper- and lower-cup sections, straight stitch them together from the upper-cup side. The reason for this is that the lower section will have slightly more ease and the feed dog will assist in holding back the fabric while it is being eased to the upper-cup section.
- After cup sections have been joined, press the seam toward the upper cup and topstitch with a regular or zigzag stitch.
- If bust cups are constructed of fused-to-fabric fiberfill, seam upper to lower as mentioned above, but press seam open and stitch on each side of seamline. Trim off all excess fiberfill before taping.

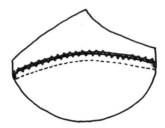

Fig. 28-2. Sewing cup seam.

ADDING FIBERFILL

If plain fiberfill is used, cut it from pattern pieces for upper- and lower-bust cups, eliminating center-seam allowance. Butt edges of upper and lower cups and stitch back and forth with a large zigzag stitch.

Construct outer and inner layer of bust cups separately. Insert fiberfill layer between. Stay-stitch around edges before proceeding with construction. When an underband of power net is used, sew it to the bust cups by stitching from the side seams in toward the center of the bra. Then press the seam toward the cup and topstitch.

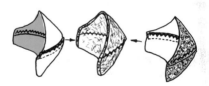

Fig. 28-3. Adding fiberfill to bra.

TAPING BRA SEAMS

Taping not only encloses the raw edges of bra seams to make them more comfortable, but also adds two more rows of machine stitching for support and shape retention. For directions see *Taped Bra Seams*, page 137. Additional tapes may be added to a bra between seams for extra support, as shown in photo.

Suggested fabric for bra tapes are:
- *Stabilized nylon*
- *Sheer nylon tricot*
- *Marquisette*
- *Purchased bra tape*

Fig. 28-4. The unfinished bra shows how bias-cut fabric, folded into tapes, may be applied not only over bra seams but between them for extra support.

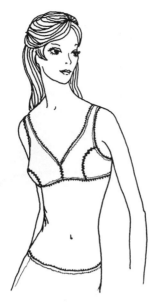

Fig. 28-5. Natural-look bra.

CONSTRUCTING NATURAL-LOOK BRAS

This type of bra differs considerably from other bras in the way it is made. Since the fabric used is a two-way stretch, seams should be stitched with a stretch stitch or small zigzag and then opened and stitched again with a wide zigzag or multiple stitch.

Follow instructions in patterns, making sure that stretch goes around the body. Elastic or power net inserts may be added for slightly more control, but generally this type is intended to have a great deal of stretch.

Some are made as "step-in" styles with no back fasteners at all, but simply to be slipped on like the top of a swimsuit.

These natural-look bras can be made fairly quickly and inexpensively and are currently popular wth the young set. They are often more pleasing worn under knit clothing than the more heavily structured kind of bra.

FINISHING AND TRIMMING BRA EDGES

Power-net sections of a bra are always finished with an elastic edge. Any trim that is to be applied should be fitted to the edges before the elastic is added so that it may be stitched to the bra at the same time as the elastic.

The edges of the cup sections may be finished in other ways, but where control is desired, plush elastic may also be used to edge sections made of tricot or other soft fabrics. Some suggestions for trimming cup edges are:

- *A soft narrow lace* may be placed between the right side of the cup and a strip of tape. Stitch ¼ inch from edge and turn tape over to wrong side of cup and stitch again along lower edge of tape.
- *Apply nylon stretch lace* to right side, grade seam of bra fabric— but not lace—and turn lace to wrong side and stitch along lower edge of lace.
- *Edge bra with shell trim* made by cutting strips of nylon sheer fabric 1½ inches wide. Fold strips in half, wrong sides together, and stitch according to directions given for Machine Shell or Mock Shell, page 145. Place shell trim on right side of bra top with the folded edge facing down toward body of bra. Stitch ¼ inch from folded edge. Grade the seam and turn the raw edges of the trim to the wrong side of bra. Fold under raw edge and stitch.

APPLYING SHOULDER STRAPS

Whenever possible, shoulder straps are applied to the edge of a bra before elastic or trim is applied so that they may be secured between fabric and elastic (or tape) when it is stitched.

SUGGESTED STRAPS FOR BRAS ARE:
- *Ready-made nylon adjustable straps* (the last 2 inches may be removed and replaced with elastic to enable them to stretch).
- *Ready-made plush-elastic adjustable stretch straps.*

- *Self-fabric stretch straps,* ribbon, plush-elastic or other self-made straps described in Chapter 27.

APPLYING ELASTIC TO POWER NET

In a bra, power net is often used in the back and underarm section to provide control and comfortable stretch. It may also extend under the bust-cup section. It should always be edged with elastic. Plush elastic is used for firm support. A narrow elastic lace may be used for a softer bra. For methods of applying, see Elastic Applications, Chapter 24.

FITTING THE BRA

The two halves of a bra are usually constructed separately. When straps are sewn in place and elastic has ben applied to the top edge, the center-front seam may be pinned or basted so that the bra may be tried on for fitting.

CHECKLIST FOR A WELL-FITTING BRA

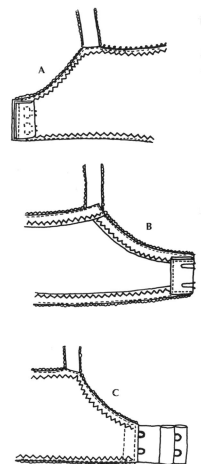

- Does bra support your bust in a normal position?
- Are cups filled out? (If not, a smaller or fiberfill cup may be needed.)
- Do you bulge above bra? (Try a larger cup size or a style with more coverage next time.)
- Does bra center touch your breastbone? (There should be no gaps between the cups. If the breasts are forced to the sides or center, the cup is too small.)
- Are you able to breathe and move easily in the bra?
- Is there proper separation between breasts?
- Do the straps provide comfort and support without cutting into shoulder?
- Does the underbust band fit snugly but not too tightly? (You should be able to run your finger easily under it. If bra rides up in front, it is too tight.)
- Does underband stay in place in back? (If it rides up, the bra is too tight.)
- Does the bra give you an attractive contour? (Center of bust should be aligned with a halfway mark between the shoulder and the elbow.)

When satisfied with fit, stitch center-front seam. Press open and topstitch and/or tape. Then apply elastic to bottom edge of the bra by same method used for top edge.

ATTACHING BRA FASTENERS

Sew the hook half of the bra fastener to the right side of the bra. Place the right side of hook half to right side of power net. Stitch close to

Fig. 28-6. Attaching bra fasteners.

hooks—about ¼ inch from edge. Grade seam and turn to wrong side on stitching line. Topstitch on remaining three edges.

Sew the eye half to the left side of bra by folding under bra ¼ inch and lapping it over the eye half. Topstitch as shown in Figure 28-6, C. If edges of hook half and eye half are unfinished, zigzag along edges to prevent fraying. If using a bra closure kit, elastic may be cut off before applying to power net.

29

TIPS ON GIRDLE-MAKING

Despite modern woman's best efforts to free herself from all repressive factors, few of us can resist trying to improve on what nature has given us. Hence some form of girdle (call it a body suit if you will) seems destined to be ever with us. For those with some previous experience of sewing on stretch fabrics, girdles are not nearly so tricky to make as they would appear.

GIRDLE PATTERNS

Girdle patterns are available from most lingerie pattern companies and some standard companies. Among them are patterns for:
- *Panty girdles*—brief, long-leg, and extra-long-leg styles—with and without reinforcing panels.
- *Plain girdles*—various styles and lengths.
- *Natural-look girdles*—designed for nylon stretch tricot.
- *Maternity girdles*
- *Garter belts*

In addition, it is possible for the home sewer to make endless variations of these patterns, such as suggested below:
- Extend a long-leg girdle to a below-knee or capri length by adding the extra inches to side and inner-leg pieces and continuing to taper leg to desired length.
- Design and add extra support panels where needed for control of figure problems.
- Make a one-piece body suit by combining a panty girdle with a camisole or chemise slip pattern.
- Use a regular panty pattern to make a brief girdle of stretch tricot, lace-patterned power net, or lightweight power net.

DETERMINING SIZE

As with ready-to-wear girdles, patterns are designed for the average figure —one in which the hips measure 9 to 12 inches fuller than the waist. Sizing is grouped as follows:

Waist	Hips	Pattern Size
24" to 26"	34" to 37"	Small
27" to 28"	37" to 40"	Medium
29" to 30"	40" to 44"	Large
31" to 32"	44" plus	X-Large

Makers of girdle patterns have designed them with a certain amount of stretch in mind. When substituting a firm fabric—with less stretch—for the fabric called for on the pattern envelope, it is necessary to use a size larger pattern. If a very soft, stretchy fabric is used, the pattern may need to be two sizes smaller.

It is important to take careful body measurements before beginning a girdle. Girdles require more attention to fitting than most other lingerie garments. Measuring will also prevent over-buying of girdle fabrics which are among the more expensive lingerie-making materials.

PATTERN ALTERATIONS

If the measurement across the hips and thighs is larger in proportion to the waist than those measurements suggested on the pattern, a simple alteration may be made without destroying the design line of the girdle. Slash the pattern from bottom of leg to waistline and spread to add the desired amount. It is not a good practice to add more than ½ inch to the side or crotch seams as the entire fit will be spoiled. It is better to select a larger size pattern.

To shorten girdle length between waistline and crotch to compensate for a low waistline, take a tuck in pattern across the entire pattern piece. Recut the side seams.

To lengthen, slash pattern, spread the desired amount, and insert piece of paper for permanent record.

GIRDLE FABRIC

For the main part of a girdle, it will be necessary to purchase a "girdle length" of one of the following fabrics. Since the greatest amount of stretch on power net is found in the direction parallel to the selvage, and girdles must be cut with the greatest amount of stretch going around the body, this may be confusing. Study carefully the *Layout of Girdle Fabric,* Chapter 22, page 130.

POWER NET: The nylon and Spandex warp knit with two-way stretch, described in Chapter 19, page 115, is available in light, medium, and heavy weight. The lighter the weight, the more it stretches. The right side has a slightly raised texture discernible to the touch. The wrong side feels smooth. Printed power nets may have the design applied to the smooth side (simply because it is easier to print) and so may be reversed for girdle making. Attractive jacquard power nets are also readily available. **STRETCH TRICOT** lends itself to the natural-look girdle. It is popular for slim young figures, for maternity girdles, for panty girdles for casual wear under slacks and jumpsuits, and for body suits. The stretch is generally with the grainline, but sometimes tubular knits have more stretch in the width, so it is wise to check before cutting.

FABRICS FOR SUPPORT PANELS

Support panels may be placed on the front, sides, or back of some girdles. They may be made of one of the following:

PREBACKED LACE: comes in colors matching those of power net. It is used for decorative panels. Has no stretch. It should not be confused with the softer padded kind of backed lace used for making bras. You may make your own panels by backing allover lace with a firm fabric such as stabilized nylon or marquisette.

POWER NET (LYCRA* POWER NET): by turning this two-way stretch material so that the greater stretch goes up and down on the girdle, excellent reinforcing panels may be made of the self-same fabric as the girdle. Jacquard patterned power net may be backed with stabilized nylon or marquisette for a more decorative panel.

SATIN ONE-WAY STRETCH (SATIN LASTEX†): also comes in dyed-to-match colors for decorative front panels. It should be cut with the stretch going up and down. This fabric ravels, so edges should be overcast before they are stitched to power net.

> [Note: to keep satin one-way stretch from curling along seaming edges, apply it to wrong side of power net but stitch from right side.]

OTHER MATERIALS NEEDED

WAIST ELASTIC:
- Plush girdle elastic is most popular choice. The usual width is about an inch wide. It will have picot trim on one edge.
- Plush lingerie elastic, in ⅜ to ½ inch widths may be used on natural-look girdles.
- Elastic lace may be used on natural-look girdles.

LEG ELASTIC:
- Stretch lace is most comfortable to use, may be any width.
- Plush elastic
- Garterless elastic eliminates need for garters, holds panty hose in place.

---

*   Tradename
†   Tradename

GARTERS: may be purchased or transferred from another girdle. Four or six are needed for holding up regular hose.

GARTER ELASTIC: may be purchased for making garter loops. It is not suitable for the waist or leg of a girdle as it does not have the necessary stretch.

CROTCH FABRIC: in girdles that have separate crotch pieces, regular tricot—cut double—is best. It may also be used on the inside leg panel. Cotton knit may also be used.

SEWING GIRDLE SEAMS

It is advisable to sew girdle seams with a zigzag or stretch stitch. If your machine does not have a stretch stitch, each seam in the power net must be stitched three times while fabric is stretched to the utmost.

A No. 90 ballpoint (or size 14 to 16) needle may be used for the heavier weight power nets. For lightweight power net or stretch tricot, a No. 80 or its equivalent is sufficient.

Thread must have stretch. A polyester, cotton-covered/polyester core, or nylon twist is preferred.

All girdle seams are stitched more than once. Recommended seams for girdle fabrics are given in Chapter 23, page 134.

Side seams and center-back seams should be taped, using self-fabric or plush elastic.

Natural-look girdles of stretch tricot do not need to have taped seams. Seams may be stitched once with a small zigzag or stretch stitch, then pressed open and topstitched down center of seamline with a wide zigzag or multiple stitch.

CROTCH APPLICATIONS

Crotches may be cut of tricot, either single or double. If cut double they may be applied by the Enclosed-Crotch-Seam method. See Chapter 23, pages 135–136.

A WELT SEAM may also be used for joining a tricot crotch or leg panel to power net.

If girdle is *long-leg style,* first join crotch to tops of inner-leg sections by placing right sides together and stitching with a stretch stitch. Turn these two seams toward the crotch and topstitch with wide zigzag or multiple stitch.

SEAMING THREE-PIECE CROTCH TO GIRDLE:
- With right sides togther, stitch the front of the crotch and inner-leg section to the front of the girdle, matching notches and stretching the power net to ease in tricot.
- Turn the seam allowance toward tricot and topstitch to the girdle using a wide zigzag stitch.

JOINING POWER NET AT CROTCH SEAM:
When a girdle does not have a separate set-in crotch, sew the two sections of power net together at the crotch seam by placing

Fig. 29-1. Three-piece girdle crotch.

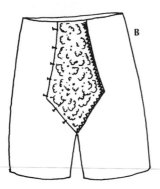

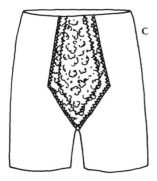

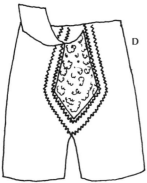

Fig. 29-2. Applying decorative girdle panel.

two right sides together and sewing with a stretch stitch. Press seam open and topstitch with large zigzag or multiple stitch.

SUPPORT PANELS

The secret of a girdle's control lies in the strategic placement of support panels. They may be added to a girdle to give extra firmness in "problem areas." A sidelong glance in the mirror tells where they are needed. A fact to keep in mind is that support panels may remove as much as 90 percent of the girdle's stretch in the area in which they're placed—depending on the fabric used. They may be decorative or they may be added strictly for reinforcing purposes. Rules for cutting out support panels are:

- If using a fabric with one-way stretch, cut so the stretch goes up and down on girdle.
- If using two-way stretch, cut so that the lesser stretch goes around the body and the greater stretch goes up and down.
- When using decorative fabrics such as lace, back panel fabric with a non-stretch material cut from the same pattern piece, staystitching the two together. (If backing material is sheer, two layers may be better than one.)
- When planning the size, number, and position of panels, consider that a girdle needs to stretch an estimated 9 inches for seating comfort.

APPLYING DECORATIVE PANELS

Use the pattern piece provided with girdle pattern or design one from lace or other decorative fabrics suggested.

- Whenever possible, apply panel to girdle before the side seams are stitched. If girdle has a center-front seam, stitch it first. Place right side of decorative panel face down on wrong side of girdle front and pin or tape in place.
- Stitch the panel to the girdle along the outer edge of panel, using a large zigzag or multiple stitch.
- Stitch again ¼ to 1 inch from the edge of the panel, using a zigzag stitch.
- From right side of girdle, carefully trim out the girdle fabric, close to second stitching line to reveal decorative fabric.
- The edges of the power net may be stitched again from the right side with an overedge stitch if desired. Or girdle fabric may be trimmed before second row of stitching is made, so that the power net can be overedged during the second row of stitching. (It is a bit more difficult to keep edges of seam smooth this way.)

APPLYING POWER-NET REINFORCING PANELS

This type of panel may be applied to the girdle during construction as in the above method, but when a panel is added purely for support, the girdle fabric is not cut away from behind or in front of it but remains for the purpose of double support. The two stretch directions then work against each other to prevent the girdle from relaxing with wear. Reinforcing panels are usually cut from the same fabric as the girdle.

- Diamond-shaped panels, with the stretch running up and down, may be stitched over "problem areas."
- Reinforcing panels may be added at problem areas after girdle is fitted. Mark on the girdle, with a soft marking pencil, the position where the panels are to be placed.
- Two-inch strips of power net, cut on the stretch, may be stitched diagonally, or crisscrossed, over stomach, hips, or across derrière for extra support. Sew in place with a stretch stitch.
- Reinforcing panels may be stitched to the *outside* of girdle, using same method of double stitching described for decorative panels. Or they may be applied to wrong side, but stitched from the right side. (This is possible because of the see-through quality of most power net.) Some feel this gives a smoother look to the girdle.

TRIAL FITTING

It is a good idea to try on a girdle for fitting after the seams are stitched and before the elastic is applied to the waist and leg. It may still be possible at this point to take in a seam or to add a triangular gusset of fabric in case you have made an error in measurement.

GIRDLE ELASTIC

APPLYING WAIST ELASTIC

Some fitters suggest a girdle waist can be as much as four inches more snug than the waistline measurement, but this is a highly individual matter. Try on girdle for fitting before applying waist elastic. If girdle comes more than ¼ inch higher than waist, trim it down.

If *plush elastic* is used, apply according to directions given on page 142. Also see, Joining Elastic Ends, page 139.

APPLYING WIDE WAISTBAND ELASTIC:
The wider girdle elastics, sometimes obtainable in 2- or 3-inch widths, may be applied as follows:
- Place elastic with plush side to wrong side of girdle edge, so that it extends ¼ inch above the top of the girdle. Have picot edge down toward body of garment.
- Stitch along top edge with wide zigzag stitch, short stitch length.
- Turn elastic to right side, and sew near bottom edge of elastic with same stitch setting.

APPLYING ELASTIC LACE TO NATURAL-LOOK GIRDLE WAIST:
- Measure stretch lace slightly less than waist measurement and apply by lapping over fabric edge about ½ inch.
- Stitch with a wide zigzag or stretch stitch.

APPLYING LEG ELASTIC

ELASTIC LACE:
Elastic lace may be applied to girdle leg by overlapping the right side of fabric while the leg seam is still open. Measurement should be same or only slightly less than leg opening.

- *For a natural-look girdle,* a narrow stretch lace may be applied by overlapping ¼ inch and stitching with a wide stretch stitch or zigzag.
- *Wider stretch lace may be lapped* ½ inch over leg opening and stitched either along bottom and top of lap with narrow zigzag, or down center of lap with wide zigzag.
- *For extra-long leg girdles,* stretch lace may overlap the girdle leg the entire width of the lace. Stitch along both edges of lace.
- *Wide stretch lace may be divided,* following the design of the lace. Use appliqué method to stitch to girdle leg, making sure to overstitch cut edge of lace to power net.

PLUSH ELASTIC:
- Apply after leg seams are completed.
- Cut elastic just slightly less than leg measurement and join ends.
- Place joint near back seam and apply as for girdle waist or bra edge.

GARTERLESS ELASTIC:
- After leg seams are stitched, measure elastic, preferably by fitting directly around leg. This type is uncomfortable if fitted too snugly. Join ends by lapping, laying a tricot tab under it as you stitch. Be sure the stretch of tricot runs the length of the joint.
- Placing joint at back-leg seam, divide elastic and leg opening into fourths and stitch garterless elastic to edge, lapping it ¼ inch over the power net. Sew with a wide zigzag or multiple stitch.

If desired, elastic lace may be sewn over the webbed part of garterless elastic for a more decorative appearance.

APPLYING GARTERS

Whenever possible, garters are sewn into a girdle before the main seams are stitched, simply because it is easier to work on the flat piece. Mark their location with pencil or chalk. (Some women prefer to have three garters on each leg—front, back, and side.)

TO MAKE LOOPS FOR DETACHABLE GARTERS:
- Cut 4-inch strips of garter elastic for each loop.
- Fold each strip across center, doubling back on itself to form loop. Place on specified marking with cut edge up toward top of girdle. Offsetting two edges will cause less of a welt.
- Cut a piece of soft knit fabric (tricot, swimsuit lining, or elastic lace), or power net the size of a quarter, to use as a stay. Place over tab ends and stitch around edges of circle and across the top of garter with zigzag stitch as shown.

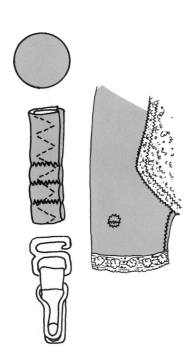

Fig. 29-3. Attaching garter loops and garters.

SELF-FABRIC LOOPS:
>   May be made easily if garter elastic is not available.
- Cut strip of power net about 1¼ inches wide, with the greatest stretch running lengthwise.
- Fold strip in thirds lengthwise.
- Stitch down middle with zigzag stitch.
- Cut into correct lengths for each garter. Fold in half and stitch across folded edge to form a slot for garters. Several slots may be stitched to make length adjustable.
>   [Note: Garters may be placed in loops with knob toward leg for a smoother look on the outside of the girdle.]

GIRDLE TRIMS

Trims made of lace and ribbon are often applied to the finished girdle. They may be appliquéd to the right side of the girdle to cover the stitching of garter loops; applied to the waistline of a sweetheart waist; or used to dress up girdle panels. They are usually made of stretch lace or a soft fabric that will not catch on a slip.

>   Some suggestions:
- Appliqués of lace or stretch lace.
- Lace flowers.
- Tiny flowers of sheer.
- Ribbon bows.

30

MAKING SLIPS OF STABILIZED NYLON

Stabilized nylon is an ideal fabric for making slips to be worn under knit garments. Patterns for full slips and half-slips to be made of this non-static material are available from lingerie pattern companies. The half-slip design features a triangular tricot gusset at the hipline to enable it to stretch. The full slip may have a tricot bodice or diamond-shaped inserts that allow for needed stretch.

>   Care should be taken in trimming undergarments of these non-cling

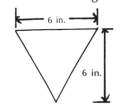

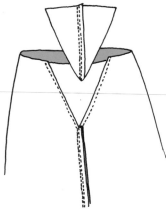

Fig. 30-1. Stabilized slip.

Fig. 30-2. Slips and half-slips made of stabilized nylon are among the most popular lingerie items to be sewn at home. They have gussets of stretch lace or tricot to enable wearer to slip them on and off. Stabilized nylon is a nonclinging fabric, perfect for wearing under knit dresses. (Photo by Thomas Hanson)

fabrics with laces or other static producing fabrics that will lessen their effectiveness. Trimming with self-fabric and the use of tailored or embroidered hems are preferred.

ADAPTING HALF-SLIP PATTERN FROM REGULAR PATTERN

A half-slip pattern designed for tricot may be adapted to stabilized nylon as follows:

- Measure hipline, allowing 1-inch ease.
- Measure length—remembering that finished slip should be about 2 inches shorter than skirt. Add 1 inch for tailored hem, or 1½ inches for embroidered hem.

CUTTING:

- Cut front and back panels from stabilized fabric, placing the pattern pieces on straight of grain.
- Cut two triangular gussets 6 inches long and 6 inches wide (8 x 8 for large size). Make certain that stretch of tricot runs across gusset.

STITCHING:

- Stitch side seams of slip, using Welt Seam; see Chapter 23, page 133.
- Turn under ¼ inch on two sides of triangular gussets. Pin gussets over the slip at the top edge on each side. Topstitch down folded edge of triangle—either zigzag stitch or two rows of straight stitching.
- Trim away stabilized fabric from behind gusset.

- Reshape back of slip by trimming away ½ inch to ⅝ inch of fabric at center back of waistline, tapering to nothing at side seams.
- Apply waist elastic, stretching the tricot in the gussets and keeping gathers in the stabilized fabric to a minimum.
- Hem slip.

FULL SLIPS OF STABILIZED NYLON

It is also possible to adapt full slip patterns to stabilized fabric by using inserts of stretchy fabric and by allowing more ease in the pattern. Patterns may be shifted and cut on the bias. Bodices may be made of tricot, or stretch lace with a sheer tricot backing (make sure that sheer tricot is placed with stretch going across the bodice). Bodice sections of tricot may be finished with narrow elastic lace.

31

SEWING KNIT SWIMWEAR

Any woman who has suffered through the frustrations of trying on ready-to-wear swimsuits will appreciate the veritable swelling "tide" of swimsuit fabrics now available from which to make her own. Sewing your own swimwear means you can find a suit that fits, in a style that's becoming, at the time of year you need it.

From the thrift angle, not only can you afford more than one suit, but matching cover-ups can be made at very little extra cost. Swimsuits for men and children, too, take relatively small amounts of fabric and both are easily fitted. Maternity swimwear—often as unattractive as it is expensive—is another bonus for the budget-minded woman who sews.

LOOKING SEE-WORTHY IN YOUR SUIT

Few women are actually satisfied with the way they look in a ready-to-wear bathing suit. When you make your own suit, you can choose a design to flatter your figure and a color that suits your skin tones. A perfect figure will look well in any style of suit. For those of us who are not so fortunate, there are tricks we can use to hide our figure faults and make our figures appear near perfect:

Fig. 31-1. (Photograph courtesy of *Singer Showcase Magazine*)

A thin figure can be flattered by a two-piece suit with a little extra fullness—gathers, perhaps, or ruffles. A maillot with horizontal stripes would also be a good choice. Don't fit it too tight.

A slightly overweight figure may be helped by a suit of vertical stripes, or piping that directs the eye upward and gives a longer, slimmer look.

The decidedly plump figure would do well to steer clear of any print, stripe, or plaid fabric. Loose knits and bulky textured fabrics should be avoided; they only make an overweight person appear larger. Choose instead a pattern that is not too brief and a firm, shape-retaining fabric. A suit in which the side seams are set slightly toward the front, or one with a definite princess-line styling, will have a slenderizing effect.

COLOR SELECTION

Think of the suit color in relation to your own coloring. Keep your skin tones uppermost in mind. People who do not tan readily will usually find a dark color more becoming as it provides contrast to the skin tones. Dark-skinned people will look well in nearly any shade from the palest to the deepest, with bright tones being equally flattering.

PATTERN SELECTION

There are many good swimsuit patterns in nearly every catalog of knit sewing patterns.

Be certain that the pattern and fabric are correlated—that you do not inadvertently use a pattern designed for two-way stretch to make a suit of a one-way stretch fabric. This is especially important in making a ladies' one-piece swimsuit. One-piece suits are almost always designed for a two-way stretch fabric.

In choosing a pattern, look for a design line that will enhance the figure. Decide whether your body's height is mainly in the leg or in the torso. (Rarely does one find a pleasing combination of both.) Design lines, carefully chosen, can help create agreeable illusions. Consider the following figure problems and ways to overcome them:

A SHORT TORSO: Gain the illusion of greater length by choosing a two-piece pattern that exposes a wide expanse of midriff. However, if the figure is on the plump side, a simple one-piece with vertical lines may be a better choice.

A LONG TORSO: One may make the torso length seem more in proportion by wearing a two-piece that offers liberal coverage. A suit in which the bra extends down to cover part of the midriff or one in which the shorts are not too low-cut will look better on this type of figure.

SHORT LEGS can be given a longer look if the suit is cut high over the top of the thigh. The higher the cut, the longer the legs will look.

LONG, LANKY LEGS are flattered by suits with a slightly longer cut to the leg. Trim, "little-boy" shorts will reduce the length of the leg.

LARGE HIPS (in proportion to the rest of the figure) can sometimes be disguised by the right choice of bikini—the idea being to separate their bigness from the top of the body by a wide sweep of midriff. However, if the figure is also plump, a solid color one-piece with boy legs (they cover a multitude of sins) is a better choice. Piping may be added for extra vertical lines.

BUST TOO SMALL: Select a suit pattern with fullness or the possibility of padding for the bra.

BUST TOO LARGE: The classic one-piece maillot with a soft natural bra is probably the best choice. If the figure is slim otherwise, a bikini with a natural top may be a good answer. Avoid padded or too-pointed inner construction. It only adds to the problem.

HEAVY THIGHS: The temptation here is to try to disguise the problem with a skirt or dressmaker shorts. Too often, however, this not only makes the suit look old-fashioned but announces to the world that you are trying to hide something. It may be wiser to select a suit style with "little-boy" shorts that stay close to the body.

32

FABRICS AND NOTIONS FOR SWIMWEAR

SELECTING FABRICS

The purpose for which the finished suit will be used should be clearly considered when you choose the fabric. While a suit intended merely for sunning might be made of a high-fashion novelty fabric, one to be worn in a swimming pool should be made of chlorine-resistant materials.

Although many woven fabrics adapt well to swimwear, we are concerned in this book only with knits.

SWIMSUIT STRETCH FABRICS are appearing in increasing numbers on the consumer fabric market. New fiber combinations, new yarn treatments, and new fabric constructions and finishes are constantly being developed to add to their appeal. Their bright colors and bold designs catch the shopper's eye as she enters a store. They may be flat surfaced or loopy in texture.

As widely diverse as they appear, swimsuit stretch fabrics generally fall into one of these three categories:

1. Stretch fabrics constructed of *texturized yarns*. Usually of nylon—Helanca stretch being a notable example—they may be found in either one-way or two-way stretch.

2. *Core-spun fabrics* which depend on elastomeric yarns such as Spandex for their shape retention in and out of water. Yarns may be nylon, cotton, polyester, or wool (or a combination thereof) wrapped around a core of Spandex. Core-spun fabrics may be found in one-way and two-way stretch.

THE STRETCH FACTOR presents the chief stumbling block the home sewer encounters when making swimsuits. Learning to recognize how much a swimsuit fabric will stretch and recover—which can vary widely—is the most important single factor for her to consider. You must determine this stretch factor before the pattern is cut out to know how much the suit will give and retract when it is put on, and just as important, how much it may "relax" or "grow" when it is wet.

A Helanca nylon two-way stretch, for example, will often "give" about 3 inches for every 15 inches of fabric width, while some of the softer, puffier knits may stretch as much as 6 inches per 15 inches of fabric. By contrast, a firm Spandex stretch fabric may only give and retract one inch for that same amount of fabric width. The stretch factor of fabric, then, must be taken into account when deciding what size of pattern to buy and how snugly the suit should be fitted; keep in mind that the higher the stretch factor, the smaller the suit size. (See Pick-A-Knit chart, Chapter 5, p. 27.)

OTHER KNIT FABRICS are also often used for swimwear. Tricot has become popular for lightweight swimwear. The nonabsorbent synthetic knits, synthetic/natural combinations may also be satisfactorily used—washability being the main criteria. Some degree of stability is also desirable for active swimwear, although even a lacy see-through raschel or sheer tricot may be made up into attractive swimwear with the use of a partial or complete underlining.

SWIMSUIT NOTIONS

The lining and notions purchased for the making of swimsuits should be as swimproof as the suit fabric. They, too, should be washable, colorfast, and quick drying.

LINING FABRICS

The most desirable lining for swimsuits is a two-stretch nylon or Banlon sold as "swimsuit lining." It is not always available in the desired color, though. Other fabrics may be used instead. Tricot is often used because it is lightweight, quick drying, and will "give" with the suit. Nylon marquisette is sometimes used as a firming-type lining, as is lightweight power net.

SWIMSUIT ELASTIC

There is a special elastic woven of Spandex and cotton available for sewing swimwear. It is off-white in color and has been treated to resist salt and chlorine. It is extremely strong, retaining its strength even when wet. It is available in ⅜-inch and ¾-inch widths. The ⅜ inch is used most often for armhole, leg, and neck edges. The ¾-inch width may be used for waistbands on men's and boy's suits . . . also for waistbands on women's two-piece suits or for a "boy-leg" effect on a girl's or woman's suit.

    Decorative elastic webbing, available in colors, stripes, and—sometimes—prints, is popular for the waistband on men's and boys' trunks. It also makes attractive, colorful belts.

SWIMSUIT BRA FORMS

Bra forms may be purchased at notion counters. They come in swimsuit sizes and may be inserted during the construction of the suit. Some women, however, prefer to buy their usual bra and build a suit around it. (Such bras should be made of nylon, polyester, or Lycra.)

    Three types of bra forms, as pictured in Figure 32-1 are:

TYPE A: individual cups molded of fiberfill or nonwoven fabric. These

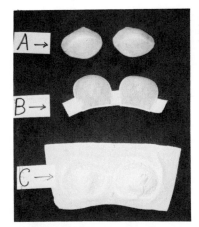

Fig. 32-1. Three types of bra forms available for sewing into swimsuits.

cups need to be bound around the edges or sewn into a bra lining before being inserted in a suit. They are handy for abbreviated bikini tops as they may be trimmed down more easily than other types of forms and are the least expensive of the three.

TYPE B: molded cups with elastic tabs. This type has an elastic band connecting the two molded cups at the center of the bust. There are also elastic tabs on the sides of the cups which can be sewn to the suit at the side seams. This type is easy to insert, but has a tendency to function somewhat independently of the suit.

TYPE C: bra panel has molded or padded cups which are set into a panel of jersey swimsuit lining. The seams are taped. Before this type of bra form is joined to a one-piece suit, the seamstress applies an elastic to the lower edge of the panel.

OTHER SHAPING MATERIALS

Lycra power net may be used either as a panel for the lower front of the suit or as an underlining for the front bodice. Quilted or fused *fiberfill; featherboning; bias nonwoven interfacing;* or *bias polyester fleece* may all be used to give body to the midriff or upper section of a suit.

CLOSURES

Zippers may be inserted in swimsuits in cases where the hips are much larger than the waist to make it easier to get in and out of the suit. Decorative zippers (with large rings) may also be inserted in the front of a suit. When choosing them, consider their strength and their resistance to chlorine and salt.

Hook-type bra fasteners are available for closure at the back of the bra of a two-piece suit.

THREAD

Use the right thread for the fabric you have chosen. A nylon, 100 percent spun polyester—or polyester/cotton core-spun thread—will provide better stretch and perform better than cotton thread when sewing swimsuit fabrics.

SEWING EQUIPMENT

A sewing machine with a *stretch* or *zigzag stitch* is a definite advantage in sewing swimwear. For heavier fabrics, a No. 14-16 (Size 80-90) needle is recommended; for lightweight fabrics, a No. 11 (or 70) will do.

A *ballpoint needle* is a near necessity. A *roller-presser foot* can be helpful on heavy fabric. *Pins* should be ballpoint or dressmaker's silk pins. *Scissors* need to be very sharp to cut stretch fabric—and those with a bent handle are apt to give a more accurate cutting line.

33

PREPARATION, LAYOUT, AND CUTTING OF SWIMWEAR

It might be assumed that fabric designed for swimwear would be pre-shrunk, but it never hurts to be doubly certain by preshrinking it yourself.

Leave stretch fabric relaxed on the cutting table for a time before cutting out the pattern so that it will assume its normal point of recovery.

One-way stretch fabric is always cut with the stretch running around the body. Two-way stretch is cut with the greater stretch going around the body.

Observe "grainline" when cutting a swimsuit.

While it may not be necessary to match the pattern of a large design at the seams, it is wise to give some prior thought to the arrangement of the design on the various pattern pieces in order to avoid a lopsided look or the possibility of drawing the eye to an unwanted point.

Leave extra fabric at the top of the strap when cutting. It may be trimmed away when the suit has been fitted if it is not needed.

Some of the flatter, smoother knits tend to run—in a manner similar to the "laddering" of hosiery. Check the fabric to see if it has this tendency by grasping it with both hands and pulling slightly. If it does, place the "laddering" edge at the bottom of the garment.

LAYOUT AND PATTERN ALTERATIONS

There are times when applying some ingenuity and originality at the cutting-out stage of making a swimsuit will result in a more stylish or a more flattering garment. A variation in style, a fabric substitution, or a fitting adjustment may mean some changes are needed. Plan for them during your layout. Then cut out the garment.

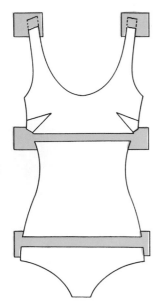

Fig. 33-1. Adjusting for one-way stretch.

Fig. 33-2. Designing a bikini.

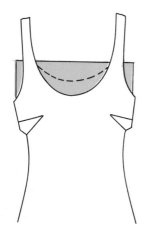

Fig. 33-3. Building up neckline.

VARIATIONS IN LAYOUT OF A ONE-PIECE SUIT:

As we've noted before, one-piece suits are designed for two-way stretch fabric—the vertical stretch is essential to their comfort.

If, for some reason, it is necessary to use a one-way stretch fabric instead, it is possible in some patterns to obtain extra vertical ease by turning the pattern pieces for the straps and the crotch so that the stretch there goes in the vertical direction.

If a pattern does not have a separate strap or crotch piece, adjustment to allow for extra stretch may be made by slashing the suit pattern horizontally under the bust, and again across the hips. Add an additional ⅝ inch at each of these points and another ⅝ inch to 1 inch at the shoulder straps (or as much as necessary).

VARIATIONS IN LAYOUT OF A TWO-PIECE SUIT:

The vertical stretch factor is less vital to the comfort and fit of a two-piece suit. Two-piece suits are often made of one-way stretch fabric. However, the pants portions of a two-piece may be adjusted to suit an individual figure. Bikini pants create a below-the-middle bulge on some individuals. Extending the top line of the bikini pants upward for 3 to 4 inches will make a hip-hugger style which is more flattering to many figures.

By the same token, pants that come to the waist, or above, give some figures a thick-through-the-middle appearance. This is particularly true for women with short torsos. Again, the top line may be adjusted . . . this time lowered . . . to a hip-hugger line with more flattering results.

DESIGNING A BIKINI:

It is also simple to adjust a pattern for swimsuit pants of the regular brief style to a bikini. Cut the waistline down 4 inches and taper up the line of the leg gradually, starting at the crotch seam, so that it is an inch or two higher at the side seam.

ADDING TO THE NECKLINE FOR A FULLER FIGURE:

For a person with a full bustline it may be desirable to cut the neckline higher than the pattern indicates.

LOWERING BUSTLINE DARTS:

- Cut pattern above dart. Set in a strip of paper to lower the dart the needed amount and to give a permanent record.
- Take a tuck under dart so waist will not be too long.

RAISING BUSTLINE DARTS:

- Take a tuck above the dart.
- Slash the pattern under the bustline and spread it apart the needed amount, inserting paper to hold sections together.

TO INCREASE SIZE OF BUST DART:

- At waistline, slash pattern across and then up through the point of the dart to the armhole.
- Slash pattern through center of dart to the point of the dart.

- Spread pattern at both places to allow for the needed increase in size of bustline and insert paper for a permanent record.
- Fold in the new dart and cut a new side-seam allowance, reshaping it to allow for the added depth of the new dart.
- Remember to adjust lining proportionately.

TO DECREASE SIZE OF BUST DART:

- Slash pattern same as above.
- Lap pattern at bustline, as shown, making dart smaller.

MAJOR ALTERATIONS:

For major adjustments, consult a good pattern alterations book. It is a good idea, when extensive fitting problems are anticipated, to follow methods of construction and lining that allow for a fitting before the side seams are permanently stitched.

Side seams are the most logical place to make adjustments. It is also possible to make a "muslin" of an inexpensive knit (with a comparable stretch factor) and work out all fitting problems on it before cutting into the more expensive swimsuit fabric.

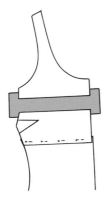

Fig. 33-4. Lowering dart.

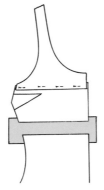

Fig. 33-5. Raising dart.

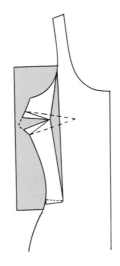

Fig. 33-6. Increasing dart.

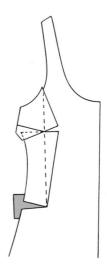

Fig. 33-7. Decreasing dart.

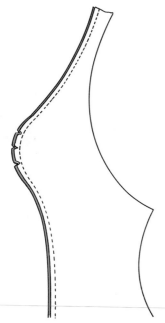

Fig. 34-1. Clipping bustline dart.

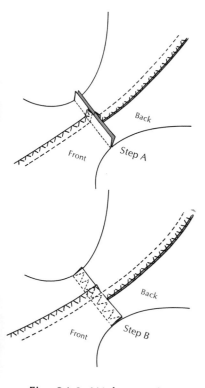

Fig. 34-2. Welt crotch seam.

34

SWIMSUIT SEAMS AND LININGS

SWIMSUIT SEAMS

It is important to "build in" as much stretch as possible when sewing seams in swimwear. A sewing machine with a 3-step zigzag or stretch stitch is most desirable. A roller-presser foot may be helpful for heavier fabrics. Be sure the needle is not dull. Adjust pressure according to the directions for your machine. It is best to test stitch seams on a sample of actual fabric you will be using.

SIDE SEAMS, CENTER FRONT AND CENTER BACK SEAMS:
See *Seams,* Chapter 7, page 39.

BUSTLINE SEAMS that are stitched vertically (such as those on a princess-style suit) may have a tendency to ripple—especially with a heavyweight swimsuit fabric. To prevent this, clip the seams carefully with trimming scissors, cutting into the seam allowance at right angles to the edge, almost to the stitching line. Make a straight or straight-stretch-stitch seam over the bustline.

CROTCH SEAMS: in suits which feature a separate section of pattern for the crotch, the "set-in" crotch may be lined at the same time that it is applied to the suit. See *Enclosed Crotch Seam,* Chapter 23, page 135.

To make a *welt crotch seam* in bikini briefs, or other suits that do not have a "set-in" crotch, turn center-front and center-back seams of suit in opposite directions before you sew the crotch seam. Trim back seam allowance to ¼ inch and press the seam toward the back of the suit. Stitch seam flat to suit, through all thicknesses.

SWIMSUIT LININGS

Whether a swimsuit is lined entirely, partially, or not at all, depends on the type of fabric used and the amount of figure control desired. As a general rule, most white suits, those made of very lightweight fabric, or those of open, lacy designs are preferable when fully lined. It's a good idea to wet a section of the fabric you've selected and stretch it across the back of your hand to see how it will look, unlined, if worn later while wet.

Many suits made of heavier fabric, and most children's suits, need to be lined only in the crotch.

A princess-style suit may be lined in the lower half of the front panel.

Lining helps a swimsuit retain its shape. Swimsuit lining fabric is more often available in white than in other colors. Tricot or Banlon knit may be substituted for regular swimsuit lining at times. Power net or marquisette is often used to give a firm quality to specific sections of a suit. Tricot is often used to line the crotch. (One pattern company recommends cutting tricot crotch lining on the bias.)

Lining should be cut—as is the outer layer of fabric—with the greatest stretch going around the body. One exception to this rule might be cutting an entire suit lining on the bias if you feel the lining fabric will restrict the two-way stretch quality of the outer fabric too much. Another exception might be an inside-front panel from which you expect definite figure control.

[Note: eliminating the lining in the shoulder straps will allow them to stretch more.]

LINING AN ENTIRE SWIMSUIT

UNDERLINING METHOD:

This technique for lining a suit treats the two fabrics—fashion fabric and lining—as one. The seams are not enclosed.

- Cut separate lining for each pattern piece, omitting lining over the shoulder.
- Place wrong side of lining to wrong side of each section of suit.
- Sew all seams, treating the two fabrics as one.
- Remove any basting before applying elastic as it is apt to inhibit the stretch of the fabric during application.

SEPARATE LINING METHOD:

Construct all parts of the suit and lining separately and then slip lining inside the suit before the elastic is attached. This method is not as highly recommended as the Underlining Method, because the seams of the swimsuit have a tendency to pull away from each other when the fabric is wet and the suit may sag more.

FULL LINING WITH HIDDEN FRONT SEAM:

This method results in an enclosed front seam. The side seams are not enclosed. It has the advantage of making fitting at the side seams easier.

- Cut suit lining for entire suit from swimsuit pattern pieces.
- Place swimsuit fronts right side to right side. Place on top of the two front-lining pieces which have been stacked, right sides together.
- Pin and stitch the center-front seam, sewing through all four layers.
- Open up lining and fabric and front seam will be concealed.
- Repeat for back section of suit.
- Join the side seams in a regular seam, doing any fitting needed before final stitching.

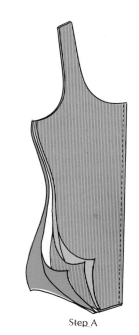

Step A

Step B
Fig. 34-3. Full lining with hidden front seam.

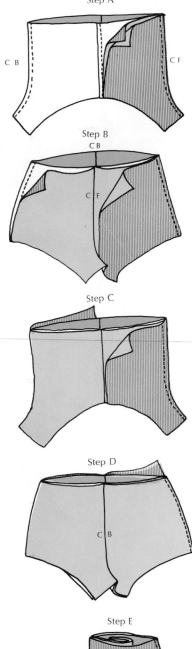

Fig. 34-4. Two-step full
lining, concealed seams.

FULL LINING WITH HIDDEN SIDE SEAMS:

This method may be used for a one-piece suit that has no center-front seam, but has a center-back seam. The center-back seam and crotch seams will not be enclosed with this method.

- When side seams are sewn, lay two layers of lining fabric over the side seam and stitch all four pieces together at once.
- Fold back lining piece over seam to enclose it.
- Repeat for other side.
- (This method may be used in a princess-line suit after the lower-front panel has been lined.)

FULL LINING WITH CONCEALED SEAM—TWO-STEP METHOD:

This method—when followed as illustrated—is ideal for lining the pants section of a two-piece suit. It may also be adapted to some one-piece suits—including the princess—by merely applying the lining, a section at a time, progressively around the suit.

- Cut lining for suit from swimsuit pattern pieces.
- Sew all seams of the swimsuit except the crotch seam and *turn suit wrong side out.*
- In suit with center-front seam, start by placing two layers of front lining (right sides together) in alignment with center-front seam of suit. Sew lining along center-front seamline—or slightly inside it—following the previous stitching. (You will be sewing through four layers.)
- Fold back lining over seam to enclose it. Smooth lining over to side seam and lay over it one section of back lining so that there are again two layers of lining over two layers of suit fabric. Stitch lining seam over top of previous suit side seam.
- Again turn lining to conceal the seam. Sew center back seam, joining in last of lining pieces in same fashion.
- Sew one of the two loose sections of lining to the remaining side-seam line.
- Wrap the remaining loose lining section completely around the suit so that the right sides of the lining sections face each other. Stitch in a final side seam along the previous stitching line. [Note: If this method is used to line a one-piece suit with a bra insert, it is recommended that the lining be sewn together separately from the suit over the bra area and then stitched into the suit from the bottom of the bra on down. Apply the bra to the completed suit before beginning to attach the lining. Carefully mark the suit seams and the lining seams so that they correspond exactly at the points where lining will begin to be joined to the suit.]

FULL LINING WITH CONCEALED SEAMS—ONE-STEP METHOD:

This is another method for lining with concealed seams. It is like the above method except that the *suit is lined as it is stitched*—in one operation. The directions below are for a one-piece suit with a center-back seam and side seams. Although many variations

 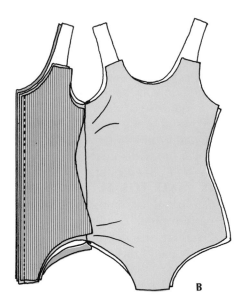 

are possible, following the exact procedure given below has one advantage: the completed suit will have both side-seam allowances facing toward the *front of the suit*. This provides a seam to which a bra form may be attached. (If no bra form is to be used, you may prefer to reverse the procedure and have the bulk of the side seams facing the back of the suit.)

• Cut lining pieces from suit pattern pieces, eliminating shoulder straps in lining.
• Stack layers for stitching the *left side seam* of suit as follows: (1) front fabric, (2) one back fabric, (3) one back lining, (4) front lining. Place fabric pieces and lining pieces with right sides together. Match the left side seam and stitch through all four layers.
• Fold out lining, smoothing the back lining over to the center-back seam of suit. *Stitch the center-back* seam in same manner. The order (from bottom up) will be: (1) other back suit fabric, (2) the back fabric you've already stitched to suit, (3) back lining already stitched, (4) other back lining. (Always keep right sides of like fabrics facing each other.)
• Turn lining over to match up with *right side seam*. Pin back lining to suit back and suit front at the side seam. Then lay the front lining over the lined back of suit so that right sides of front and back lining are facing each other. Line up edges of all four pieces and stitch remaining (right) side seam.
• Stitch crotch seam, also, while fabric pieces are in this position.
• Now reach inside suit and pull it right side out.
• Try suit on for fitting before shoulder straps are joined. If bra form is to be used, insert it between lining and suit front during fitting to ascertain its proper placement. Secure bra form to the side seams before applying elastic to neck and arm edges.

Fig. 34-5. Full lining, concealed seams, one-step method.

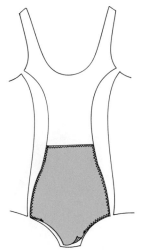

Fig. 34-6. Support panel (Princess suit).

Fig. 34-7. Support panel with concealed front seam.

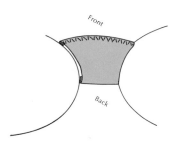

Fig. 34-8. Front crotch lining.

PARTIAL LININGS

LINING FRONT PANEL IN PRINCESS-LINE SUIT:

Many women's suits—particularly those with a princess line—are lined only in the lower front. This lining may be of power net, for the purpose of supporting and flattening the tummy.

Swimsuit lining may also be used. So may a piece of self-fabric. A stabilized fabric may be inserted here as long as it does not cover too wide an area, for it will naturally inhibit the stretch of the suit. (See Chapter 29, p. 170, for principles of support panel.)

SUPPORT PANEL FOR SUIT WITH NO CENTER-FRONT SEAM:

- Cut panel of lining or power net, using swimsuit center-front pattern piece or pieces from front-crotch seam to waistline.
- Overcast or stitch along waist edge of lining if desired.
- Apply panel directly to wrong side of suit as you would an underlining. Stay-stitch to suit fabric within the seam allowance, using a stretch stitch.

SUPPORT PANEL WITH CONCEALED FRONT SEAM:

- Stitch the two sections of lining to front seam in an enclosed seam, as shown.
- Then stitch side-front seams. Do not attach lining to suit at waistline.

LINING FRONT CROTCH ONLY (for suit with no center-front or center-back seam and no separate crotch piece):

The simple addition of a front-crotch lining may be all that is needed in suits of fairly heavy material. It may be applied during the suit's construction.

- Using the swimsuit front pattern piece as a guide, cut a front-crotch lining, deciding in advance how high up the front of the suit you want the lining to extend.
- Match seam edges of suit front and back at crotch, right sides together.
- Pin the crotch lining with right side to wrong side of suit back, matching seam edges. Stitch the crotch seam through all three layers.
- Turn the crotch lining to the front, pin it in place, stitch with a stretch seam along the edge. The crotch seam will be hidden.

LINING CROTCH IN A SUIT WITH CENTER-FRONT AND CENTER-BACK SEAMS (One-Step Method):

This is a trade technique that is fast and easy to apply. The crotch lining is sewn in as the suit is constructed. However, the lining is not stitched to the suit at its upper edge so it is possible that it will be something of a "sand trap" if worn at beaches.

- Cut four sections of crotch lining, using the front and back sections of the pattern piece as guide, deciding in advance how deep you want the crotch lining to be.

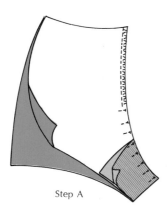

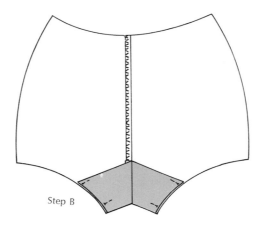

Step A

Step B

Fig. 34-9. Lining crotch—
trade method.

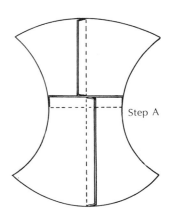

Step A

- Place the two front-crotch pieces, right sides together, on top of two front-swimsuit sections. Line up the seam edges and stitch entire center-front seam—stitching through four layers as you approach crotch seam.
- When suit front is laid flat and pinned, the crotch seam will be hidden.
- Apply crotch lining to back section in same manner, if desired.
- Join the crotch seam, using a welt seam, trimming away excess fabric.

LINING CROTCH IN A SUIT WITH CENTER-FRONT AND CENTER-BACK SEAMS (Two-Step Method):

This is a method for applying a crotch lining to a suit that has no separate crotch piece, but is seamed at center front and back.
The crotch lining is stitched to the suit after it is constructed and the stitching line at the upper edges of the crotch lining will appear on the outside of the suit.

- Decide in advance how far up front and back of suit the crotch lining should extend, and cut lining, using the front and back pattern pieces as a guide. (There will be four pieces to the crotch lining.)
- Sew center-front, center-back, and crotch seams of suit, but leave side seams open. Sew center-front, center-back and crotch seams of lining in same manner. Press seams in opposite directions to stagger bulk.
- Pin crotch lining to inside of pants, wrong sides together, matching seam lines.
- Turn under raw edges (or leave unfinished) and stitch along front and back edges with a stretch or zigzag seam, stitching through swimsuit fabric. (Leg edges will be stitched when elastic is applied.)

EXTRA CROTCH LINING FOR SUIT THAT IS LINED OR UNDERLINED:

This is an extra, or *shadow*, crotch lining that will help protect

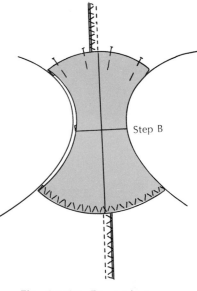

Step B

Fig. 34-10. Four-piece
crotch lining.

Fig. 34-11. Shadow crotch lining.

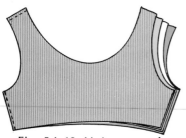

Fig. 34-12. Lining top of two-piece suit.

the lining fabric in a suit and/or eliminate the possibility of "see-through" in lightweight or lacy fabric.

• Cut crotch lining from pattern pieces.

• Apply by one of the above methods, stitching crotch lining to the lining or underlining fabric, instead of the suit fabric, before lining is stitched into suit.

CONCEALED SEAM LINING FOR TOP OF TWO-PIECE SUIT WITHOUT BRA:

This method may be used to line the top of a girl's or child's suit or a misses' two-piece suit in which a braless look is desired.

• Using the pattern as a guide, cut a lining for the top portion of a little girl's swimsuit.

• Place the fabric pieces for suit front and back, right sides together. Place front and back lining pieces, right sides together. Stack layers as follows: suit back, suit front, lining front, lining back.

• Pin so that all seams match and baste at side and shoulder seams. Try on suit for fit.

• Stitch side and shoulder seams using zigzag stitch.

• Turn garment right side out and seams will be hidden.

• Apply elastic to unfinished edges.

For *tips* on lining *men's and boys' swim trunks,* see Chapter 42.

35

SHAPING YOUR SWIMWEAR

The no-bra or natural look—although the current fancy of fashion—is not everyone's cup of tea. (If it were, Rudi Gernreich's 1964 topless version of the swimsuit would have swept the country!) Most women prefer a little firmness added to the top part of a swimsuit. This bit of "shape insurance" may be obtained in various ways—depending upon the amount of control or shaping desired.

For minimal firmness, merely underline the bra portion of your suit with a washable, nonwoven fabric and construct it according to the pattern directions.

For maximum control, purchase a washable bra form and insert it in the suit. See *Swimsuit Bra Forms,* pages 179–180.

THE BRA PANEL

One of the most popular bra forms is the bra panel. It gives support and, when properly applied, has the ability to stretch and move with the suit.

TO INSERT IN A TWO-PIECE SUIT:
- Place the bra panel, with seamed side up, on a table or your lap.
- Place the swimsuit front, right side up, over the panel. The highest point of the bra panel should come directly under the fullest part of the swimsuit.
- Smooth the jersey out to the edges of the swimsuit and pin the suit to the bra, placing pins in a circle around each bra cup. (Some people like to use a knee as a basis for this operation.)
- Baste-stitch the bra panel in place, around the entire cup. Then baste the jersey to fabric around the neck, the armhole, and the lower edge of the swimsuit bra.
- When the suit has been tried on for fit, trim away excess jersey and proceed with attaching swimsuit elastic.

TO INSERT IN A ONE-PIECE SUIT:

When a bra panel is used in a one-piece suit, an elastic is stitched across the bottom of the jersey to hold the panel in place at the rib cage. The elastic then hangs free of the suit.
- Before stitching the panel to the suit, measure a piece of elastic that is about 1 inch less than the front body measurement, or just tight enough to hold bra to body. If elastic is stretched too much it will pull the side seams inward, causing the suit front to bulge. (Plush elastic may be used.)
- Stitch elastic (plush side inward) to the jersey, about ½ inch below the lower edge of bra cups. Trim excess jersey below elastic, close to the stitching.
- Proceed as pattern directs, sewing panel into side seams and leaving bottom of panel hanging free.

MAKING YOUR OWN BRA PANEL:

If a bra panel is not available, one may be made, using power net or swimsuit liner and individual molded bra cups.
- Cut a partial lining of power net or swimsuit lining fabric, using the front bra section of the swimsuit pattern as a guide. Do not include the front shoulder strap.
- Sew any dart seams the same as those of swimsuit.
- Place individual molded bra cups directly over fullest portion of lining. (You may wish to hold the lining up to your body for the correct placement.) Pin them in position and baste to lining.
- Cut away the lining inside each bra cup, leaving a ¼-inch seam allowance.
- Using a crosscut binding of tricot or other soft, folded binding, tape bra cups in place. Starting at side seam, pin binding tape flat across top of cup; miter at inside point; pin under cup; miter; then pin up to underarm seam. Stitch binding in place. See Taped Bra Seams, Chapter 23, page 137.

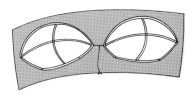
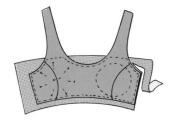

Fig. 35-1. Applying Type A bra panel to two-piece suit.

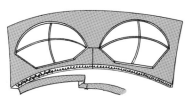
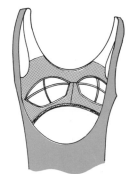

Fig. 35-2. Inserting Type A bra panel in one-piece suit.

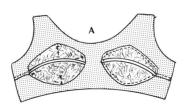
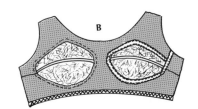

Fig. 35-3. Making Type A bra panel.

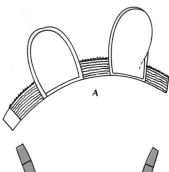

Fig. 35-4. Applying Type B bra form.

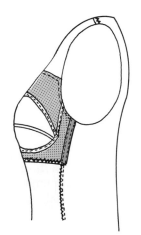

Fig. 35-5. Adding feather-boning.

- Sew soft elastic along lower edge of lining for a one-piece suit.
- Pin bra lining to top front of suit and stitch in place.

INSERTING MOLDED CUPS WITH ELASTIC TABS (REMOVABLE BRA FORM)

This type of bra form may be made removable. It may be lightly tacked to the side seams and center-front lining, or merely safety-pinned or attached with snaps. This will enable you to remove it to another suit or replace it easily if it becomes soiled or misshapen. A person with a large ribcage may find that the elastic inserts are too short for the bra to reach the side seams of a suit without their pulling. If this is the case, simply add an extension of elastic—either at both ends or in the center, as needed.

It is also advisable to catch stitch this type of bra form to the suit at the top of each cup to hold it more securely in place.

OTHER BRA TREATMENTS

If additional firmness is desired in a swimsuit bra, featherboning may be stitched to the inside of side seams or—in a princess-line suit—over the curve of the bust. Stitch a tape—one that is slightly wider than the boning—to the seam. Slide the boning under the tape. Plastic boning may be cut to the length desired. Round off the ends of the boning before inserting. Or buy and insert pretaped featherboning.

MINI BRA CUPS:

For the lass with a less full-blown figure, it is quite simple to make a soft mini-cup that will give slightly more shaping to the suit than if it were merely underlined.
- Cut a circle of fiberfill approximately 5 inches in diameter for each cup.
- Slash circle from edge to exact center and overlap until the correct bust size is obtained.
- Place a strip of linen, twill, or bias, or strip of fabric under seam to reinforce it and stitch with a zigzag as shown.

TEENY CUP:

For a young miss whose figure has not yet rounded out, but

whose beginning development and budding modesty require a bit of soft shielding in the bust area of a suit, a mere wisp of a bra may be suggested by:

- Cutting two circles of lining fabric: one approximately 3 inches in diameter, the other, 3½ inches.
- Stitch the two circles together around the edges and insert between suit and lining—stitching to wrong side of suit lining.

Step A

Step B

Fig. 35-6. Mini bra cup.

36

ELASTIC FOR SWIMWEAR

Swimsuits made for active wear require special elastic—as an incident in a midwest city early in the swimsuit, home-sewing evolution proved.

A class of eager seamstresses sewed regular rayon elastic into their suits then trooped jointly to the local "Y" to christen their finished creations with a mass plunge into the pool.

Proud spirits were somewhat dampened when half the class surfaced from the dive minus their swimsuits!

Swimsuit elastic—woven of Spandex and cotton—is quite firm. Indeed, it can cut into the flesh if wrongly applied. The length to use is determined by the size of the opening , but in most cases it is stretched somewhat so that the actual number of inches is slightly less than that of the suit opening.

The degree to which elastic is stretched as it is stitched to a suit may be influenced by the intended function of the suit . . . suits meant for diving, for instance, need tighter elastic. The best way to judge the length is to try the suit on and fit the elastic to it, pulling until it is comfortably snug.

Tips for distributing the amount of stretch in swimsuit elastic for the various openings are given below:

NECK EDGES: on most patterns, elastic is stretched as it is applied to the lower edge of the front and back neckline. For a good, firm fit, shorten the elastic from 1 to 3 inches as it is applied to the curve of the neckline. Suggested formula: allow ½ to ¾ inch of elastic for each inch of suit fabric at lower edge of front and back neckline.

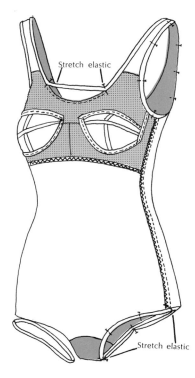

Fig. 36-1. Distributing fullness in elastic.

ARMHOLE EDGES: elastic is usually not stretched as much for an armhole as for the neck or leg. It may be only a fraction of an inch shorter than the arm opening. It is important here that the amount of stretch applied to the shoulder strap area be equal to the amount applied to the inside, or neck, edge. If it is not, the strap is apt to twist.

LEG EDGES: little or no stretch need be applied as elastic is stitched across the front of a leg opening. The stretching is done in the back, under the buttocks. A leg elastic that is too tight can be particularly cutting.

WAIST ELASTIC: should be snug, but not so tight that it will roll. One pattern maker suggests that the measurement of the elastic around the waist be divided so that 1 inch is subtracted from the measurement across the back and applied to the front waist, on the assumption that the average waistline measurement is one inch less in the back than the front.

APPLYING SWIMSUIT ELASTIC:

Swimsuit elastic may be enclosed in a casing, but most people prefer to apply it directly as follows:

- Join elastic ends by overlapping if opening is circular. See Chapter 24, page 139.
- Pin elastic to inside of suit, lining up elastic with raw edges of fabric.
- Stitch along outer edge using either (a) stretch stitch, (b) overedge stitch, (c) zigzag stitch, or (d) straight stitch. Stretch where indicated by pattern guide or use tips given above. If a straight stitch must be used, stretch fabric and elastic to prevent thread breakage in future when stress is put upon elastic.
- Turn fabric and attached elastic over once to the inside of the suit. This forms a hem the width of the elastic.
- Working from the wrong side, make a second row of stitching along inside edge of elastic. A stretch stitch or wide zigzag is most advisable. If straight stitch is used, a second row is advisable. Care must be taken to apply the same amount of stretch for each row of stitching.
- Overlap stitching on circular edges—sewing beyond the starting point.
- The more advanced seamstress may attempt the second row of stitching from the right side of the suit.

WIDE DECORATIVE WEBBING is used mainly for men's and boys' trunks, but may be applied as a waistband on a woman's two-piece suit. For method, see Chapter 42, page 228.

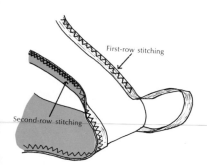

First-row stitching

Second-row stitching

Fig. 36-2. Applying swimsuit elastic.

37

TRIMS FOR SWIMWEAR

Unless your swimsuit is to be strictly functional, you'll want to look for the fashionable trims that do so much to set it off.

Most of the fancy touches currently seen on ready-to-wear suits are simple enough to duplicate, but remember to keep the trimmings consistent with the rest of the suit. Fabric used for trim needs to have approximately the same degree of stretch and recovery as that of the suit fabric. If it does not, the trim may either limit the freedom of the suit or—by failing to return to shape after dunking—leave the suit looking puckered and droopy.

BANLON TRIM

Banlon trim, which is available in colors, stripes, and prints of various widths, may be used to smarten up a swimsuit. It is a knit and will hold its shape when wet if it is stretched as it is applied to the suit fabric. It will accommodate buttonhole making without the need of reinforcement. It should always be applied with a zigzag stitch to retain its stretch.

Banlon trim may be bulky. It does not miter, seam, or overlap smoothly. It is most satisfactorily used when the cut ends can be enclosed in a seam allowance.

It may be applied to a suit in place of elastic, but does not impart the same degree of stretch to the garment. If applied to the waist of a suit, it is usually used in conjunction with a zipper or drawstring for proper fit. If applied to a bra top, the suit usually has a hook or other closing device.

The most commonly used type of Banlon trim is a fold-over tape which is applied to edges as follows:

APPLYING BANLON FOLD OVER TRIM:
- Working from the wrong side of suit, unfold the Banlon trim and place one edge of it along the raw edge of suit so that the edge of the fabric falls directly under the crease in the Banlon.
- Machine-baste the Banlon in place, stretching it considerably and shaping it to the contour of the suit as you baste.

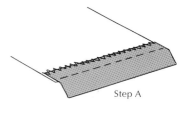
Step A

Step B

Fig. 37-1. Applying Banlon trim.

- Using a zigzag or stretch stitch, sew along the inner edge of the Banlon trim next to basting, stretching slightly as you sew.
- Turn the Banlon trim over the fabric edge to the right side of the garment. Trim suit fabric, if necessary, to make a perfectly even fold.
- On the right side of the suit, topstitch along the edge of the Banlon trim using a zigzag or decorative stitch—again stretching the Banlon as it is stitched.

STRETCH CORDING

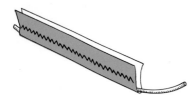

Fig. 37-2. Stretch cording.

A cording of contrasting or matching stretch fabric and elastic cord may be used to accent seams or to face edges of a suit.
- Cut straight strip of stretch fabric, having the length of the strip running in the direction of the fabric's greatest stretch.
- Fold strip in half lengthwise, wrong sides together, inserting elastic cord in fold.
- Stitch with narrow zigzag close to cord, being careful not to catch cord with needle. (An adjustable zipper or cording foot is helpful here.)

INSERTING STRETCH CORDING IN SWIMSUIT SEAM:

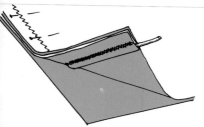

Fig. 37-3. Inserting stretch cording in seam.

- *Pin* strip of covered cording to right side-seam edge of one garment section—matching raw edges—and *stitch* with narrow zigzag close to previous stitching line.
- Place second section of garment so that right side of fabric faces right side of fabric to which cording has been applied. (Cording will be between layers.) Match seam edges and pin.
- Turn work over so that previous stitching line will be visible to use as a guide. Stitch along the previous stitching line, again using a zigzag stitch to preserve the garment's stretch. (This seam will join the garment sections.)
- After seam is joined, seam allowances may be trimmed and over-edged for added strength.

APPLYING STRETCH CORDING AS EDGE TRIM:

- Apply stretch cording to seam allowance of outer edge of garment, following directions as detailed above.
- Grade seam by trimming edges to different widths and then understitch them with a narrow zigzag close to cording—using a zipper foot.

CUTOUT HOLES

That occasional flash of flesh, visible through cutout holes, can make a plain swimsuit an attention-getter. Holes may be round, oval, pear-shaped, or you-name-it. They are easily added after a suit is completed.
- Decide on location, size, and shape of cutout. Mark the exact outline on the *wrong* side of suit with a chalk or pencil.

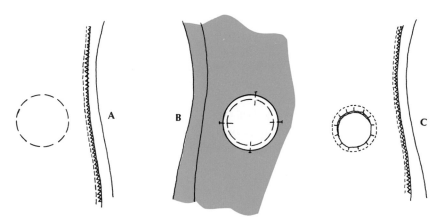

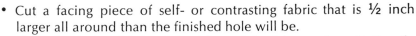

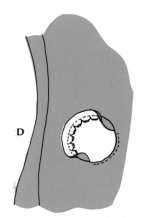

Fig. 37-4. Cutout holes.

- Cut a facing piece of self- or contrasting fabric that is ½ inch larger all around than the finished hole will be.
- Place the facing fabric, *right* side to *right* side, on the suit directly over the marking for the cutout hole. Center it from the wrong side and pin or tape it firmly in place.
- Stitch from wrong side of suit, following the pencil or chalk line.
- Remove pins and trim the fabric away from the center of the hole, leaving ⅛-inch seam allowance. Slash the seam allowance at regular intervals up to the seam line.
- Turn the facing to wrong side of suit and topstitch from the right side. Contrasting thread or a decorative stitch may be used for extra accent.

TRIMMED CUTOUT HOLES:

To accentuate cutouts, trim the holes with a narrow binding of stretchable fabric in a contrasting color or with purchased Banlon trim. Prepare and apply bindings as directed for Fold-over Banlon or Stretch Cording (see this Chapter), French Binding Chapter 25, p. 144), or Hong Kong finish (see Chapter 25, p. 146).

Mark the hole where you want it and cut to the exact size and shape. Then bind raw edges with trim. As you apply binding, leave enough trim at ends to either overlap or turn under for a neat finish.

or

Leave additional length at both ends of binding so that it may be tied in a bow at the top or bottom of the cutout hole.

BAND TRIM

To make band trim, use self-fabric or choose a contrasting fabric with a stretch factor similar to that of suit.

- Cut fabric for bands so that the fold will follow the direction of the greatest stretch. Cut the fabric twice the width of the desired finished band, plus ½ inch for seam allowance.

Fig. 37-5. Cutout holes.

Fig. 37-6. Band
trim.

Fig. 37-7. One-
piece maillot.

Fig. 37-8. Two-
piece maillot.

- Fold band lengthwise, wrong sides together, and pin with edges even.
- Apply as an edge trim by matching raw edges of folded band with raw edges of right side of suit. Stitch ¼ inch from edge—preferably using an overedge stitch.
- Fold band so that it stands out away from suit and press seam allowance down toward suit.
- Narrow band trim may be used to pipe seams in the same manner as given for Stretch Cording (see this Chapter, p. 196).

RINGS

Rings may be used effectively on some swimsuits. Look for novel rings in sewing-notions departments or try the drapery-hardware department for ideas. Unbreakable plastic rings are the most practical.

They may be inserted at the center-front seam of a bikini bra and at the side seams of bikini briefs. You may need to adjust your suit pattern to fit the rings. If the suit material is a lightweight knit, it may be gathered onto the ring for a soft effect. A heavier fabric may need to be tapered slightly toward the seam edge to fit the ring.

Turn under the fabric seam edge to form a casing over the ring—adding or subtracting width from the normal seam allowance, depending on the thickness and diameter of the ring.

LOOPS

Fabric loops made of spaghetti cording (see Chapter 27, p. 159) may be used in place of button closures or as an attractive simulated button closure for the front of a suit.

MAILLOT LACINGS

Lengths of cording or other lacing may be run through a series of eyelets to form maillot lacings on the front or sides of a suit. Lacings may be purchased or made of spaghetti cording (see Chapter 26, p. 152).

If you're daring—and your figure justifies the exposure—try designing a deep V plunge at the front neckline or side seam of a suit for maillot lacing.

Cut a facing for the proposed V, marking the stitching line on the wrong side of the facing with a pencil or chalk. Widen the gap at the top or curve the seam, if desired. Stitch and then slash down center to the depths of the V. Turn facing to inside—topstitching or understitching edges for more stability—and mark location for grommets.

For a less startling effect, fake maillot lacings can be achieved by merely inserting two vertical rows of grommets down the center of the suit and threading laces through them.

BELTS

Belts can dress up either one- or two-piece suits. They made ride on the hip or snug in the waist. A two-piece suit of contrasting fabric may be tied together by having the top and belt of one fabric and the shorts of another fabric.

    Belts that are purchased should be washable.

    Belts may be made of Banlon trim, decorative elastic webbing, or of self-fabric or contrasting fabric. Washable buckles may be purchased.

    Make belt loops of self-fabric.

ZIPPERS

A suit of simple design may be enhanced by a zipper-front closing. If you wish to play up the zipper, select one with large teeth and a sizable ring or pull tab and apply it with an exposed method. (See Chapter 9, p. 56.) Be sure that you don't stretch the swimsuit fabric while putting in the zipper as the zipper tape does not stretch.

BOW KNOTS

Fabric may be extended at center-cup sections of pattern, or at side seams of bikini pants, so that it may be tied in a bow knot rather than stitched in a seam. Use lightweight or drapable fabric.

    Extensions should be faced with self-fabric or fabric of a coordinating color and similar drapability to that of the swimsuit fabric.

    The length of the tie ends depends on personal preference. They will need to be at least 5 inches to be knotted, or shorter ends may simply be lapped and sewn permanently with a narrow band of self-fabric placed over the seam to simulate a knot.

Fig. 37-9. Zipper.

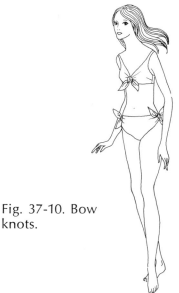

Fig. 37-10. Bow knots.

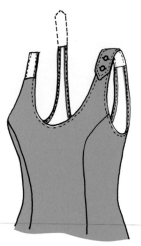

Fig. 38-1. Adjustable shoulder strap.

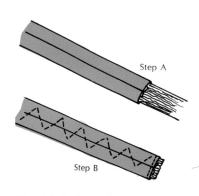

Step A

Step B

Fig. 38-2. Stretch straps.

38

STRAPS AND CLOSURES FOR SWIMWEAR

STRAP TREATMENTS

ADJUSTABLE STRAPS

Adjustable straps are a comfortable feature for many women's suits as well as an economy measure for growing girls' suits.

FRONT-BUCKLING STRAPS:

Make the following adjustments in the suit pattern:

- Cut off the front shoulder strap where you want the buckle to be, leaving enough seam allowance to attach buckle.
- Take the piece you cut off the front pattern piece and tape it onto the back-strap pattern piece.
- Cut out back of suit, adding the extra length to the strap so that it will extend down over the shoulder to the front of the suit and slide through the buckle. Make the end pointed or round it off so that it will slip through buckle.
- Cut a 3-inch facing of firm fabric and stitch it, right sides together, to back-strap extension. Turn right side out.
- Cut facing and apply in same manner to front.
- Topstitch all the way around strap and facing as you apply elastic to rest of suit. (This keeps strap ends from curling.)
- Attach buckle to front strap.
- Make eyelets in back strap.

FRONT-BUTTONING STRAP:

Follow the above directions with the following exceptions:

- Cut front suit strap as usual.
- Extend back strap the amount necessary for overlap.
- Make 2 buttonholes, 1 inch apart on extended back strap.
- Attach 2 buttons to front strap.

NARROW STRAPS

For a more abbreviated look you may wish to eliminate the wide shoulder straps that are often a part of the front and back pattern piece and substitute narrow straps.

To do so, the pattern will need to be restyled slightly. Eliminate the existing strap at top of front and back bodice, reshaping the top bodice line.

Unless straps are the adjustable or string type to be tied at the shoulder, or halter fashion at back of neck, sew them securely at the back of the suit. Then try on suit to determine correct length before attaching strap to front of suit.

The following are narrow strap suggestions:

SELF-FABRIC STRETCH STRAPS:

These straps are made by inserting a narrow swimsuit elastic into a fabric casing to give straps a combination of ease and security.

- Cut straps on lengthwise stretch twice the width of the elastic, plus ½ inch for seam allowance. Make them 1 inch longer than desired finished strap.
- Fold fabric in half, right sides together, and stitch ¼-inch seam along raw edge.
- Turn strap right side out.
- Cut swimsuit elastic 2 inches shorter than strap length. Thread elastic through casing, placing seam allowance down middle of underside of strap. Stitch across one end to secure elastic.
- Stretch elastic and pin even with other end of casing.
- Stitch down center of strap with a large zigzag stitch, beginning at stitched end. Stretch elastic to fit straps.

SPAGHETTI STRAPS:

- Cut strips of fabric 1 inch longer than needed and approximately 1 inch wide.
- Fold fabric lengthwise, wrong sides together, over a strip of cord. Secure fabric to cord at one end. Stitch, close to cord, using a cording or zipper foot.
- For a flat strap, trim seam allowance. For a rounded strap, leave excess fabric in seam.
- Pull cord and turn strap right side out.

VARIATIONS:

- Bows: Make shoulder straps of spaghetti long enough so they may be cut and tied in a bow at the shoulder. Front section should be shorter than back section so that bow may be tied toward front for most comfort.
- Long string tie for low-cut back: For low back interest, recut pattern as shown, adding at the same time loops through which narrow straps may be threaded. Cut the fabric tab deep enough so that it can be folded over and stitched securely. The front of the suit may also be abbreviated somewhat. This type of suit does not need to have elastic applied to the upper edge. Crossing the straps before threading them through the fabric loops in the back will keep the suit fitted to the body.

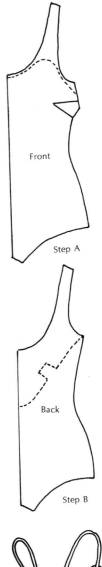

Front

Step A

Back

Step B

Step C

Fig. 38-3. Low back interest.

BANLON ONE-PIECE SHOULDER STRAP AND TRIM

Fig. 38-4. Banlon one-piece shoulder strap. Underarm trim.

A continuous strip of fold-over Banlon trim may be used to trim the center front of a suit bodice and to form a shoulder strap, all in one operation.

- When cutting out suit, eliminate shoulder straps, reshaping the top of bodice.
- Apply Banlon trim to underarm section of suit first, using method given on page 195, stitching first on the wrong side of suit and then on the right side. Begin and end underarm trim at the point on the bra where straps would normally be attached.
- Starting at the center front and working both ways, baste trim to front section of suit, catching in ends of underarm trim.
- Try on suit to determine length of trim needed for straps over shoulder—stretching for a comfortable fit. Pin in place to fit the individual.
- After fitting, continue to sew trim across back of suit, catching in the opposite ends of underarm trim.
- Topstitch around entire edge, sewing the trim to itself over the shoulder area. Use a flexible stitch and stretch the Banlon as you sew.

SELF-FABRIC BAND TRIM may also be used for this one-piece application.

- For underarm section, cut band trim and apply as directed on page 197.
- For the portion of the trim that is to extend over the shoulder, widen the band to a width that is half again as wide as the finished trim.
- Fold the strip for front and shoulder, wrong sides together, and place it along the right-side edge of the suit, keeping the wider portion exactly at the end of the underarm trim. Sew the band to the front-neckline edge with an overedge seam, stopping exactly at the end of the bodice section.
- Trim away ¼ inch from each side of the strap portion so that pieces will fold into 3 layers that are the same width as the finished trim.

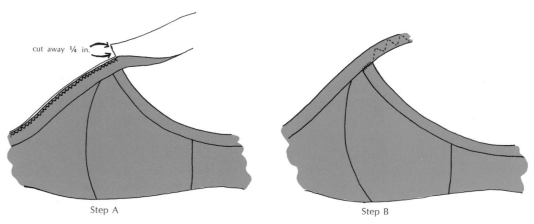

cut away ¼ in.

Step A   Step B

Fig. 38-5. Applying self-trim and strap.

- Stitch with a wide zigzag through the center of the straps (and around entire neck edge, if desired).
- Bar tack to reinforce the point where two sections of trim meet.

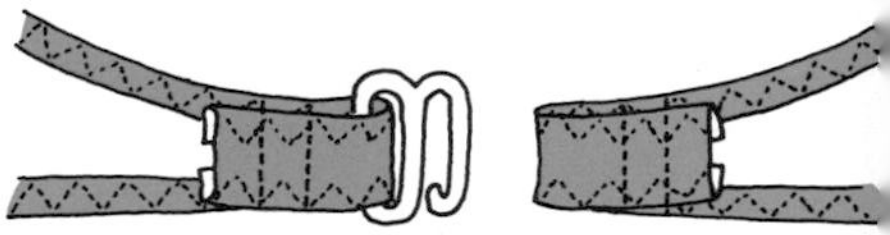

Fig. 38-6. Bra closure.

CLOSURES

SWIMSUIT BRA HOOKS

To apply purchased plastic hook to back of bra in a two-piece suit:
- Pull end of right half of bra through the closed part of the hook. Fold bra fabric to inside of bra and stitch close to loop, using a straight or zigzag stitch.
- Reinforce with a second row of stitching.
- Turn left back of bra to inside and finish with two rows of stitching, ½ inch from the folded edge, to form a slot for fastener.
- Trim off any excess fabric extensions.

ZIPPERS

For applications, see *Zippers,* Chapter 9, pages 53–61.

Fig. 38-7. Zipper back closing.

OTHER BACK CLOSINGS

The back sections of a swimsuit bra may be faced and machine buttonholes or fabric loops may be applied to one half, and buttons to the other (see *Buttonholes,* Chapter 9, p. 53).

Fig. 38-8. Button back closing.

39

SEWING PANTS THAT FIT

Pants or slacks are part of every woman's wardrobe today, worn on every conceivable occasion from playing sports to entertaining at a formal evening party.

Obviously, pants must fit to be both fashionable and comfortable, and one reason pants frighten the home sewer is that they can't be

altered once they've been cut. For this reason, it is best to design and make a *test basic pants pattern* which can be used to make any design of pants you want, or to check against the measurements of a commercial pattern.

Keep in mind that in sewing knit pants, it is the *stretch* of the knit that will determine the amount of ease allowed, as well as your own personal preference. Bear in mind, too, what the pants will be used for— are they for skiing or for city wear? Finally, it's best not to fit pants too snugly. Remember Ogden Nash's immortal words:

> Sure, deck your lower limbs in pants,
> Yours are the limbs, my sweeting.
> You look divine as you advance,
> Have you seen yourself retreating?

MEASURING YOURSELF FOR PANTS

The first step in making pants is to have someone take your measurements. Wear the undergarments you usually wear with pants. Tie a piece of linen or twill tape comfortably around your waistline. Take the following measurements:

WAIST: Measure as snugly as you like, waistline of pants.
HIGH HIP: Measure on top of hip bones, 2 to 4 inches down from waistline.
HIP: Place pins on side seams at fullest part of hips, usually 7 to 9 inches down from waistline. Measure over pins. Record distance down from waistline.
LEG:

> *Thigh:* Measure fullest part of leg. Record inches down from waistline. For large thighs, may wish to check the thigh measurement when seated.
> *Knee:* Measure around knee.
> *Calf:* Measure around calf. Record inches down from knee.
> *Instep:* Measure over instep and across the heel.

CROTCH DEPTH: Sit erect on a straight hard chair. Measure from waist to chair.

CROTCH LENGTH: While standing, measure from waistline in front to waistline in back. (A drapery weight works well for this—then measure the weight.) If your figure is irregular, you may wish to take a front and back crotch measurement.

SIDE LENGTH: Measure at side from waist to center of knee, waist to ankle, or to any additional pants length desired.

DECIDING ON THE BASIC PATTERN

Generally, it is better to *select a pants pattern* by the hip measurements since it is easier to make waistline than hipline adjustments. However, if your hip measurement is not more than 2 inches larger than the hip measurement designated on the pattern for your waist size, you can choose a pattern according to your waist measurement.

PREPARING PATTERN FOR MEASUREMENT

Adjust the flat pattern *before* making your test garment of fabric similar to fashion fabric.
* Draw hip measurement on pattern the correct number of inches below waistline according to your body measurements.
* Draw crotch position on pattern by drawing a line perpendicular to grain line at widest part of crotch. (See Fig. 39-1, B.)
* Determine location for thigh measurement by measuring down from waistline.

SUGGESTIONS FOR EASE

Measuring inside of the seam allowances, *check the flat pattern measurements* with the body measurements. Allow for ease. Below are listed some suggestions for ease which should be added onto body measurements:

WAIST: For personal comfort, or, snug waist measurement plus 1 inch.

HIGH HIP: 1 inch.

HIP: 1 to 2 inches.

THIGH: 1 to 2½ inches (for slim and stretch pants, knees [bent]—1 to 2 inches; ankle, 1 to 2 inches; instep, 1 to 2 inches).

CROTCH DEPTH (*SEATED MEASUREMENT*):
* Small sizes (hips below 35 inches)—½ inch
* Medium sizes (hips below 38 inches)—¾ inch
* Large sizes (hips over 38 inches)—1 inch
[Note: For stretch fabrics, reduce in half. Reduce slightly for knits with moderate stretch. Since it is difficult to determine the amount of stretch of the knit fabric, you may add an extra 2 inches on front and back from point of crotch tapering to notch. This allowance may be used in fitting, removing what is unnecessary.]

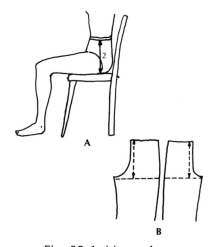

Fig. 39-1. Measuring crotch depth.

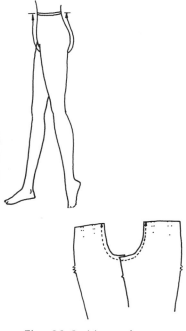

Fig. 39-2. Measuring crotch length.

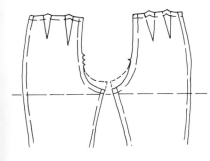

Fig. 39-3. Adding allowance to crotch for fitting.

CROTCH LENGTH (*STANDING MEASUREMENT*):
- Allow about 1¼ to 1½ inches—the amount of ease depends on your figure.
- *Front crotch:* ½ to ¾ of an inch.
- *Back crotch:* ½ to 1 inch.

[For example: *for an average figure,* the amount of ease *in front seam* may be ½ to ¾ of an inch; and *in back* ¾ of an inch. For a *prominent tummy,* the *front crotch* may allow 1 inch ease, and *the back,* ½ inch. For a *large derrière,* may allow 1 inch ease for the *back crotch seam* and ½ inch for the *front.*]

SIDE LENGTH: Check side length measurement according to style you desire to construct.

[Note: For most knits, an added 1 inch ease provides comfort. If the knit fabric has a great deal of stretch, you may choose a pattern ½ to 1 size smaller, particularly if the pattern is designated for wovens or as being "suitable for knits."]

COMMON ALTERATIONS

TO LENGTHEN OR SHORTEN IN THE CROTCH AREA: cut and spread, or fold-in the desired amount on the designated line on your pattern.

TO LENGTHEN OR SHORTEN THE LENGTH OF THE PANTS: cut and spread, or fold-in the desired amount on designated line on pattern.

TO INCREASE OR DECREASE WAISTLINE: add or decrease on center and side seams—¼ the amount on each seam, tapering to hip on side seam and to the notch on center seams.

FIGURE DIFFERENCES AND POSTURE DIFFERENCES

It is important next to *note the "attitude" of your figure*—i.e., your figure differences and posture differences. If your figure falls into any of these categories, allow extra fabric when cutting the test garment. Remember, you alter *where* you need it.

ROUND PADDED HIPS: curve the side seam to conform to body contour.

FLAT STRAIGHT HIPS: taper gently from hip, removing part of curve of side seam.

PROTRUDING HIP BONES: add a short dart above the hipbone to release fullness for the protruding bone.

PROMINENT TUMMY: add more length at front waistline seam; decrease front darts and let out side- and center-seam allowances if needed.

FLAT TUMMY: decrease length of crotch at front waistline seam; eliminate a front dart and take in CF and side seams to decrease width.

LARGE DERRIÈRE: add more length at back-waistline seam for

more back rise; more length to back-crotch seam; and may add a dart at waistline (thus creating hip fullness). When the dart is added, you may need to let out back-side seams, tapering from hip to waistline.

FLAT DERRIÈRE: lower the waistline ¼ to ½ inch at the CB seam, tapering to nothing at side seam. May decrease inner leg seam ¼ to ½ inch.

LARGE THIGHS: a small amount is added on inside seam, half on front and half on back. Larger amounts are added on both inner and side seams.

Fig. 39-4. Pressing creases.

STITCHING AND PRESSING

Stitch your test garment as you will later sew your fashion garment. However, baste-stitch the test garment to aid in fitting. After it is stitched, check the fit and make any necessary alterations on your commercial pattern.

- *Press in creases:* Fold each pants lengthwise right side out so seam edges meet. Stretch up and outward toward the lower point of the crotch seam. Begin *front creases* below darts and end *back crease* at crotch length.

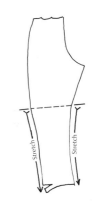

Fig. 39-5. Stretching front piece.

- *Join and stitch side seams:* On some patterns the lower-back legs are slightly longer which helps prevent "baggy" knees. If your pattern has not provided for this, stretch front pieces by pressing side- and inner-leg seams from about 3 inches above knee to 3 inches above hem. Cut off ¼ to ¾ inch at bottom along hemline:

  > 5 feet 3 inches—remove ¼ inch
  > 5 feet 4 inches—remove ½ inch
  > 5 feet 5 inches—remove ¾ inch

Stitch seam keeping the front of the pants *up* on the sewing machine, easing the back onto the front. Leave opening for zipper if side zipper is being used.

- *Press side seams over a ham:* In the front, press up and outward and in the back, down and outward. This shapes the pants, providing "shape" where needed.
- *Stitch inner-leg seams:* Press open.

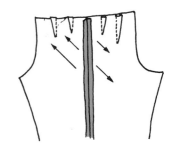

Fig. 39-6. Shaping side seams.

- *Stitch center crotch seams:* Turn pants leg inside out, slipping one leg inside the other with the right sides of fabric together. *Stretch when sewing in lower curve of back seam only.* Clip seam at notch or about 2 inches below hipline. Press seam open above the clip. Trim seam below the clips to ¼ inch to ⅜ inch. Stitch a second row of stitching ⅛ inch from the first row. This seam stands up. May reinforce this bias seam by stitching a 7-inch piece of linen tape or seam tape folded—3 inches to the front of seamline and 4 inches toward the back of the inner-leg seam.
- *Waistline:* If a *waistband* is used, ease about 1 inch of pants to waistband. Usually the ease is distributed in the hip area where more fullness is needed. *Elastic waistbands* are common for fashionable knit pants. See Chapter 14, pages 92–98. Be sure to allow

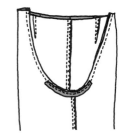

Fig. 39-7. Tape bias crotch seam.

Fig. 39-8. Fitting waistline of pants.

Fig. 39-9. Faced waistband.

extra fabric at top of pants if pants top is to fold back for the elastic casing (1½ inches). A tip for fitting waistline of knit pants is to tie a piece of linen tape around your waistline over the pants. Adjust the pants for a smooth fit. Chalk or pin to mark the waistline.

• *Wide decorative elastic webbing* may be used in place of a waistband. For application, see Chapter 42, pages 228 and 229–230.

FACED WAISTBAND

A faced waistline is used for hip-huggers. Stay the waistline with linen, twill, or seam tape. Place one edge ⅛ inch over the seam line. Ease pants onto waistband with right sides together. Stitch seams through tape, facing, and garment. Grade seams and press toward the facing. Understitch facing to keep from rolling. Turn to inside of pants. Turn in ends and tack to zipper tape. Tack facing at seamlines and darts

or

stitch by machine in seamline at side seams on right side of garment.

PANTS HEMS

The length of the pants is determined by fashion and shoe-heel heights. Hems, by hand or machine, or cuffs are fashionable (see Chapter 15, p. 102). A double-stitched hem (see Chapter 15, p. 101) is good for heavier double knits. Most hems are tapered longer at CB to as much as ¾ inch. Taper seam in hem area (see Chapter 15, p. 103). A shaped facing is sometimes applied in the back.

CHECKING THE FIT

When checking the fit of pants there are a few pointers which will be helpful to remember:
• The closeness of the fit is determined by the current fashion and by personal preference.
• Consider the activities for which the pants will be worn.
• Stretch in knits allows for easier movement. Do not use the stretch for fit.
• If the pants are smooth when standing, the waistband will not remain on the waistline when seated.
• So—sit, walk, and stand in your pants. Lift your arms. Check waist, hips, and legs for comfort and appearance. Check crotch width and length. If you have met the criteria, you have created pants that fit!

EXTRA TIPS FOR MAKING PANTS

DESIGNING PATTERN VARIATIONS:

FOR BELL BOTTOMS: add equally on each side of leg on both legs, flaring from knee to bottom of pants.

FOR A SLIMMER KNEE: taper from hip to knee and flare from knee to bottom.

FOR PAJAMA OR PANTS SKIRT: begin at hip on outside seam and at the crotch on the inside seam and enlarge to hemline, flaring gradually.

TO TAPER LEGS OF PANTS: draw a straight line from hip to bottom of leg on outside seam, and on inside seam if tapering a considerable amount.

IF USING A REGULAR PATTERN FOR SKI PANTS: adjust pattern length according to the stretch of the fabric. If 9 inches of fabric stretches lengthwise to 10½ inches (or a 1½-inch stretch), then a yard would stretch 6 inches—that is, 1 inch per 6 inches in length. Therefore, shorten the pattern above and below the crotch 1 inch for every 6 inches in measurement.

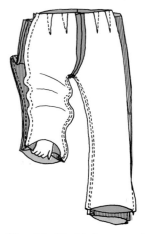

Fig. 39-10. Lining pants.

UNDERLINING:

Bondeds and some stretchy knit fabrics may be underlined to prevent "baggy" knees or "rump spring." In some cases, just the knees are underlined. See Chapter 10, page 65.

LINING:

- Make lining seams slightly larger than pant seams.
- Turn pants and lining wrong sides out. Align inside-leg seams and placket, if there is one. (See Fig. 39-10.)
- Permanent-baste the lining and pants inner-leg seams together.
- Turn pants right side out by running hand inside of pant leg and grasping one side of pant and lining. Pull through lining. Repeat for other leg.
- Hem lining separately.

or

- A lining can be made and dropped into the pants and attached at the waistline.

or

- Make a separate pants liner (see Chapter 18, p. 113).

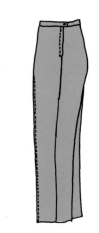

Fig. 39-11. Stitching creases.

STITCHING CREASES:

If a front crease is stitched, stitch with a *single needle* ⅟₁₆ inch from pressed crease through the hem. (See Fig. 39-11.)

A *double needle* may be used to stitch a crease. This is done after pressing the crease before the garment is assembled. Tighten upper tension slightly. Stitch on right side of pants with pants flat along crease on the front. This crease is not as sharp as stitching with a single needle on the fold.

PLACKETS:

An invisible-zipper fly front is a common placket opening. Buttoned fly fronts present a casual look. Zippers may be inserted with slot application in front openings of lap application in side. They are usually machine-stitched.

SHIELD:

A *crotch shield* for reinforcement may be made of cotton/polyester fabric. Trace curve of crotch and cut about 3 inches wide and

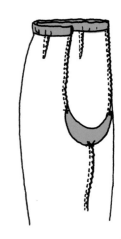

Fig. 39-12. Crotch shield.

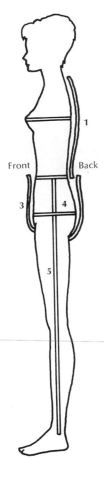

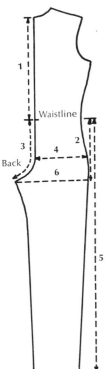

5 inches long. Zigzag or overedge raw edges and tack at crotch seam and inner-leg seam. (See Fig. 39-12.)

JUMPSUITS AND PANT-DRESSES

Jumpsuits may be sleek and slim, or dramatic and flowing in jersey. They may have bibs, or may be short or long. The hemline may be gathered as in knickers, cuffed as in boy shorts, tapered as in bell bottoms, or flowing as in a skirt.

To *select your pattern size* for a jumpsuit, choose it according to your bust measurement.

Check the following personal body measurements and add suggested ease. This should equal flat pattern measurement. If not, add or subtract the amount needed. You must keep in mind the stretch of the knit and the desired closeness of fit. (See chart, p. 211. The numbers in Fig. 39-13, A and 39-13, B correspond to the numbers in the chart on p. 211, with the exception of number 2 in the chart. Number 2 corresponds to Fig. 39-1, A, p. 205, and Fig. 39-13, B, 2.)

MARK THE FOLLOWING ON PATTERN TO CHECK THE MEASUREMENTS:

- Draw a line from crotch point to side seam at right angles to grainline (Fig. 39-13, B, 6).
- Draw in waistline.
- Draw in hipline (Fig. 39-13, B, 4).

CHECK PATTERN MEASUREMENTS:

- Check back-waist length according to number 1 (Fig. 39-13 and chart, p. 211).
- Check crotch depth on number 2 (Fig. 39-13, B and chart, p. 211).
- Check crotch seam for front and back on number 3 (Fig. 39-13 and chart, p. 211).
- Check length on number 1 and 5 (Fig. 39-13 and chart, p. 211).

MAKE NECESSARY PATTERN ALTERATIONS BEFORE CUTTING FASHION FABRIC:

You may line or underline just the bodice of a jumpsuit or pant-dress. Tricot or Underknit are good choices. The entire garment may be lined by constructing the lining and attaching to neck and armscye before finishing.

The jumpsuit or pant-dress, too, is a "fun" garment to fashion in knits. Do try one—tailored in stable knits or sumptuous in printed tricot or jersey!

Fig. 39-13. Measuring jumpsuit.

MEASUREMENTS

	Personal Measurements	Ease	Pattern Measurement	Total needed + or −
1 Back waist length (Prominent neck bone to waist)		up to ⅜″		
2 Crotch depth * (Sit on chair and measure from waist to chair) 36 inch hips—½ inch 37 inch hips—1 inch		½-1″		
3. Crotch seam (Measure crotch from front to back while standing) Front—From waist in front to a point between legs close to body where inside leg seams will be located. Back—Subtract front from total crotch-seam measurement.		1″ 2″		
4. Hip Ease varies according to style. See pattern for amount allowed.		According to style		
5. Length Waist to ankle or to desired length.				

*See Fig. 39–1, p. 205 and Fig. 39–13, B, 2.

40

SEWING THE KNIT SKIRT

Knit skirts are simple to make and are so versatile in the fashion picture. They may be straight, pleated, or A-line, or feature godets—yes, even a complete circle skirt drapes beautifully.

CHOICE OF FABRIC:

The double knits cling less, sit-out less and may be constructed using a ⅝-inch or more seam allowance. Press the seams open for a smooth fit over the hips. Other knits may be used if desired (see Chapter 1).

FIT OF GARMENT:

Generally speaking, the knit skirt should provide 1½ to 2 inches ease at the hipline and at the waist 1 inch ease. This means that 1½ to 2 inches is *added* to your hip measure *inside* of the seam allowance. This will provide the "high-fashion" fit. However, for a stretchy knit, less ease may be needed.

FABRIC LAYOUT:

Be sure to lay the fabric with the most stretch going around the body. Watch for shading of fabric (see Chapter 5, pp. 26–28).

WAISTBAND AND PLACKET:

If an elastic waistband is desired for a "pull-up" skirt, the waistline measurement of the skirt should be 1 to 2 inches larger than *your* waist measurement. This allows it to stretch to pull over your hips.

If your hips are over 12 inches larger than your waist, you may desire to use a zipper application.

If an elastic waistband is used, cut fabric crosswise for band. (See Chapter 14 for waistbands.)

PLEATS OR GORES:

Pleated or gored skirts are adaptable for firm, stable knits. Gores or pleats may be topstitched close to the edge. *Press the seams open* in hemline and casing at top of skirt.

A trade technique used to secure the inside of the pleat through the hem is to stitch from the fold of the hem, tapering to stitching of the seamline.

MACHINE STITCHING:

Stitch the skirt seams from the bottom up, stretching slightly. Use a stretch or zigzag stitch if one is available or a straight stitch (see Chapter 7).

HEMS:

Allow approximately 2 inches for a hem. The hemline pattern design usually tapers in slightly at the hemline to prevent flaring. The thickness of the hem against the tapered line will provide a straight line from the fashion side of the garment. (For hem finishes, see Chapter 15.)

PRESSING:

Press side seams over a ham from the bottom up. "Round" or shape over the hip area. Press open if a plain seam is used. Press toward the back of the skirt if a knit seam is used. (See Chapter 7, pp. 40–41.)

SWEATER BODY SKIRT

A skirt may be fashioned from a sweater body piece of fabric.

PREPARATION OF FABRIC:

Cut the fabric open and steam press. Relax until thoroughly dry.

DESIGN:

Use the *ribbing* either at the waistline for a casing or at the hemline on a hem. For a smoother look, put in *darts* and add an *attached waistband*. Taper the side seams from the hip up, keeping the lower side seam fairly straight.

41

TAILORING KNIT COATS AND JACKETS

Knits are adaptable for the high-fashion outer garments of the 1970s—the coat for the dress-coat ensemble, the bicycle jacket accompanying knickers, the blazer with the pleated skirt, the hiking jacket with the flare-leg pants, the sleeveless cardigan with the jump suit, or the tunic wraparound with the cuffed pants.

Knits, especially the double knits, tailor beautifully. They are adaptable for coats and suits for men, women, teens, and children. The garments may be tailored so that they are washable or dry-cleanable— "structured" or "unstructured." The fiber, yarn, fabric construction, the finish, the findings, and the method of tailoring used, may be varied to achieve the fashion look you desire.

SELECTION OF PATTERN, FABRIC, AND TRIMMINGS

Double knits in wool, polyester, or blends are suitable for tailoring. Simple designs usually are more effective.

Jackets and coats are *not* usually *underlined* unless the knit fabric lacks firmness. You may wish to underline with cotton/polyester or light-weight commercial underlining if the structured or couture look is desired.

Hair canvas is a suitable *interfacing* for men's and women's jackets and coats which are to be dry-cleaned. For washable polyesters, choose washable canvas of polyester/rayon blend or bias featherweight or light-weight nonwoven interfacing or an iron-on interfacing.

To *line washable polyester suits* or coats, choose a washable lining. A stabilized nylon knit, tricot, polyester crepe, a silk/synthetic blend print or similar washable fabric is a good choice. Always wash lining fabric before application. For *wool or wool-blend knit garments,* any light-weight, drapable fabric like polyester crepe, silks, synthetic, tricots, or stabilized nylon knit may be used for lining.

For selection of *thread* see Chapter 3, pages 18, 36–37; for *zippers* see Chapter 4, pages 23–24; and *tape* see Chapter 4, page 24.

To *prepare fabric,* see Chapter 5.

For constructing *buttonholes* and *pockets,* see Chapter 9. Instructions are given for buttonholes in a seam, with or without a facing. Also the patch/window method is illustrated for bound buttonholes. Instructions for patch, welt, flap, and in-a-seam pockets are found in Chapter 8.

SEAMS

Shoulder seams in coats and jackets should be taped. Necklines may be machine-stay-stitched or taped. Often, just the back neckline is stayed with tape. Armscye seams are sometimes taped on garments which will receive hard wear. Plain, unfinished seams are used for garments which are lined. If an unstructured, *unlined garment* is being fashioned, finish the seams with overedging, zigzag, or the Hong Kong finish (see Chapter 25, p. 146) for an elegant look.

INTERFACING

FRONT INTERFACING

To *cut,* place the facing pattern on top of the front jacket pattern. Cut the interfacing across entire shoulder seam, down the armscye onto 2½ to 3 inches on side seam. At lower edge of facing, cut interfacing ¾ inch wider than the facing, extending in a curved line to the side seam.

Iron-on interfacings may be pressed onto the facing or to the front

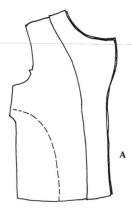

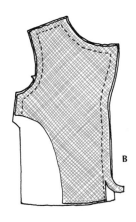

Fig. 41-1. Interfacing. *A,* cutting front interfacing; *B,* attaching interfacing to underlining.

if a line doesn't show. Sometimes the entire front of jacket is fused with interfacing for a firm, tailored look.

If the garment is *underlined,* stitch the interfacing to the underlining 1 inch from edge. Trim interfacing close to the line of stitching.

To *remove seam bulk from front interfacing,* lay a piece of cotton/polyester fabric under the front, neck, and shoulder edge of the interfacing. Stitch 1 inch from front, neck, and shoulder edge. Trim away interfacing close to line of stitching.

BACK INTERFACING

For a structured knit jacket, you may desire a *back shoulder interfacing.* If stretch is desired, use tricot; for stability, use cotton/polyester, stabilized nylon, or a lightweight commercial interfacing or underlining.
- Use the back jacket pieces for a pattern. Trace around the neck and armscye.
- At center back place a mark at 5 inches from neck, and, at underarm, 2½ to 3 inches from armscye.
- Connect the latter two markings with a curved line.
- Attach interfacing in neck, shoulder, and side seams.

COLLARS

Collars in knits may be interfaced or not, unshaped or shaped by machine-padstitching or hand padstitching, just as in wovens. The choice is dependent on the desired effect and the type of knit used, and whether one desires to use the time for a custom or couture effect, or prefers to use trade or quickie techniques.

Terms used for collars in dressmaking are: *fall,* portion of collar which falls from the breakline to the outer edge of the collar; *stand,* portion of collar between creaseline and neck edge; and, the *breakline,* or creaseline, which is the foldline of the collar.

MACHINE-PADSTITCHED COLLAR FOR SUITS OR COATS

This method resembles hand padstitching for shaping, more than most prescribed methods presently used.

The undercollar, as well as the interfacing, should be cut on the bias with a seam at center back.

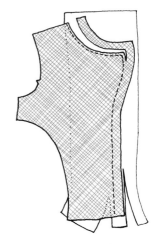

Fig. 41-2. Removing seam bulk from interfacing.

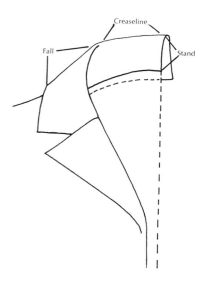

Fig. 41-3. Terms for collar.

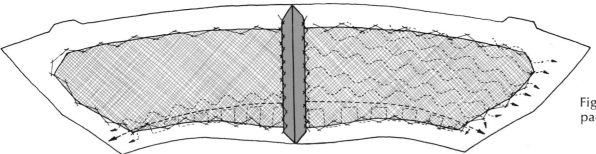

Fig. 41-4. Machine-padstitched collar.

Sewing with the New Knits

PREPARE THE UNDERCOLLAR:
- Stitch the center-back seam of the undercollar. Press open.
- Trim center-back seam to ⅜ inch. Angle-trim at ends.

PREPARE THE INTERFACING:
- Remove ⅝ inch from the neck edge of the interfacing.
- Remove ⅝ inch from the center-back seam.
- Remove ¾ inch from ends and outer edge of interfacing.
- Cut diagonally at outer corners.

ATTACH INTERFACING TO UNDERCOLLAR:
- Place the interfacing on the wrong side of the collar.
- Push the center-back seam allowance of interfacing under the CB seam allowance of the collar. Catch stitch the CB seam with a regular size stitch.
- Using a large catch stitch, attach the interfacing to the undercollar around the outer edges.

SHAPE AND MACHINE-PADSTITCH COLLAR (Fig. 41-4):
- Machine-stitch the breakline* of the collar from the CB toward the front-neck edge using a small machine stitch, about 20 s.p.i.
- Shape collar over a ham or a collar roll.
  SHAPING ON A HAM:
  - Fold stand under on breakline stitching.
  - Begin by placing steam iron on outer edge of collar. Curve collar with left hand while moving iron on grain up to fold of collar.
  - Continue process until collar curves. Do half a collar at a time.
  SHAPING ON A COLLAR ROLL:
  - Tie a piece of linen tape in loop end so collar roll simulates neckline curve.
  - Pin breakline of half of collar to curve.
  - Steam collar. Allow to dry. Steam again.
  - Repeat the procedure on other half of collar.
- Machine-padstitch the stand of collar with a regular machine stitch, perpendicular to the breakline in a rectangular pattern beginning at the CB and working to CF on each side.
- Machine-padstitch the fall, using the same directional stitching as used by professional tailors for hand padstitching. Begin at CB and stitch parallel to the breakline in rows about ⅜ inch to ½ inch apart. Use a serpentine, three-step zigzag, or a regular machine-stitch.
- Shape-press again.

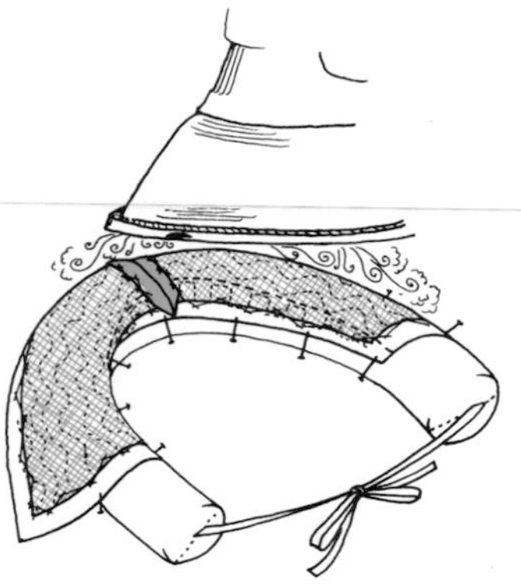

Fig. 41-5. Shape-press collar on collar roll.

---

* To determine the breakline, baste the undercollar to the garment. When the collar rolls into position, mark the fold line. This is the breakline. Do not guess!

HAND PADSTITCHED COLLAR

For the couture method, the collar may be padstitched by hand.

PREPARE THE UNDERCOLLAR:

  Same as above.

PREPARE THE INTERFACING:

  • Lap seam allowance on top of seam allowance at CB. Stitch.

  • Trim seam allowances close to line of stitching.

ATTACH INTERFACING TO UNDERCOLLAR:

  • Place the interfacing on the wrong side of the collar.

  • Hand baste the interfacing to the undercollar at the breakline.

HAND PADSTITCH:

  • *Padstitch just to the seam allowances.*

  • Padstitch the *stand* by beginning at CB and continuing to the right-front seam allowance. Begin again at CB and padstitch to the left.

  • Fold collar stand under the collar at the breakline.

  • Beginning at *right-collar point,* padstitch near the breakline to CB, returning to point. Do not turn collar around. Continue until half of collar is completed.

  • For *left half of collar,* begin at CB on breakline and continue to point, returning to CB without turning collar.

  • Shape collar on collar roll or ham. See directions above.

APPLICATION OF UNDERCOLLAR TO JACKET:

  • Attach the shaped, interfaced undercollar to the jacket at the neck edge, clipping where necessary.

  • Begin at CB and terminate stitching ⅝ inch from end of collar at seam allowances. Trim seam allowances to ⅜ inch. Press seam open.

  • Understitch undercollar seam allowance to undercollar.

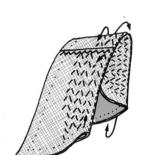

Fig. 41-6. Hand pad-stitching collar.

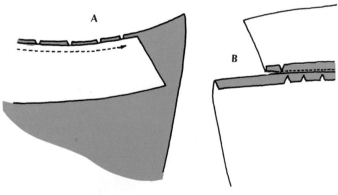

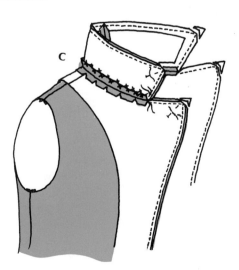

Fig. 41-7. Attaching undercollar, *A,* applying undercollar to jacket; *B,* under-stitching undercollar seam allowance; *C,* application of upper collar and facing to garment.

APPLICATION OF UPPER COLLAR TO FACINGS:

* Stitch back-neck facings and front facings at shoulder seam. Press open. Trim seam allowances to ⅜ inch.
* Attach upper collar to neck edge of facings, beginning at CB and terminating the stitching ⅝ inch from the end of the collar at the ⅝ inch seam allowance.
* Clip facing where necessary. Trim seam allowances. Press open. OPTIONAL: Catch stitch loosely the upper-collar seam allowance to the upper collar. If stitches show on the right side, *omit.*

APPLICATION OF UPPER COLLAR AND FACING (Fig. 41-7, C, p. 217):

* Seam upper collar at CB if it has a seam. Press seams open. Trim to ¼ inch.
* Pin a ⅛-inch tuck or tailor's blister just back from point or curve of upper collar and at point of lapels on the facing. This provides fabric ease for upper collar to roll back over undercollar and the facing to roll back as a lapel.
* Place right side of collar and facing to garment. Match CB and points of collar at end of collar notch.
* Machine-stitch collar from CB to neckline seam. Retrace or tie threads. Repeat on other side.
* Turn seam allowance up and begin sewing at end of notch and stitch facing to the garment.
  [Note: *If collar and lapel are pointed,* take one or two stitches diagonally across the corners. When turned, a point will result rather than a knob.]
* Press seams open. An edge presser works well. Trim uppercollar and garment seams to lower part of lapel to ½ inch, and undercollar and facing seams to base of lapel to ¼ inch. On the lapel, trim facing seams to ½ inch and garment seams to ¼ inch.
* Roll collar into position. Using hand stitches, attach the upper- and undercollar seam allowances togther at CB between the shoulder seams.
  [Note: If garment is unstructured with no lining and no back-neck facing, attach bias tape of nylon or polyester between the shoulder seams, covering the seam. See Fig. 41-8.]

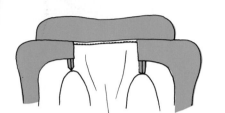

Fig. 41-8. Unstructured suit—attach bias at back neck edge of collar.

SLEEVES

To set sleeves, see Chapter 13, pages 88–90. Armscye seams may be double stitched for added strength.

Lined knit garments may have sleeve hems interfaced. (See Chapter 15, p. 101.)

A sleeve shape or "pad" may be used at the top of the sleeve to add roundness and a smooth line to the shoulder-cap area. It lifts the cap of the sleeve and gives support. It does not substitute for the shoulder shapes which support the shoulder area. In a tailored knit garment, the sleeve shape may be referred to as a "sleeve head" or a "sleeve welt."

SLEEVE SHAPE FOR KNIT DRESSES AND UNLINED GARMENTS

Use self-knit fabric, polyester all-bias fleece, or lightweight, bias non-woven, depending on the desired effect.

- Cut the shape the same as the sleeve pattern between the notches over the cap.
- From the high point of the sleeve, measure down approximately 2½ inches. Taper from this point to the notches. Mark front and back on the shape, as there are no notches on the shape.
- The lower edge of the sleeve cap may be finished with an over-edge or zigzag or left unfinished.

INSERT THE SLEEVE SHAPE:

- Turn the armscye-shoulder seam into the sleeve.
- Working from the inside of the sleeve, lift up the seam allowance. Insert the shape against the wrong side of the sleeve, matching the high point of the shoulder. Extend the ends of the shape to the notches in front and back. Ease the shape over the cap.
- Permanent-baste the sleeve shape on the seam allowance, very close to the line of machine-stitching.
- Turn garment to the right side, pushing the armscye-sleeve seam into the sleeve. The sleeve shape cushions the crown of the sleeve.

SLEEVE HEAD OR WELT

The sleeve head or welt is used in the shoulder-cap area for lined garments and men's sport coats.

USE POLYESTER ALL-BIAS FLEECE:

On knits which are to be dry-cleaned, cotton sheeting, lamb's wool, or heavy cotton flannel on the bias may be used.

LIGHTWEIGHT PADDING:

- Cut the fabric 1 inch wide and 8 or 9 inches long.
- Place the padding strip between the sleeve and the armscye-sleeve seam.
- Permanent-baste the *center of the strip* in the seam allowance, just inside the stitching line.
- The strip usually extends between the notches on men's wear, but may be trimmed off shorter for more lightly tailored wear.

HEAVIER PADDING:

- Cut fabric 3 to 4 inches wide and 12 inches long.
- Fold back 1 inch lengthwise. Machine-stitch.
- From the inside, push the sleeve-armscye seam up.
- Place the *smooth side of the sleeve head* or welt toward the wrong side of the sleeve. Keep the folded edge of the padding to the outer edge of the seam allowance.
- Extend the sleeve head lengthwise between the notches.

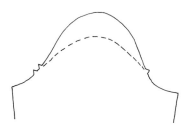

Fig. 41-9. Sleeve shape for knit dress.

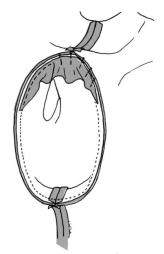

Fig. 41-10. Attaching sleeve shape.

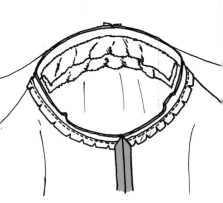

Fig. 41-11. Inserting sleeve head or welt.

• Cut off the excess.
• Permanent-baste to the seam allowance just inside of the armscye-sleeve stitching line.

Turn the garment to the right side, pushing the armscye-sleeve seam into the sleeve. The sleeve head folds back on itself, padding the crown of the sleeve.

SHOULDER SHAPES

Lightweight, washable shoulder shapes may be inserted in lined jackets or coats. These are thin, mold to the body, and are easily constructed.

• Pin the front and back pattern pieces together on the shoulder seams by lapping the seam allowance.
• Place tissue paper over the shoulder area of pattern pieces.
    BACK:
    • Measure 4 to 4½ inches down back-armscye curve. Mark.
    • Measure in 1½ inches from neckline at shoulder. Draw a line 2 inches down, curving to meet the first marking.
    FRONT:
    • At the neckline continue down front 5 inches, curving slightly away from the neck edge.
    • Measure down 4¾ inches on front armscye and connect the two lines.
    • Cut out tissue pattern.

CUT AND MARK THE SHOULDER SHAPES:

• Cut one or two layers of a medium- to heavyweight nonwoven interfacing, making one layer ⅛ inch smaller.
• Cut one layer of polyester fleece. (More if more padding is desired.)
• Mark shoulder line on interfacing.
• Place fleece down with two layers of interfacing on top. Machine-stitch the three layers together with the interfacing up. Do not pin or baste.
    RIGHT SHAPE: Beginning at armscye, stitch across the shoulder seam, pivot, continue down neck edge to bottom edge of front, shaping the pad while stitching. Continue stitching across bottom front, up armscye, along back curve, and complete with a second row of stitching across the shoulder seam.
    LEFT SHAPE: Repeat for second shoulder pad.
• Fit shoulder shape to garment by placing shape on figure. Put on garment, matching shoulder seam of garment to shoulder seam of pad as nearly as possible. Pin in position at shoulder and in front and back. Remove garment.
• Attach shoulder shapes by stab stitching the pad to the garment at the shoulder line. Swing-tack at front and back of shapes.

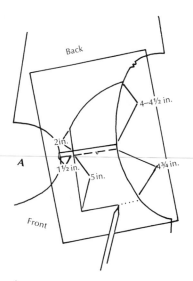

Fig. 41-12. Drawing pattern for shoulder shape.

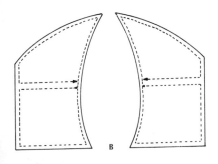

Fig. 41-13. Stitching shoulder shape.

HEMS

Hems on unstructured garments are not usually interfaced but structured garments are. To interface hem, see Chapter 15, page 101.

HEM-FACING FINISH

To complete the hem-facing, you may follow your pattern instructions. There are, however, two machine methods for finishing the hem-front facing at the hemline for coats, jackets, suits, long vests, or tunics. Basically, the bulk is removed, but in *Method A the garment may not be lengthened, while in Method B, the garment may be lengthened.*

METHOD A:
- Mark the hemline. Press fold line lightly.
- Pin the front facing to the garment at the front and along the bottom edge.
- Stitch the facing to the right coat-front seam, beginning where the collar is attached to ⅛ inch below the marked hemline. Pivot and stitch horizontally 1 inch, staying ⅛ inch below the hemline. Pivot and stitch to the bottom seam allowance (usually ⅝ inch). Pivot again and stitch to ⅝ inch from the inner edge of the facing.
- Press seams open. Grade coat-facing seams, leaving the garment seam slightly longer. Trim lower-front corner diagonally; clip into corner. Trim seams to about ¼ inch along 1 inch horizontal line and to ¼ inch to bottom of coat. Along bottom edge of coat, trim the *facing only* to ¼ inch.
- Fold *right sides* of facing together along the bottom stitched line of the coat hem. Stitch from previous stitching to ⅝ inch from the top of the hem if the garment is to be *unlined*. For a *lined* garment, stitch up from the hemline to point where lining is to be attached to the facing. Trim seam to ¼ inch and trim diagonally at corner. Clip in ⅝ inch at end of stitching on facing.
- Press.
- Turn coat-facing hem into position.
- Repeat on left coat front.
- Hem the garment. The lining may now be attached to the extended facing seam allowance.

METHOD B:
This hem technique is one used in trade in which the entire hem through the facing can be hemmed in one operation with the blind hemmer. The bulk is removed from the hem, yet the garment may be lengthened.
- Follow the pattern when cutting the front facing.
- Establish the hem line. Press lightly. Turn under ⅝ inch and press at top of hem.

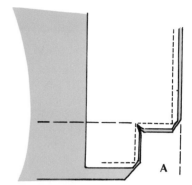

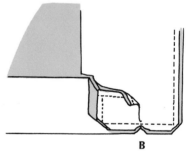

C
Fig. 41-14. Machine Method A for hem-finish (garment may or may not be lengthened).

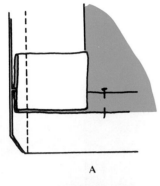

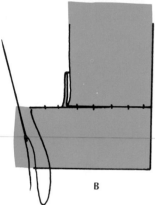

Fig. 41-15. Machine Method B for hem-finish.

• Turn the right side of the hem to the right side of the garment, folding along the lightly pressed marked hemline.
• Pin facing to front of garment with the right sides together to within 4 inches from the bottom of the garment.
• Fold a pleat across the facing by aligning the fold of the pleat even with the top of the hem; and the lower raw edge of facing to the raw edge of the hem allowance.
• Stitch the facing to the garment down the front to the bottom through the pleat and hemline. Trim the lower corner at an angle.
• Turn and press.
• Hem may be interfaced. Hem along the entire hem through the facing to the garment-edge seamline.

LININGS

The lining for a washable knit coat or suit should be compatible with the outer fabric. Some good suggestions for washable linings are: Underknit (nylon); Ciao (woven polyester); Qiana (woven or knit nylon); and nylon-tricot knit fabric. Be sure that the lining is opaque so that the seams do not show through.

Lining fabrics such as crepes and twills may be used for knit garments which are to be dry-cleaned. To provide the extra "give" across the back, add an extra-deep pleat in the back of the lining. Of course, any of the linings mentioned previously for the washable knit fabrics may also be used.

COMBINATION HAND-MACHINE METHOD FOR LINING KNITS

MAKE THE FOLLOWING ALTERATIONS TO THE COMMERCIAL LINING PATTERN:
• Add ⅜ inch at the underarm of the sleeve, tapering to the notches in front and back.
• Add ⅜ inch at the lower armscye, tapering to the notches on both the front and back of the jacket. This prevents underarm "pull."
• Check for a pleat at the center back.
SUIT HEM: Cut lining ½ inch longer than the marked hemline.
COAT HEM: Cut lining 1½ inches longer than marked hemline. This provides for a 2½-inch hem. This will make the coat lining 1 inch shorter than the coat. The lining will be hemmed separately.

IF A LINING PATTERN IS NOT INCLUDED:
Use the jacket pattern pieces to cut a lining. Make the following additional alterations to those for using a commercial lining pattern.
• Add a 2-inch pleat in the center back.
[Note: Add 1 inch to the fold.]

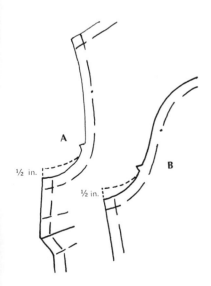

Fig. 41-16. Cutting additions for armscye and sleeve of lining.

- Place the facing pattern on top of the front-jacket pattern. Mark along the front-facing line. Removing the facing pattern, extend the marked line 1¼ inches toward the front edge for a cutting line. This allows for a seam allowance of ⅝ inch plus a ⅝-inch lap onto the facing.
- If the jacket pattern has a back-neck facing and you desire to use the facing, cut the back lining 1¼ inches above the lower-facing line. To eliminate the facing, cut the lining to the neck edge the same as the jacket back, except for allowance for the CB pleat.

STAY-STITCH:

- Stay-stitch the front edge, armscye, and back-neck edge at "⅝ inch minus."
- Press back ⅝-inch seam allowance along the stay-stitched lines. Clip on curved edges to the stay-stitching.

STITCH DARTS AND SEAMS:

- Stitch the bust darts and any other vertical darts and seams other than the underarm seams. *Do not stitch back-shoulder dart.*
- Run a machine-basting along back shoulder to ease in back-shoulder dart if there is one.
- Fold in a ¾-inch release dart at the middle of the shoulder on the front. The fold falls toward the armscye with the pleat underneath, turning toward the neckline. This provides ease over the bust area: Baste-stitch on the seam line to hold the dart. Hand stitch either with a bar tack horizontally about 2½ inches down from the shoulder—or—catch or feather stitch horizontally—or—catch or feather stitch vertically for about 1½ to 2 inches.
- Fold in, pin and baste pleat at center back of lining. The fold line will turn to the right and the pleat underneath will fold to the left. Stitch across the top of the pleat in the seam allowance at the neck edge.
- Fasten the lining pleat with either the bar tack or feather stitch at the top—the same as the shoulder dart. Another stitching is added at the waistline.
- Machine-stitch shoulder seams and underarm seams.
- Stitch sleeve darts. Press. May ease in sleeve darts the same as the back-shoulder dart. Stitch sleeve seams. Press open.
- Stitch a row of machine-basting on the seamline of the cap of the sleeve from notch to notch. Pull up lower thread slightly to fit sleeve of the garment-body lining.
- Stitch in the top half of the sleeve lining into the garment lining from notch to notch. Press the seam allowance into the sleeve.

PRESS:

Press lining thoroughly before attaching it to the garment.

ATTACH SLEEVE LINING SEAMS:

- Turn the sleeve lining inside out. Pull the jacket sleeve inside out.

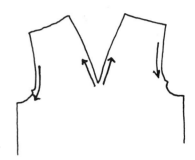

Fig. 41-17. Staystitching.

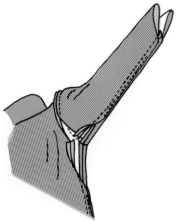

Fig. 41-18. Permanent-baste garment—sleeve-lining seams.

- Place the wrong side of the sleeve lining to the wrong side of the jacket sleeve.
- Permanent-baste the two seam allowances together, leaving them free 3 inches from the armscye and 3 inches from the hemline.
- Turn the lining back over the sleeve and the jacket sleeve back into the armscye.

ATTACH UNDERARM SEAMS:

- Place the wrong side of the lining against the wrong side of the jacket. Fold back the front lining to the side seam. Align the seam allowance of the lining to the jacket lining, matching notches.
- Permanent-baste the two seams together, leaving about 2 inches free at the armscye and at the hemline.
- Repeat this procedure for both seams.

JOIN SHOULDER SEAMS:

- Align the lining front-shoulder seam allowance to the jacket-shoulder seamline.
- Permanent-baste the front-shoulder lining to the shoulder shapes. Catch through the jacket-seam allowance if possible.
- Permanent-baste lining-seam allowances and garment-seam allowances together for 2 inches on each side of the shoulder seam.

ATTACH JACKET LINING AT ARMSCYE:

- Pin the armscye of lining to jacket-sleeve line from *notch to notch*.
- Permanent-baste as close to the seamline as possible toward the cut edge.

PIN FRONT AND BACK NECKLINE OF LINING:

- Smooth the lining toward the front.
- Lap the pressed-back edges of front lining over the edge of the facing.
- Pin in position, allowing ease in the bust area.
- Pin, baste, or hand baste.

PIN BACK NECKLINE INTO POSITION:

- Match fold of pleat to the CB of jacket.
- Pin clipped seamline to collar-neck seam allowance.
- Pin-baste or hand baste.

HAND STITCH OUTER EDGE OF LINING:

- Slip-stitch the lining around the front and back neck from hemline to hemline.
- Leave about 3 inches free at hemline.

COMPLETE UNDERARM SLEEVE LINING:

- Trim jacket-lining seam allowance from notch to notch to ¼ inch plus.
- Fold back the lining seam allowance at underarm, matching to jacket. Pin and baste.

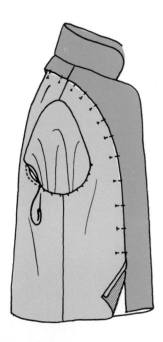

Fig. 41-19. Attaching jacket lining at armscye and front facing.

- The extra allowance added on the lining allows the lining to go up over the ¼-inch standing underarm-seam allowance. This eliminates the sleeve lining "pull."
- Slip-stitch into place with small stitches for added strength.

HEM THE JACKET OR COAT LINING:

JACKET:

- Trim off lining so that it is ½ inch longer than the jacket.
- Press back ½ inch.
- Pin the pressed fold 1 inch up from the lower edge of the jacket. Slip-stitch.
- Press the lining down into position, forming a ½-inch release pleat at the hemline.

COAT:

- Sew a 2½-inch hem in the coat lining, or hang it so that it is 1 inch shorter than the coat.
- After the remaining 3 inches of the lining is attached to the facing, make a 1-inch French tack between the hem and the lining at each of the side seams.
- Complete the remaining 3 inches at the lower-front edge of the lining with hand stitches.

HEM THE SLEEVES:

Use the same procedure for the sleeve lining hems as for the jacket lining hem above.

COUTURE METHOD FOR LININGS

This method is similar to the combination method except that the sleeve lining is set by hand around the entire armscye. This is somewhat more difficult for the beginner, but for the seamstress who enjoys couture finishes, this is a preferred procedure.

The sleeve lining is not stitched into the sleeve at the upper half of the armscye. It is set after the body lining is attached. Permanent-baste together the seam allowances of the coat and coat lining around the armscye, close to line of stitching.

SET THE SLEEVE LINING:

- Attach the sleeve lining and garment sleeve seams with a permanent basting, leaving the seam allowances free at both ends for about 3 inches.
- Stay-stitch on the seam allowances of the sleeve lining armscye. Use a basting stitch over the cap between notches.
- Pull up the ease over the cap so the lining fits into the armscye. Clip and turn under the seam allowance of the sleeve lining.
- Pin-baste the sleeve-lining armscye into the garment, matching underarm seams, notches, and the top of the sleeve.
- Hand stitch, using a small whipping stitch, a backstitch, or a slip stitch. Be careful that the stitches do not penetrate the outer fabric.

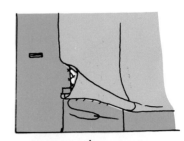
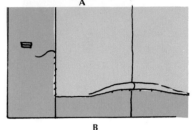

Fig. 41-20. Hemming jacket lining.

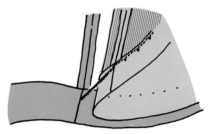

Fig. 41-21. French-tack coat lining at hem.

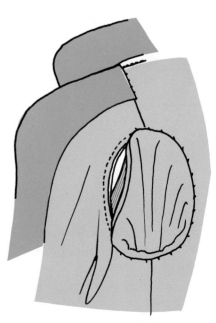

Fig. 41-22. Setting sleeve lining—couture method.

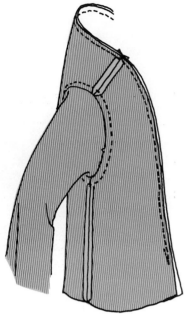

Fig. 41-23. Machine method of lining.

MACHINE METHOD FOR LININGS

This method is the quickest of all methods and is used in the trade. It is used for boxy jackets, coats, and children's garments, and for garments which will be machine washed frequently.

- Sew the entire lining together, including setting the sleeves, darts, etc.
- Machine-stitch the front- and back-neck edge of lining to the facing, by placing the two right sides together. Begin at CB and stitch toward each hemline, leaving 3 to 4 inches free at the hemline.
- Attach the underarm seams of lining and garment using machine basting.
- Stab stitch the garment to the lining at the shoulder seam.
- The *sleeve lining hem* may be finished by hand.

or

- Stitch the lining hem to the sleeve hem before attaching the lining to the garment.

42

SEWING KNITS FOR MEN

Women *and men* are sewing garments at home for men. Knit shirts, turtlenecks, and pullovers are fashioned using the same techniques as described in Chapters 1 to 16. Be sure to change the direction of the plackets—remember the men's garments button *left over right*.

MEN'S SWIM TRUNKS

Some construction variations are necessary when sewing swim trunks for men and boys.

LINING MEN'S SWIM TRUNKS

Men's and boys' suits may be lined or be partially lined. Most of them have at least a partial front lining. Swimsuit lining fabric, heavy tricot, stretch nylon, or cotton knits may be used.

Fig. 42-1. Men's supporter.

Step A

SUPPORTER FOR MEN'S OR BOYS' TRUNKS:

Rather than making a full front lining, a simple supporter may be made and added to the front of any boy's or man's bathing suit.

- Choosing from one of the recommended lining fabrics, cut a rectangle of fabric that is 9 inches wide (7 inches for boys) and the depth of the suit from waist to crotch seam. (You may desire to make the supporter shorter than the suit—for boys, approximately 3 inches shorter.)
- Taper sides of rectangle so that it is only 4 inches wide at the bottom.
- Starting at center of lower edge, make a dart that is ½ inch deep, tapering to nothing about half way up the rectangle. Trim the dart.
- Finish side edges of lining and insert in front of swimsuit, with dart centered at center of crotch seam. Stitch lining to crotch seam. The top will be joined with waistband.

PARTIAL FRONT LINING FOR MEN'S AND BOYS' TRUNKS:

- Using the front-pattern piece as a guide, cut a lining panel that is 4 inches wide (smaller for boys), measuring from the center front.
- Sew center-front seam of lining, using a stretch stitch. Overcast side edges with overedge stitch.
- Pin lining to wrong side of suit, matching center seams. Catch the lower and upper edges in the crotch and waistline stitching.

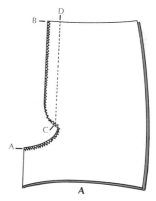

Step B

Fig. 42-2. Men's partial front lining.

FULL FRONT LINING FOR MEN'S AND BOYS' SUITS:

Linings may be made for men's and boys' suits by the same method as those used for women's and girls' suits, see Chapter 34.

FALSE FLY FRONT FOR MEN'S AND BOYS' SUITS:

Many men's and boys' ready-to-wear bathing trunks have a false fly at the center-front seam. It is more practical for active swimwear than a true fly opening and more masculine appearing than merely stitching straight up the center front seam. To make a false fly:

- Place the two front sections right sides together.
- Starting at the crotch, stitch the center-crotch seam. Starting at (A) and continuing on around the outer edge of the fly extension to the waistline (B), use a stretch or overedge stitch. (If straight stitch is used, stretch fabric while sewing.)
- Stitch center-front seam from base of fly extension (C) to waistline (D), making the seam ¼ inch closer to the edge of the fly extension than a normal center-front seam would be.
- From right side of suit, fold fly extension on inside of suit toward left leg of suit, leaving a ¼-inch tuck at center front to simulate a true fly opening.
- Topstitch through three layers of fabric, outlining the fly. End stitching with a triangle to secure base of fly, as shown in Figure 42-3, B.

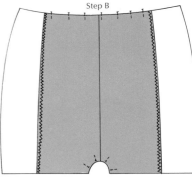

A

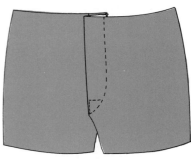

B

Fig. 42-3. Men's false-fly front.

WAISTLINES FOR MEN'S SWIM TRUNKS

WIDE DECORATIVE WEBBING:

Used mainly for men's and boys' trunks. May also be applied as a waistband on women's pants. To apply to trunks:

- Trim down waistline of pants the width of the elastic webbing, leaving a ¼-inch seam allowance.
- Measure elastic to fit waist comfortably—not too tight as it is very firm and has a tendency to roll.
- Join ends of elastic to form a circle, using a plain seam. Overcast cut edges to prevent fraying and to give a smooth finish.
- Divide the swimsuit top into equal portions.
- Apply the webbing to the waist of trunks by *either* of the following methods:
  - Overlap elastic ¼ inch on right side of suit and stitch with stretch stitch,

    or

  - Seam with a plain seam (overedge or zigzag finish), right sides together, and then flip webbing up into position.

FRONT DRAWSTRING:

Step A

A waistband may be made more adjustable by the addition of a drawstring. A drawstring in a casing may be applied around the entire top of a suit, but a better fit is usually obtained by applying elastic to the back waistline and using the drawstring only in the front portion of the trunks, as follows:

- Apply elastic to back half of suit. If enclosing elastic in a casing, allow extra fabric when cutting out suit back. For applying webbing, see directions above.
- In cutting out suit front, allow at least 1 inch for casing at top of suit.
- Make 2 machine or hand-worked buttonholes ¾ to 1 inch apart at center front within the casing.
- Cut 2 lengths of swimsuit cording long enough to tie in a bow. (Braided shoelaces may be used.)
- Stitch one end of each cord within the seam allowance of the casing, having the length of the cord toward center of suit.
- Thread the two loose ends of cord through buttonholes to right side of casing.
- Fold casing to inside of suit and stitch in position. Then stitch side seams. (Or if casing has been used in back, sew the side seams before stitching casing in position all the way around.)

Step B

Fig. 42-4. Men's front drawstring waistband.

OTHER WAISTLINE VARIATIONS:

- Apply regular swimsuit elastic (stitched and turned) across the back and apply decorative webbing to front waist,

  or

- Finish top with a hem, add belt carriers and a snug-fitted belt, perhaps made of elastic webbing, *or*

- Apply swimsuit elastic all the way around as for woman's suit. (Simple for small boys.),

or

- Make a waistline casing and insert elastic or drawstring.

MEN'S TRICOT PAJAMAS

The "man in your life" will be thrilled with tricot pajamas, trimmed with piping and a monogram on the pocket.

PAJAMA TOP:

For the neck finish, follow the directions for V-neck insert, Chapter 12, page 81. Remember to have the front lap left over right.

Tape the shoulder seam and back neck seam with a lengthwise strip of tricot 1 inch wide and length of shoulder and neckline + 2 inches. Fold under ¼ inch on each side of tape. Placing wrong sides together, stitch along folded edge, keeping both tape and fabric relaxed.

PAJAMA PANTS WITH EXTENDED FLY FRONT:

If the pattern fly is a separate piece, tape it to the pajama bottom and cut in one piece as an extension.

- Turn under the edge of the fly front ⅛ inch and topstitch.
- Sew the front crotch seam using a "welt" seam, French seam, or the zigzag overcast seam, being certain to reinforce the stitching at the fly end of the seam.
- Clip the seam allowance at the bottom of fly to ⅝ inch.
- Turn back the left-front fly along center-front marking. The right side remains flat and underneath the left front. Pin in place through all layers of fabric.
- Check the right side to make sure the fly opens correctly.
- Topstitch the fly front through all layers of the fly.
- Sew the back crotch seam. Sew the inner-leg seam.
- Hem the legs using a tailored hem. Apply waist elastic.

ELASTIC WEBBING FOR PAJAMA PANTS:

Elastic webbing may vary in resilience so take this into consideration when determining the amount to cut for waistline. Unless it is unusually soft it can usually be fitted to the waist measurement, allowing an extra ½ inch for joining.

It may be applied to the waist of pants by a trade technique—leaving the back seam open until after it has been stitched to top of pants and then incorporating it in the seams as it is stitched,

or

the ends may be joined by one of the methods given lingerie elastic and applied as follows:

METHOD A:

- Turn under upper edge of pants ½ inch to inside.

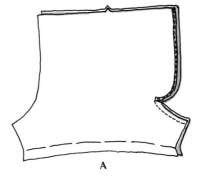

A

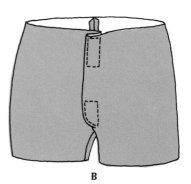

B

Fig. 42-5. Extended fly front for men's pajamas.

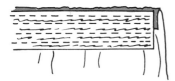

Fig. 42-6. Applying elastic to pajama pants—Method A.

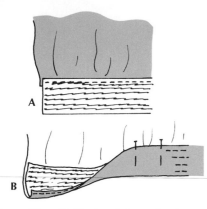

Fig. 42-7. Applying elastic to pajama pants–Method B.

- Quarter elastic and pants and pin elastic to inside of pants, placing one edge of webbing ¼ inch below the fold, so that it overlaps raw edge of tricot ¼ inch.
- Stitch along the upper edge of elastic, through all three thicknesses, stretching to fit quarter marking.
- Stitch again along bottom edge. Then stitch two more rows between so that there are four rows of stitching in all.

METHOD B:
- This method provides its own casing; it is smooth, and serves to hide webbing which is not readily available in colors.
- Allow extra fabric (the width of the webbing) at top of pajama pants when cutting out pattern.
- Lap webbing and upper edge of pants ¼ inch. Stitch, stretching to match quarter marking.
- Turn webbing over to wrong side of garment.
- Turn again, the width of elastic, and stitch through all thicknesses on same edge of elastic as before.
- Make another row of stitching along top of casing and two evenly spaced rows between.

MEN'S DOUBLE-KNIT SPORTS COATS

If the double-knit sports coat is of wool or polyester and is to be dry-cleaned, the same findings and hand-padstitching techniques may be used as are used in tailored wool woven garments.

> FRONT: hair canvas
> COLLAR INTERFACING: linen canvas
> UNDERCOLLAR: Melton
> POCKETING: silesia
> INTERFACING SLEEVE HEMS: wigan
> SHOULDER PADS: cotton or wool pads
> STAYS: linen tape and wigan
> LINING: twills or rayon or polyester wovens

To fashion this garment so it may be hand washed or machine washed, some "quickie" techniques and washable findings may be substituted.

> FRONT: Use washable canvas of synthetics, or fuse a woven or nonwoven interfacing to facing in lapel area, to jacket front or to entire jacket front.
> COLLAR: Fuse a lightweight woven or nonwoven to upper/undercollar.
> UNDERCOLLAR: Self-fabric or synthetic flannel-like fabric.
> POCKETING: Substitute woven Dacron/polyester or stabilized nylon taffeta.
> INTERFACING SLEEVES: Bias woven Dacron/polyester or bias nonwoven.

STAYS: Iron-on strips of woven or nonwoven fabric for break-line, vent edges, hems, front edge, etc. May use strips of nylon taffeta.
SHOULDER PADS: Use foam pads or make pads using polyester fleece.
LINING: Tricot, Underknit, or polyester woven fabrics.

MEN'S DOUBLE-KNIT SLACKS

The pattern-counter books carry many slack patterns with excellent instructions. Slacks may be made washable or dry-cleanable depending on the fabric and findings. Washable waistband findings, woven Dacron/polyester or stabilized nylon taffeta for pockets, and heavy zippers for fly fronts are available at your favorite fabric store.

OTHER GARMENTS

Continuing to apply the techniques of knit sewing, there are still other pattern designs available for men. Do try some of these:
- Men's nylon tricot or cotton briefs
- Knit hip-huggers, bell bottoms, knickers, shorts, or bib overalls
- Knit vests: single or double breasted
- Knit shirts and jackets
- Knit neckties, cummerbunds, etc.
- Knit robes and smoking jackets
- Knit jumpsuits, short or long

So—pick a knit, select a pattern and follow the know-how, using couture or quickie techniques to create a knit fashion.

APPENDIX A
THE HISTORY OF KNITS

FROM HAND KNITS

Knitted fabric is a fairly recent innovation in the fabric industry, yet the interlocking stitch we call "knitting" (perhaps after the fisherman's netting) is one of the oldest craft techniques known to man. Almost all primitive peoples were—without knowing it—using the knitting concept when they knotted grasses together to make mats, baskets, and nets.

Knitting was a considerably more complicated concept for men to comprehend and to apply to natural fibers than the more simple idea of *weaving*. The act of crossing two sets of grasses or reeds (or—later—yarns) at right angles and interlacing them into an early version of weaving now seems elementary compared to the principles involved in man's efforts to form a single set of reeds (grasses, yarns) into a series of connecting loops that would produce the first rough forms of knitted cloth.

The oldest piece of knitted fabric known to exist is a swatch of woolen cloth dated at 256 A.D., found by Yale University and the French Academy of Inscriptions and Letters at Dura-Europas (Syria). It was identified as being of the Crossed Eastern Stitch pattern—a form of knitting known to have been done by nomadic peoples of North Africa. These early practitioners of the craft were the first known to have worked on frames.

Though the Scots are often credited with being the first to hand knit with wool, heavy woolen socks have been uncovered among other hand-knitted articles in Egyptian tombs. They are dated by authorities at anywhere from the fourth century B.C. to the third century A.D. There is ample historical evidence, also, to support the theory that knitting was a wide-ranging avocation of Europeans near the latter part of the first millennium A.D. The Viking tombs of Scandinavia contain knitted fragments. And an example of a ninth century Spanish altar cloth, now in the Ashmolean Museum of Eastern Art at Oxford, appears at first glance to be brocade. But on closer examination, it proves to be a knit of the Arab traditional "crossed stitch" pattern.

Hand-knitted garments are known to have been popular in England by the twelfth century. The word *cynattan* (meaning to tie or to knot) was first introduced into the English language in 1442. At the time, the material it described was a coarse net which was produced by primitive wood or bone needles. Hand knitting spread rapidly throughout Europe within a few generations.

. . . TO MACHINE KNITS

The history of machine-knitted fabric has more definite beginnings. The first knitting machine was made in 1589 in England. Its inventor was a clergyman in Nottingham named William Lee. (Legend has it that he wanted to free his fiancé—an avid knitter—from her needles to allow her more time to spend with him.)

Lee's machine was a complete original. A flatbed type with spring-beard needles, it could knit eight loops to an inch of width. This produced too coarse a mesh to be practical, but in time the machine was improved to make twenty loops to an inch. Nine years after his invention became a reality, Lee finished a pair of silk stockings and presented them to Queen Elizabeth I.

The knitting machine was immediately recognized as the most important innovation in textiles since the development of the hand loom thousands of years earlier. It could produce at ten times the speed of hand knitting. In fact, the panic produced by the thought of its potential to replace hand knitting—and thus cause widespread unemployment—prevented Lee from ever receiving the patent he repeatedly sought from Queen Elizabeth for his remarkable invention.

Modern knitting machines still operate on the same general principles established by William Lee. The hand-knitting machine, operated by one person, which makes garments one section at a time, has come down to us practically unchanged since Lee's day.

Stockings were to remain the staple product of the Reverend Lee's type of machine for more than two hundred years. Only at the beginning of the nineteenth century did hosiery-making companies start turning out underwear on knitting machines. First men's, then women's. The advances in design were accomplished mainly through fiber changes—a progression that included Egyptian cotton, silk and wool, spun silk, and even cashmere.

In 1758, another Englishman, Jedediah Strutt of Derbyshire, developed a device which would produce ribbing in knit cloth. His invention was known as the Derby Rib Hosiery Frame. It put machine-knit fabrics in close competition with hand-knit products. After that, improvements in knitting machines became more frequent. Before the end of the eighteenth century, the rotary frame and the warp frame were to appear—doing much to improve the quality of machine-knit fabric.

A circular knitting machine—invented by Marc Brunel in 1816—was later improved upon by Peter Claussen in 1845.

The latch needle was patented by Matthew Townsend in 1847. Instead of the usual barb on the needle hook, it featured a half-hook which opened and closed by means of a swinging latch.

The high powered Cotton machine (patented by William Cotton) came into the picture in England in 1864. It has undergone many refinements, but its principles remain today. A large, noisy machine, it forms loops faster than the eye can see, knitting and shaping the fabric automatically. It was the basis for our modern full-fashioning machines.* It has become an instrument of amazing versatility.

Since the introduction of power drive over a hundred years ago, knitting machines have continued to be improved and developed to a point undreamed of by the Reverend Lee in the sixteenth century. Today's knitting process is a very complex and sophisticated system that can be programmed by computers. Working speeds on warp machines have increased from 300 to 1,000 courses per minute in the last twenty years alone.

THE IMPORTANCE OF FIBER

Knits were hampered in reaching their full potential by the limitations of the fibers needed to produce them. Natural fibers were often irregular, hairy, and weak in spots. Knitted fabrics, particularly those made of a single chain of fiber, were only as strong as their weakest link.

Overcoming the inadequacies of natural fibers has occupied man for centuries. Historically—except for silk—yarn was a combination of short fibers joined into a long continuous thread by spinning. Wool, cotton, flax, and other vegetable fibers all grew in short fibrous tissue and had to be spun together to make yarn.

Scientists in the textile field continually sought to develop processes and finishes that would make yarns more even, smoother, and stronger. (Mercerized cotton; worsted spinning wool.)

However, while man was fighting to overcome the drawbacks of natural fibers, he had also become accustomed to their many virtues. The unevenness of natural yarns gives them a "living" quality that people like. They feel pleasant to the hand. They are comfortable when worn next to the skin because the various protuberances in the yarn keep it away from the skin—except at the point of the protuberance—and prevent it from feeling clammy.

The development of synthetic fibers utterly disrupted the knit fabric picture. Modern technology had triumphed over nature. Suddenly, the fabric industry was given long, continuous filament yarn with which to knit, yarn that was small, clean, uniform, and rodlike.

But the very virtues of the synthetics originally contributed to drawbacks in their use. They were so even, so smooth, and so uniform that they lacked the "living" tactile quality to which we had become accustomed. The knit fabrics produced from them often felt clammy and "dead."

Among the first attempts to correct this were efforts to chop the synthetic fibers into short lengths and then spin them together again to

---

* Full-fashioned knitted goods can be identified by the fashion marks near the seams that appear at the points where stitches have been decreased. Illustrative of full-fashioned knitting were the sweaters worn at the turn of the century by the so-called Gibson girls. Stylishly full fashioned, they had fitted waists and beautifully puffed sleeves.

approximate a natural fiber. But this solution seemed to be a step backwards. After all man's efforts to overcome the inadequacies of nature by giving smoothness and strength to textile yarns, he was negating his achievements by again making yarn less strong, less smooth, and less regular.

Texturizing proved to be one of the answers. Working with the knowledge that most synthetic fibers are thermoplastic (and therefore can be reformed by heat), fiber technologists went back to the laboratory and developed new techniques for crimping and twisting fibers so they would take on permanent irregularities without needing to be chopped. Thus they satisfied man's traditional requirements—producing fabric that was pleasant to the touch, comfortable to the skin, and with greater bulk and coverage than the original non-textured synthetics had offered.

Textured polyester—originally developed in England—was slowed in reaching the market place by the appearance of undesirable horizontal lines which occurred in a repeat pattern throughout the fabric. These lines would often be darker or lighter than the fabric itself. They were caused by complex problems, mainly involving the yarn's ability to absorb dye. Once these problems were overcome, by careful quality control, the polyester knits took the public's fancy and cornered a sizable share of the knit interest in both ready-to-wear and over-the-counter fabrics.

Stretch yarns entered the picture soon after du Pont invented nylon in 1939. Research teams began to explore the concept of stretchable yarns made of the new nylon fiber. They wanted a means of giving faster recovery to knits as well as taking the rigidity out of woven fabrics.

The first practical stretch fabrics came out as woven fabrics in European ski wear during the late 1940s, but American research was not far behind. The research into the thermoplasticity of nylon and Dacron polyester laid the foundation for today's *heat set yarns*. With the invention of Lycra—the world's first *Spandex fiber*—another whole new stretch concept was born.

All these strides—plus additional ones in the areas of yarn and fiber finishes and inventive use of patterning—have led to the present widespread use of knitted fabric.

ENTER THE HOME SEWER

While the fabric industry was keen to produce knits of all types for clothing manufacturers, they were slow to recognize the potential market for over-the-counter piece goods (more recently known as consumer fabrics). It was the determination of home sewers themselves that brought about a change of attitude on the part of manufacturers and retailers of fabric and finally caused knit fabric to be made available for home sewing.

A backlash movement occurred in the late Sixties. Women began to show their resentment of an increasingly mechanized society. There was a great deal of talk about "creativity," "self-expression," and "doing your own thing." What past societies had done out of necessity, this one began doing out of choice. Various types of handcraft became popular, and sewing topped the popularity poll. According to *McCall's National Piece Goods Sales Survey*, in 1968 the American home sewer bought $1.76 billion worth of retail fabrics.

Decision making—like the politics of the era—had moved into the streets. Women no longer accepted the clothing retailer's clichés such as "nobody's wearing that now," or "we don't carry bathing suits this time of year." If she couldn't buy what she wanted when she wanted, the lady would make it herself. But she wanted the same fabrics to work with that were being featured in ready-to-wear fashions. Knits were the "in" thing. Yet knits were not available to her. The idea persisted that knits must require some sort of exotic sewing equipment or they would be available to buy.

It remained for a few determined and curious women to pave the way for the knit sewing boom. One of these was a housewife living in Eugene, Oregon—Mrs. Ann Person. She was teaching art and giving sewing lessons when she was given a box of knit scraps—mill ends of wool knit and trim in jacquard prints—from a Portland knitting mill. After studying the knit garments being sold in retail stores at the time, she took her fabrics to the sewing machine and began unlocking some of the "secrets" of sewing knits. She, and others like her, dispelled any myths about the inability of home sewing machines to handle knits. Mrs. Person's efforts aroused so much interest among her friends and sewing students that, by 1967, she had opened the first of a chain of stores featuring knits and lessons on how to sew them. Her method is known as "S-T-R-E-T-C-H-and SEW."

THE LINGERIE SEWING BOOM

Just as West Coast women got into knit sewing early through their proximity to factories making swimwear and apparel knits, the women of Minneapolis/St. Paul profited from the Munsingwear (makers of lingerie) company's factory fabric-outlet store. The availability of the fabrics and findings for lingerie sewing in Minneapolis/St. Paul gave these women a head start on the rest of the country. Those who were interested evolved techniques and patterns—based on what was available in ready-to-wear. They were quick to share their knowledge with others. Courses of instruction were offered by adult education teachers at the Young Women's Christian Association (YWCA) in Minneapolis. By May of 1969 it was estimated that more than a thousand women had taken one or more of the lingerie sewing courses at the Minneapolis "Y."

The Eastern Woolen Company (St. Paul), which is an adjunct to a fabric wholesaling business, became the first to offer coordinated lingerie fabrics and findings, both wholesale and retail. The new business flourished without benefit of promotional advertising. Its success inspired Mr. Irving Rothschild (who had been engaged to supply Eastern Woolen with lingerie goods) to give up his fabric export business and form the Sew Easy Lingerie Company.

In April 1969, Standard Fabrics, Minneapolis-based converters, opened their Rose E. Dee division. They offered retailers the first complete program of instruction along with a coordinated lingerie package. It included a stock unit for display of the lingerie goods for an initial investment of $900 to $1200.

In the meantime, three Minneapolis area stores began selling lingerie fabrics by mail to out-of-state buyers: Kieffers, Eastern Woolen Company, and The Tricot House.

THE PATTERN LAG

Pattern companies were lagging behind the new sewing trend, so Minneapolis seamstresses made their own brown-paper patterns ("Ruboffs" of r-to-w lingerie traced onto grocery wrapping paper). Half slip and panty patterns sold for $1.00 apiece, with little or no instruction to accompany them. Small pattern companies were quickly formed to produce, print, and sell lingerie patterns.

From these modest beginnings, the lingerie sewing phenomenon continued to grow steadily. At last, taking their cue from the home sewer, textile companies began offering a wide selection of consumer fabrics and trims for lingerie. Such manufacturers as Beaunit, that had long been supplying tricot for the lingerie trade, began offering retail goods. And major pattern companies finally realized the impact of the trend and began cooperating with fabric companies in offering a variety of stylish patterns.

Space limitations made many fabric store owners either unable or unwilling to stock tricot fabric initially. Tricots originally came only in 108-inch widths on long cylindrical bolts. An awkward width to cut and to sew. In many cases, small shops scooped the large fabric stores by going in exclusively for tricot, stretch, and other knits.

When wholesalers began splitting tricot into narrower widths, doubling and rolling it, it became easier for both the store owner and the home sewer to handle. [The home sewer who selected a yard of 108-inch-wide fabric to make a slip had enough fabric left over to make another slip and two or three pairs of panties—but not all women appreciated this redundancy of color.] It also made it sound more economical to advertise by the yard. The narrower widths could be offered at lower prices.

Armo, a division of Kayser-Roth, came out with a compact store display unit called a Gingerbread House. The fixture—which fits into four running feet of space—features a reference library of patterns produced by commercial companies, 24 bolts of fabric in narrower widths, and the matching trims. The entire package could be put in a store for $400.

INSTRUCTION AND INFORMATION

As the clamor for instruction increased, neighborhood classes, begun in family recreation rooms, came up out of the basements and were taken over by adult education departments in schools, city recreation departments, and University extension programs. Department and fabric stores also learned they could generate a volume of sales by offering lessons in sewing tricot.

Sewing machine centers—finding that sales depended more and more on a machine's ability to handle sheers and tricots—began including lingerie sewing as a part of the machine instruction. The Viking Company (Husqvarna Vapenfabriks of Sweden), for instance, were responsible for the first appearance in this country of Kerstin Martensson in 1965. Miss Martensson, an experienced instructor in European trade techniques and fashion design, did a great deal to kindle interest in knits with her lectures and demonstrations dealing with methods of sewing on knits and stretch fabrics. Her patterns, designed for Sew-Knit-N-Stretch, Inc., and her subsequent series of instruction books proved to have great impact, both commercially and educationally, tipping off a rash of sewing books and articles delving further into the intriguing subject of knit sewing.

ADVANCES IN SEWING MACHINES

Advances in home sewing machines cannot be overlooked in terms of the important role they played in accelerating the knit sewing boom. Since World War II, when foreign trade policies relaxed to open the doors to foreign sewing machines, exporters have shipped hundreds of thousands of European-made machines into the United States each year. The capability and versatility of all home sewing machines have continued to improve yearly.

Technical advances that have contributed greatly to the popularity of home sewing in recent years are:
- *Improved pressure and feeding ability:* Many machines now function uniformly, sewing all types of fabric, regardless of weight, with little or no adjustment of tension and pressure settings.
- *Pattern stitching:* Zigzag, stretch, three-stage, or a variety of decorative stitches are conveniently controlled by easy-to-insert and removable cams, or by cams permanently built into the machine mechanism.
- *Non-tangle bobbin mechanism:* Machines will not jam or lock, even when stitching on sheer or sleazy fabrics.
- *Free arm:* Helpful for sewing circular seams and hard-to-get-at areas.
- *Ballpoint needle:* Needle with a rounded point, advantageous in sewing many knits, available for most machines.

APPENDIX B
THE CONSTRUCTION AND CHARACTERISTICS OF KNITS

LEARN THE KNIT JARGON

In knitted fabrics, the basic principles of hand knitting are applied to manufactured knit fabrics except that the knitting is done by intricate machinery. In contrast to woven fabrics, knitted fabrics are made by using needles which form *one* or more yarns into a series of interlocking loops. To fabricate the loops, needles are used. For jersey and rib knits, a *latch needle* with a swinging finger closes as the yarn is pulled through a loop to form a new loop. Tricot, Simplex, and milanese utilize a *spring-beard needle* which has a spring hook which resembles a beard. The latter is capable of producing smaller loops for finely fabricated fabrics. Knitting machines produce either *flat* or *circular* knit fabric.

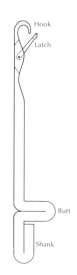

Fig. B-1. Latch needle.

The rows of stitches which run across are referred to as *courses* and the vertical stitches as *wales*. *Gauge* or *cut* is a measure of texture in knitted fabrics, expressed by the number of needles on the machine bed per unit of width across the wales. In some cases it refers to the number of needles *per inch and one-half*. In circular and most flat knitted fabrics, it refers to the number of needles *per inch. The higher the gauge number, the finer the texture of the fabric.* Low gauge numbers indicate the use of coarse needles.

The term *gauge* is commonly used when referring to flat-knitted, full-fashioned fabrics. *Cut* is the knitting term used for circular and other flat-knitted fabrics. For example: a double knit of 16 cut is knit on a machine with 16 n.p.i. (needles per inch). Double knits are now made on a 22–24-cut machine and referred to as 24-cut knit. It possesses more loops per square inch and has a higher stitch density than a knit of 16 cut. This is similar to more warp (ends) and filling (picks) yarns in a woven fabric. To illustrate: a 16 cut would be similar to a woven Shetland fabric (soft, lightweight fabric with a raised finish) and a 24 cut in double knit would be similar to a fine worsted woven sharkskin.

In knit goods, the count of cloth (number of yarns in the warp and filling) is stated in terms of the number of *wales* together with the *courses*.

Fig. B-2. Spring-beard needle.

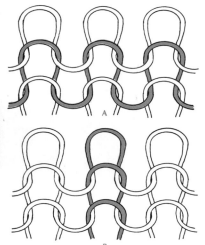

Fig. B-3. Jersey fabric, A, courses, B, wales.

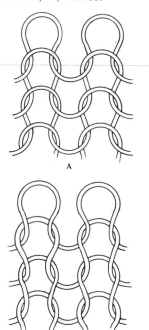

Fig. B-4. Plain knit, A, right side, B, wrong side.

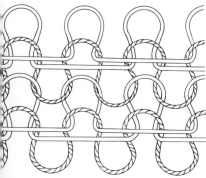

Fig. B-5. Circular knit.

CONSIDER THE CONSTRUCTION

Knits are classified into two general types: *Filling* or *weft* knits and *warp* knits. The filling knits use one continuous yarn forming courses across the fabric. The fabric may be made by hand or by machine. Warp knits use a series of yarns forming wales lengthwise or vertically.

WEFT OR FILLING KNITS

The three basic types of weft machines are *plain, rib,* and *purl.* Each of these machines is made to produce both flat or circular (tubular) knits. **JERSEY (PLAIN):** The basic knitting stitch is the jersey stitch. The plain jersey is the fastest to produce, but the jersey machines are the least versatile. The hand knitter calls the jersey stitch the *stockinette* stitch. Since the loops are formed in one direction, jersey fabric is characterized by vertical ridges (wales) on the right side and horizontal ridges (courses) on the wrong side. Jersey derived its name from the turtleneck sweaters originally worn by the English sailors and fishermen from the Isle of Jersey off the coast of England. Jersey sometimes is referred to as *balbriggan* stitch after the hosiery and underwear fabrics made in Balbriggan, Ireland.

There are basically two types of jersey knitting machines, the *flatbed* and the *circular.* The *flatbed* machine is used for making fully shaped garments or full-fashioned shaping. It is slow and the fabric curls easily. Intarsia* patterns in the designs of flowers and diamonds have recently been developed on these machines. The *circular* machine is the fastest method of producing filling knits and is referred to as the "workhorse" of the industry. It is the least complicated machine; however, it is limited in pattern potential. On this machine fabrics for underwear, seamless hosiery, men's shirts, and fabrics for bondings are made. A variety of plain knitting in a circular knit construction is a type of run-resistant knit. Also pile fabrics, velours, and all types of striped jerseys are knitted on the jersey circular machine. One of the future uses for this machine may be knitted continuous draperies.

RIB: There are basically two types of rib-knit machines—*rib-flat* and *rib-circular.* The *flatbed* machine is utilized when a fabric must have a selvage or start, as in full-fashioned collars and cuffs; for trim in dresses, plackets, and pockets; and most turtleneck collars. The machine does not produce volume, but is important in producing full-fashioned trim.

The *rib-circular* is used for *rib-knit fabrics* and *double knits.* The latter has revolutionized women's wear in the last ten years. It produces with speed and is capable of design flexibility. It also can take textured,

---

* *Intarsia,* derived from the Italian word meaning "inlay," refers to a flat knit—usually in geometrical patterns in solid colors with both sides of the fabric alike.

spun, and filament yarns and the resulting fabric is stable and doesn't curl. The machine, however, is complex. There is also fabric waste when the tube fabric is trimmed.

The rib stitch is characterized by vertical ribs or wales on both the face (right) and the back (wrong) sides of the fabric. A 4 x 2 rib means that the rib is 4 loops of stitches wide and has 2 loops between ribs. If two wales alternate, it is called 2 x 2 or Swiss rib. Rib knits are made on a rib-circular machine. This stitch has excellent crosswise elasticity, is heavy and durable. It is used for wristbands and waistbands, underwear and socks for children and men, as well as for trims.

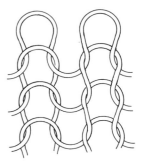

Fig. B-6. Rib stitch.

Variations of the rib stitch include the *full-cardigan* stitch. It is a bulky rib knit which looks the same on both sides. It has the appearance of a stretched jersey fabric.

The *half-cardigan* is a variation of the full cardigan in which the construction on the wrong side of the fabric is the reverse of the front. The *rack stitch* is another variation, featuring a herringbone pattern on the right side.

Fig. B-7. Interlock stitch.

The *interlock* stitch appears as two 1 x 1 rib fabrics having the same appearance on both sides. The fabric possesses excellent lengthwise "give" and limited widthwise "give." It is also soft, firm, and absorbent. It is used for fine gauge sweaters, knit shirts, and sportswear. Mock piqué is also made on the interlock knitting machine.

The *cable stitch* is characterized by small groups of plain wales twisted with one another in rope-like fashion. It is a popular construction for sweaters and sweater knits for garments.

The *double knit* is made with a double set of needles giving double thickness to the fabric. Both the face and the back of the fabric have a finished appearance. In fact, it is difficult to distinguish the right from the wrong side unless the fabric is patterned or textured. Even though it is made on circular machines, it is usually delivered split. The fabrics hold their shape, are wrinkle resistant and durable.

There are many forms or *variations of double knit construction*. One type is the *double piqué* in which the surface may have a honeycomb or diamond effect. It is produced in a variety of colors, textures, and gauges. *French double piqué* is made with a coarser loop than the *Swiss double piqué*. *Birdseye back* or jacquard fabrics in lightweight double knit are available in 24 cut. *Moratronik* machine equipment is available which can produce unlimited sizes in patterns and can change a pattern design in three minutes. Textures in the form of blisters or reliefs are available. *Matelassé* knits are an example of this fabric. *Double jersey* appears with a fine rib on the face and a fine jersey on the reverse. Ribs appear in *Ottoman knit* which has rounded horizontal ribs on the face and a flat knit on the back. A *bourrelet* construction features a ripple stitch formed by knitting and tucking or knitting and welting, forming loops across the surface.

PURL: The purl stitch in knitting may be made on either the flat or circular machine. Since the purl machine moves leftward, this construction

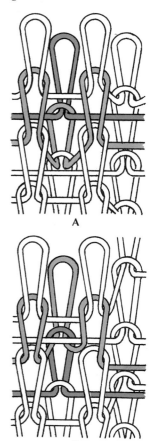

Fig. B-8 Piqués, *A*, Swiss double piqué; *B*, French double piqué.

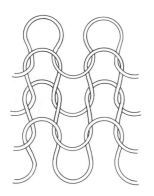

Fig. B-9. Purl or link.

is also known as "links-links" from the German word meaning leftward. The purl stitch is rounder and puffier than the jersey stitch and it looks the same on the face and the reverse side. It is said that the stitch resembles a pearl. The fabric has excellent stretch both crosswise and lengthwise. It is widely used for children's and infants' wear and ladies' wear.

The *purl-flat* machine holds needle beds which lie in the same plane, the same needle moving back and forth to produce the fabric. Stitch transfer is possible so patterns may be fabricated. Lacy and open effects are obtained by using stitch transfer through a racking operation. It is used primarily for sweaters and ladies' outerwear. It is also used for making classic cable stitch tennis sweaters, the Irish fisherman knit sweaters, and other higher priced knit sweaters. The high fashioned *Kimberly knit* dresses are made on the fine 10-gauge machine. The fronts for cut and sewn sweaters are often made on this machine and the backs on the circular.

The *purl-circular* machine produces a fabric on a cylinder. It does not have the ability to produce fancy patterns requiring stitch transfer. It is the slowest producer of the weft machines, but versatile, for it can knit, rib, plain, or purl on one garment. It is used for high volume, lower priced sweaters, some dress fabrics, and men's socks.

WARP KNITS

Warp knitting provides the fastest means of producing knit cloth. A cloth which is 169 inches wide can be fabricated at a rate of 1,000 courses per minute and 4,700,000 stitches per minute or 40 square feet of fabric per minute. Because of the popularity of warp knits, new construction techniques are increasing their versatility. The warp yarns generally run lengthwise. The yarn is prepared as warp on beams with one or more yarns per needle. The bearded-type needles make parallel rows of loops simultaneously and are then interlocked in a zigzag pattern. This "cobweb-like" mesh does not ladder (drop stitches) because loops interlock both ways in the fabric. It may be made flat or tubular, but most are made on the flat machine. The fabric is smooth, wrinkle and shrink resistant, strong, possesses abrasion resistance, and may be sheer. It is less elastic than a filling knit. Some of the types of warp knitting are: tricot, raschel, milanese, Simplex, and crochet. The products made on a warp machine vary from hairnets, to girdle and lingerie fabrics, to rugs.

TRICOT: The brightest future for tricot seems to be its use for menswear and for fashion garments for women. It has broken out of the lingerie image.

Tricot fabric has fine vertical wales on the face and crosswise ribs on the back. The machine to fabricate tricot was invented by an Englishman named Crane in 1775. The fabric produced gets its name from the French word *tricoter,* which means *to knit.* Tricot possesses high tear strength, is resilient, crease resistant, lightweight, run resistant, and

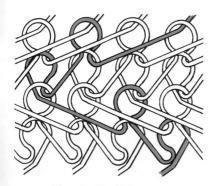

Fig. B-10. Tricot.

stable. It also has controllable elasticity and does not fray. It is used for lingerie, for bonding and laminating fabric, for dresses, blouses, uniforms, shirts, nightwear, loungewear and insulated underwear, as well as for industrial uses.

Much of the versatility of tricot (or raschel) comes from yarn guides, mounted on guide bars which extend across the width of the machine. The guides wrap a sheet of warp yarns around a set of needles and simultaneously form a row of stitches forming a course. Each guide bar controls a separate sheet of warp yarns. All warp machines have at least one guide bar, but single-bar machines are usually not commercially practical. In a single bar the yarn is knitted in one direction and then in reverse. In a two bar, there are two sets of yarn, one knitted in one direction and the other in the opposite. Two-bar machines are usually used for plain fabrics; three-bar for dimensional effects; and for ornamental fabrics, the four-bar machine is utilized. The tricot machine may have up to 18 bars and the raschel up to 48 bars for lace work. The limitation of the tricot machine is its inability to utilize spun and coarser yarns.

Fig. B-11. Raschel.

RASCHEL: The raschel machine is a versatile machine which produces jacquard patterns with intricate eyelet and openwork designs using latched needles. It is capable of stitching and laying-in yarns through the use of multiple bars. It can make lacy fabrics that are either stable or elastic. It can produce dense fabrics, either rigid or with stretch, and even makes plush and carpet fabrics. Power net fabrics for foundation garments and thermal knits for underwear are raschel knits. The use of raschel also includes fabric for intimate apparel, blouses, dresses, curtains, and trims. Netting, also raschel, is used for bridal veiling (replacing bobbinets), as well as for fish nets and laundry bags. Because of the interesting surface effects, it is used for outerwear. In 1971, the Borg Textile Company introduced a line of raschel knit coatings including the hand-knit look, plain and fancies using spun, high-bulk acrylic, some with polyester filament in the back ranging from 17 to 24 ounces in weight. Raschel knits provide interesting textures for men's tailored knits as well as for women's wear.

KETTEN-RASCHEL: Ketten-raschel is also referred to as chain raschel. It is also a variation of the tricot knit, but produces a coarse gauge of 14 to 20 n.p.i. (needles per inch) on widths 90 to 120 inches. Using bearded needles, the fabric produced is finer and has a better "hand" than raschel. The fabrics produced may have raised pattern effects in one or more colors by using a shell-stitch construction.

MILANESE: Milanese knit is fabricated by the use of two sets of yarns using bearded needles but no reversing of direction. Each set of yarns is knitted in one direction, one toward the right, the other toward the left. This diagonal crossing of the two sets of yarns makes the diamond effects on the back which characterizes the fabric. A fine rib shows on the face. It is superior to tricot in split and tear resistance, smoothness and elasticity. It is used for women's underwear, blouses, and gloves.

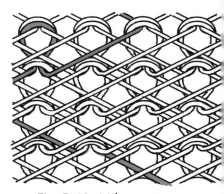

Fig. B-12. Milanese.

SIMPLEX: Simplex knits are produced on a machine using spring-beard needles. The machine is somewhat like two tricot machines back to back. The gauge ranges from 28 to 34 on fabrics fabricated in width of 84 to 112 inches. It is a reversible double fabric with the same ribbed appearance on both sides. It is chiefly used for gloves, handbags, sportswear, and slipcovers. Eyelet and openwork may also be made on this machine. Simplex knits have the weight of a double knit, but the price is lower.

PILE KNITS: The high (deep) pile fabrics (fake or fun fur) may be knit, too. [Flocking, tufting, and weaving are other methods used to produce deep pile fabrics.] The dominant method of producing these fabrics is by knitting. One of the fastest and most economical methods is the *sliver knit*. The background of the fabric is knit with yarns, usually Dynel or sometimes cotton, to reduce the cost. The pile is made from slivers which are picked up by the needles along with the ground yarn and are locked into place as the stitch is formed. The color is produced in the fiber through stock or solution dye processing. The steps in the production of the pile knit include:

- Heat setting to shrink the ground fabric and to expand the diameter of the individual face fibers.
- Tigering to remove surplus fiber from the face of the fabric.
- Shearing to desired height.
- Electrofying to impart luster.
- Applying finishing techniques such as printing to achieve surface effects.

Another method which is faster and newer is to use *circular loop knitting*. In this process, a finished yarn is used for the pile and it is interlaced with the backing. The backing is usually a basic jersey stitch with the pile yarns laid in and left floating over two or more wales in the filling direction. The loops are then cut, sheared, and finished.

Circular loop knits are also used for baby towels and wash cloths in a fabric called *knitted terry*. It is softer and more absorbent than woven terry, but does not conform to shape well. *Velour* is another circular knit, but is a cut pile. It is a fashion fabric used for men's shirts and women's apparel. The latter two fabrics have cotton backing yarns with low twist and are larger in size.

The high pile knits, or fur-like fabrics, are used for shells (outer surface of coats) or for liners (inner surface of coats). When purchasing knits you will note the difference in the two fabrics.

The shells are usually heavier and denser than the liners; however, the fabrics used for liners are sometimes used in less expensive ready-to-wear apparel. A denser pile can be obtained from sliver knits because the amount of face fiber is not limited by yarn size or the distance between the yarns as in weaving. The woven pile fabrics are less pliable than the knit pile fabrics for, when the former is folded back, the backing is apt to show (grin).

SEARCH FOR VARIETY IN FIBERS AND YARNS

FIBERS

Nearly every fiber, man made or natural, can be used for a knitted fabric. Cotton and wool lead in the production of the natural fibers while polyesters and acetate lead among the synthetics. In warp knits for apparel, production of the fibers falls in this general order from the highest to the lowest: acetate, nylon, polyester, acrylics, cotton, and rayon. In the circular knits, cotton ranks the highest, with polyester, acrylics, nylon, wool, acetate, and rayon following in descending order. Blends are also common.

See chart, *Know Your Knits,* which lists the fibers and trade names in addition to special features of each fiber, its use and its care. (See Chapter 1, p. 3.)

YARNS

Knit fabrics may be placed into categories based upon the yarns and combination of yarns which are used for construction.

FILAMENT YARN is a fine, smooth yarn, produced from man-made fibers and consists of continuous parallel filaments which are twisted slightly. They produce a slick "hand." Fabrics produced from these yarns need considerable care in production to avoid fabric snags or the development of pills during wear. The yarns have no protruding ends so they shed lint, resist pilling, and shed soil. Fabrics fabricated from these yarns may be so compact they lack absorbency for comfort.

Filament yarns may be constructed in many shapes. The shape affects the sheen of the fabric because of the reflectance pattern. A round cross-section reflects like this because of the smooth surface:

Some other types of cross-sections are: "H's," I-beams, tri-lobals, and pentalobal. Pentalobal reflects like this:

It is possible to make filament yarns very fine which, in turn, produce sheer fabrics. The size of fineness of the yarn is referred to as *denier.* Some sizes of yarns used for particular fabrics are:

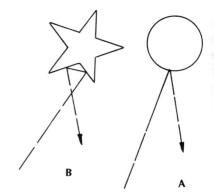

Fig. B-13. Reflecting light, *A,* Pentalobal yarn; *B,* Round yarn.

> 15 denier for hosiery
> 40 to 70 denier for tricot lingerie, blouses, and shirts
> 140 to 520 denier for apparel
> 520 to 1040 denier for upholstery and yarn for carpets

Lightweight yarns of 68 denier/24 filament are sheer and used for blouse fabrics while 180/64 is a good pants weight. Ideal for men's knitted sports shirts is 135/50 denier.

SPUN YARNS are made from staple fibers which are short. These yarns are used for fabrics in which absorbency, bulk, and warmth are desired. The spun yarn is also more comfortable on a humid day as the fiber ends

hold the yarn away from skin contact. These yarns impart a high degree of cover, a traditional hand, and resistance to pilling, snagging, and pulling.
COMBO YARNS: Warp knitting has used a combination of the two yarns, filament and spun, but it is a concept now being used in weft knitting also. Spun yarns can be used in the front bars for surface effect and, in the back bar, a variety of yarns may be used which have value in terms of fabric economies, weight, aesthetics, and performance. For example, various yarns may be used to increase run resistance, add bulk or durability, stretch, crease retention, etc. The combo knits offer more comfort in wearing, a crisper hand, and more pattern variety.
TEXTURED AND STRETCH YARNS: Filament yarns have certain disadvantages such as static build up, poor "hand" (dead feeling), poor cover (opacity), and low absorbency. Thus, filament yarns are texturized so they are no longer closely packed, but have loops, curls, coils, or crimps which impart *bulk, stretch,* and *surface texture.* Few yarn texturizing processes are necessary on spun yarns.

The *bulk* type yarns are either loop or crimp. The resulting yarns have some elasticity, but not as much as stretch yarns. A registered trademark of *crimp-type* bulk yarn is *Textralized,* used in Banlon development by Joseph Bancroft and Sons. An example of *loop bulk* is Taslan by E. I. du Pont de Nemours & Company, Inc.

Stretch yarns are constructed from filament yarns which are twisted 50 or more turns-per-inch and heated until the fiber's memory is set and then untwisted. When the yarn is made into cloth, the yarn tries to return to the coiled state, thus imparting "stretch" to the fabric. Agilon, of Deering Milliken, and Helanca, a Heberlein patent, are two examples of registered trade names of stretch yarns.

The textured *"set"* yarn is false-twisted, heat set, wound loosely, and heat set again by steaming. This removes the stretch from the yarn but stabilizes it with bulk and texture.

Texturized and stretch yarns provide texture and stretch both for an aesthetic appearance and for comfort in knit fabrics.

KNIT FABRIC FINISHES

Knit fabrics have finishes applied to them to minimize some of the disadvantages such as shrinking, static, lack of stability, etc.
SHRINKAGE: Several compressive shrinkage techniques have been applied to cotton knitted goods and have proved to be quite effective. Pak-knit was developed and patented by Compax Corporation and this finish guarantees less than 1 percent shrinkage. Another is Redmanized by F. R. Redman Co. and another is Perma-sized finish.

The Wool Bureau and the International Wool Secretariat has developed a process called the IWS Superwash. It is being used on a variety of wool knits making them completely machine washable and dryable.
ANTI-STATIC: Some anti-static finishes have been developed for synthetic yarns which are fairly effective. Those finishes do not eliminate the static but dissipate it more quickly. They make the yarn more hydrophilic

(water attracting) so it releases soil and retains whiteness. Other claimed advantages for these finishes are better opacity, luster, and "hand." Some finishes used are: 22N (Monsanto), Antron III (du Pont), and Staticaway (Celanese).

Collins and Aikman claimed to have developed the first non-static nylon tricot called "cling-free," according to the standards of AATCC. It included two 40 denier tricot fabrics (dull, matte-face and satin face) in Allied Chemicals' Capralon nylon. They were designed to eliminate the "ride"—the cling bulking of nylon worn under knits and over panty hose.

LAMINATED KNITS: A laminated knit fabric consists of a layer of knit attached to a layer of foam laminate (polyurethane). In about 1958, dress-weight jersey laminated to foam became quite popular as a coat fabric. This is the first time a fabric made popular in an inexpensive line was later upgraded. The foam stabilized the knit. The fabrics had body and drapability. The warmth of the fabric was directly in relation to the thickness of the foam, the fiber content, and the knit construction.

Delamination has been a problem with some laminated knit fabrics. Also, sometimes the knit is applied "off grain."

Lamination is accomplished basically by heat bonding or adhesive bonding. In the heat method the foam is heated until tacky and applied to the knit between rollers. The adhesive method adds stiffness to the fabric and is not too durable to dry-cleaning and washing. Bondaknit by Abasco Fabrics, Inc. is an example of a knitted fabric laminated to Scott Apparel Foam.

BONDED KNITS: In 1961, bonded fabrics were launched with a wool flannel bonded to an acetate jersey. One may find woven fabrics bonded to knits, knits to knits, knit-sew fabrics to knits, and lace to knits.

One advantage to bonding is that a sleazy fabric can be bonded to

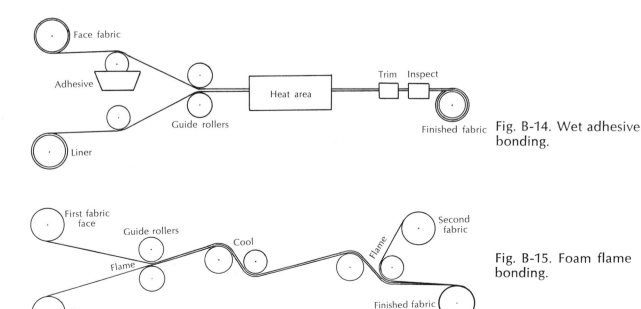

Fig. B-14. Wet adhesive bonding.

Fig. B-15. Foam flame bonding.

another fabric and result in a "new" fabric of excellent quality. However, some bonded fabrics do bag and delaminate.

The two basic methods for bonding are *wet adhesive bonding* and *foam flame bonding*. In the former method, the adhesive is applied to the wrong side of the face fabric and the liner fabric is joined by passing through rollers. In the latter process, polyurethane foam is made tacky on both sides and then applied to both fabrics. This method produces a stiffer fabric. Acetate tricot is most often used as the lining fabric.

The companies involved in fabrics which are bonded have worked desperately hard to improve the consumer image of bondeds through better performance standards. Many guarantee their fabrics against separation, colorfastness, etc. Some examples are Coin-bonded of Coin International, Certifab Guarantee and Certifab Plus of Collins and Aikman, and Celebond by Celanese.

THE FUTURE FOR KNITS

FABRIC PRODUCTION: According to recent estimates made by the editors of *American Fabrics* magazine, the knit share of the total consumption of apparel fabrics may—by the year 1975—be as high as 45 percent. Knitting, then, will be practically on a par with weaving in the textile industry.

MORE MACHINES AND FINER CUTS: In the early Sixties there was scarcely a single double-knit plant in the United States. By 1971 there were approximately ten thousand of them—many of them operating double-knit machines imported from Germany, England, France and Switzerland, and Japan. At this writing, one company has introduced a 32-cut plain double-knit machine and it is expected that by the mid-Seventies, a 30-cut jacquard double-knit machine will be available for industrial use. However, we must remember that the higher the *cut,* the less stretch the knit fabric possesses.

ELECTRONICALLY CONTROLLED MACHINES: One new knitting machine is electronically controlled, guided by a small magnetic tape cassette, which sets a pattern programmed by computers. The operator "designs" at a keyboard and sees the pattern on a video screen as it is being entered on the tape. The operator also gets a paper printout. It takes about 20 seconds to change cassettes. Other new machines operate with punched films.

NEW FIBERS: In the decade of the Seventies, knits have also begun showing their metal. Metex Corporation has introduced fabrics made of knitted stainless steel, copper, aluminum, tungsten, gold, and other kinds of metals not usually considered fashion ingredients. It is claimed that a filmy fabric of tungsten may be made as sheer as the sheerest nylon stocking.

NEW KNITTING TECHNIQUES: Another new dimension in warp knit fabric production has been the *insertion of weft yarn in a warp structure*. It is used on both tricot and raschel machines. This technique provides added textural interest to the knitted fabric since spun, textured, or even slub yarns can be introduced into the warp knit. The resulting knit fabric combines the advantages of wovens with those of warp knits. Some examples of these fabrics are: Spunway (TMW), Division of North American Rockwell; Weft Lock (Crompton & Knowles/Liba); and Weftomatic (Karl Mayer/J. P. Stevens). Another new warp knitting machine is Mayer's Co-We-Nit. The resulting fabric is a combination of weaving and knitting.

ULTRASONIC SEWING: In 1971, the art of sewing by high-frequency sound waves was tested, researched, and pilot runs were made. The single best application was expected to be the double-knit polyester. Ultrasonic sewing would fuse the knit fabric rather than fastening it with thread. It is expected to cut costs by eliminating thread and needle inventories, machine "down time," and the training of operators.

NEW QUALITY CONTROLS: During May of 1971, the board of KTA (Knitted Textile Association) took the first step toward approving a set of ground rules for evaluating the quality of knitted fabrics. KTA accounts for more than 80 percent of the nation's knitters, so this was considered a strong move. The evaluation system was adapted from one developed by the U.S. Army Laboratories in Natick, Massachusetts.

The rating was based upon a point system. Fabrics up to 64–66 inches wide may have up to 50 points chargeable against 100 linear yards and still be rated first quality. Greater widths are charged proportionately. Points are assigned for dropped-needle defects, slubs, streaks, off-shading, etc.

The development of a standard signifies the maturing of the knit industry and their concern for understanding between buyer and seller as to what constitutes an acceptable piece of knit fabric.

COTTAGE INDUSTRY: John Carr Doughty, a British knit designer and technologist, has proposed a plan for developing cottage industries for knitting, similar to those developed for weaving. Original designs may be used on manually operated knitting machines which cannot be produced on automated machinery. This may be an answer for utilizing unskilled labor in the developing areas of the world.

Yes . . . knitting has come a long way from knit one, purl one. . . .

Index